Cold Cases

Evaluation Models with Follow-up Strategies for Investigators

Second Edition

Cold Cases

Evaluation Models with Follow-up Strategies for Investigators

Second Edition

James M. Adcock, PhD
The Center for the Resolution of Unresolved Crimes
East Longmeadow, Massachusetts, USA

Sarah L. Stein, PhD
The Center for the Resolution of Unresolved Crimes
Springfield, Massachusetts, USA

CRC Press
Taylor & Francis Group
Boca Raton London New York

CRC Press is an imprint of the
Taylor & Francis Group, an **informa** business

CRC Press
Taylor & Francis Group
6000 Broken Sound Parkway NW, Suite 300
Boca Raton, FL 33487-2742

First issued in paperback 2019

© 2015 by Taylor & Francis Group, LLC
CRC Press is an imprint of Taylor & Francis Group, an Informa business

No claim to original U.S. Government works

ISBN-13: 978-1-4822-2144-2 (hbk)
ISBN-13: 978-0-367-86909-0 (pbk)

Library of Congress Cataloging-in-Publication Data

Adcock, James M.
  Cold cases : evaluation models with follow-up strategies for investigators / James M. Adcock, Sarah L. Stein. -- Second edition.
      pages cm. -- (Advances in police theory and practice)
  Includes bibliographical references and index.
  ISBN 978-1-4822-2144-2 (hardback)
  1. Cold cases (Criminal investigation) 2. Criminal investigation. I. Stein, Sarah L. II. Title.

HV8073.A5285 2014
363.25--dc23   2014032654

Visit the Taylor & Francis Web site at
http://www.taylorandfrancis.com

and the CRC Press Web site at
http://www.crcpress.com

To all the victims and the surviving families of the 185,000 unresolved homicides (since 1980) and the detectives charged with investigating such horrible crimes.

James M. Adcock, Ph.D.

To my family: Uni, Papa, Kristin, Christopher, DeDe, and Hal. I love you with all my heart. I couldn't have made it without you. Also to Kim and Molly: the two most beautiful angels in heaven.

Sarah Land Stein, Ph.D.

To our success and the damnation of our enemies.

Richard Walter
New Orleans, July 2008

Contents

Section I

GETTING STARTED: HOW DO WE PREPARE TO REVIEW AND CONDUCT COLD CASE INVESTIGATIONS?

Section II

THE EVALUATION PROCESS

Section III

FOLLOW-UP INVESTIGATIVE STRATEGIES

10   Suspectology: The Development of Suspects Using Pre-, Peri-, and Post-Offense Behaviors   **151**

RICHARD WALTER, SARAH L. STEIN, AND
JAMES M. ADCOCK

11   Investigative Interviewing: Issues and Concerns Relating to Cold Cases   **177**

JAMES M. ADCOCK AND SARAH L. STEIN

Series Editor's Preface

While the literature on police and allied subjects is growing exponentially, its impact upon day-to-day policing remains limited. The two worlds of research and practice in relation to policing remain disconnected, even though cooperation between the two is growing. A major reason for this is that the two groups speak different languages. The research work is published in hard-to-access journals and presented in a manner that is difficult to comprehend. On the other hand, police practitioners tend not to mix with researchers and remain secretive about their work. Consequently, there is little dialog between the two and almost no attempt to learn from one another. Dialog across the globe, among researchers and practitioners situated in different continents, is of course even more limited.

I attempted to address this problem by starting the International Police Executive Symposium (IPES), www.ipes.info, where a common platform has brought the two together. IPES is now in its 20th year. The annual meetings, which constitute most major annual events of the organization, have been hosted in all parts of the world. Several publications have come from these deliberations and a new collaborative community of scholars and police officers has been created whose membership runs into the several hundreds.

Another attempt was to begin a new journal, aptly called *Police Practice and Research: An International Journal* (PPR), which has opened the gate for practitioners to share their work and experiences. The journal has attempted to focus upon issues that help bring the two onto a single platform. *PPR* will complete its 15th year in 2014. It is certainly evidence of a growing collaboration between police research and practice that *PPR*, which began with four issues a year, expanded into five issues in its fourth year and, now, is issued six times a year.

Clearly, these attempts, despite their successes, remain limited. Conferences and journal publications do help create a body of knowledge and an association of police activists, but cannot address the substantial issues in depth. The limitations of time and space preclude larger discussions and more authoritative expositions that can provide stronger and broader linkages between the two worlds.

It is this realization of the increasing dialog between police research and practice that has encouraged many of us—my close colleagues and I connected closely with IPES and *PPR* across the world—to conceive and implement a new attempt in this direction. I am now embarking on a book series, "Advances in Police Theory and Practice," that seeks to attract writers from all parts of the world. Further, the attempt is to find practitioner contributors. The objective is to make the series a serious contribution to our knowledge of policing as well as to improve police practices. The focus is not only on work that describes the best and most successful police practices, but also work that challenges current paradigms and breaks new ground to prepare police for the 21st century. The series forges comparative analyses that highlight achievements in distant parts of the world as well as comparisons that encourage an in-depth examination of specific problems confronting a particular police force.

In this second edition of *Cold Cases: Evaluation Models and Follow-up Strategies for Investigators*, Dr. Adcock and Dr. Stein have taken their experience to another level and provided the reader with new information and two new models that can be very useful to police agencies in solving cold cases. One of these new models focuses on the physical evidence that may exist in an investigation while the other provides concepts for investigating a missing person's case that is believed to also be a cold case homicide. Furthermore, they have included a chapter from their colleagues at the Police Academy in the Netherlands that demonstrates another perspective and view of resolving the problem as taught through an educational environment.

It is hoped that through this series it will be possible to accelerate the process of building knowledge about policing and help bridge the gap between the two worlds—the world of police research and police practice. This is an invitation to police scholars and practitioners across the world to come and join in this venture.

Dilip K. Das, Ph.D.
Founding President
International Police Executive Symposium
http://www.ipes.info

Series Editor
Advances in Police Theory and Practice
(CRC Press/Taylor & Francis Group)

Series Editor
Interviews with Global Leaders in Police,
Courts, and Prisons
(CRC Press/Taylor & Francis Group)

Series Editor
PPR Special Issues as Books
(Routledge/Taylor & Francis Group)

Founding Editor-in-Chief
Police Practice and Research: An International Journal
(Routledge/Taylor & Francis Group)
http://www.tandfonline.com/GPPR

Acknowledgments

I wish to express my deepest appreciation to all those persons and their respective agencies who have contributed to *Cold Cases: An Evaluation Model with Follow-up Strategies for Investigators*. I wish to acknowledge each individual for his or her professional expertise, suggestions, comments, and so on, who have either contributed to this work or encouraged me to complete this phenomenal task. I have listed these people alphabetically, and please forgive me if I unintentionally omitted someone.

Before I list all those fine people, I feel it is imperative that I acknowledge the efforts and contributions of my coauthor Sarah L. Stein. It was at the Henry C. Lee Institute of Forensic Science (HCL), colocated at the University of New Haven (Connecticut), that she suggested we start conducting pro bono reviews of cold cases from local police departments as part of the Cold Case National Institute of Justice grant HCL had obtained. For those of you who do not know her, she is an extremely smart young lady whose intuitiveness in this type of work goes well beyond expectations, belief, and, in many cases, the experiences of others. She is a natural when it comes to conducting case reviews and being able to pick out the nuances of information others did not see, not to mention her innate ability to identify and correlate behavioral information of potential persons of interest. She is in fact many years ahead of her age, one of a kind, and a must-type for any evaluation team of unresolved homicides.

I need to also give a special thank you to R.A.M. Hulshof, H.A.M. Heijmerikx, J.C. Knotter, and Y.M. Spoormans and their supervisor Henk Walles, my colleagues at the Dutch Police Academy in Apeldoorn, the Netherlands. Over the past couple of years, they have been very insightful and worked with me on the issues concerning the solving of cold cases worldwide, not just in the United States and the Netherlands. Teaching there has been a joy, and every time I talk in front of one of their classes of detectives I learn something new. Furthermore, they wrote Chapter 8 to discuss cold cases in an educational environment from the Police Academy. Last, I want to further thank Ms. Spoormans for the patience she exhibited while she served as the conduit through the writings of their chapter and subsequent revisions. A job well done. These are great people and thanks to each one of you.

I want to thank the following:

With assistance and contributions from: R. A. M. Hulshof, H. A. M. Heijmerikx, J. C. Knotter, Y. M. Spoormans, Albert B. Harper, Richard Walter, Arthur S. Chancellor, and Grant D. Graham, Sr.

Joe Buckley, CEO of Reid & Associates, The Reid Technique of Interviews and Interrogations, Chicago, Illinois. We met through a mutual colleague, and Joe was very helpful and patient with me as I worked on the chapter regarding interviews and interrogations.

Heather Coyle, Ph.D., professor at the University of New Haven, Connecticut, who specializes in DNA, and significantly contributed to the cold case seminars at HCL and was a great supporter of this project.

Dilip K. Das, Ph.D., chair, Department of Criminal Justice and Law Enforcement, Coppin State University, Baltimore, Maryland. If it had not been for Das's suggestion and subsequent encouragement to write this book for his book series, Advances in Police Theory and Practice, it probably would not have ever happened.

Marc Dorsett of Marc Dorsett Designs, www.marcdorsett.com. Prior to this book Marc was very helpful with a couple of other designs I needed. In this book he has been absolutely phenomenally patient and very creative with his work, from all the diagrams/figures in the book to the spectacular cover.

Jim Gannon, formerly of the Morris County Prosecutor's Office, New Jersey, came to one of the Institute's cold case seminars and was very helpful with providing his standard operating procedure (SOP) for establishing and operating a cold case unit.

Albert B. Harper, Ph.D, J.D. In addition to being extremely supportive of this project, Al agreed to write the chapter on forensic science and cold cases. Over the years he has been a great friend and colleague.

Robert Keppel, Ph.D. He is one of a kind who probably knows more about murder and the investigative process than anyone else. While Bob was not directly involved with this book, he did significantly contribute through all the research he has done on the topic. I enjoyed working with him at the University of New Haven and wish him all the luck and good health in the future.

Henry C. Lee, Ph.D. Again, one of those who did not directly contribute to this book but who by his mere presence at the cold case seminars was a delight to see and hear. You cannot attend a Lee lecture without learning something, and it was he who got the Institute the grant money for the Cold Case Project at the University of New Haven. Without that opportunity and subsequent experiences, this book would not have been possible.

Eddie Majors, cold case detective, Tulsa, Oklahoma. Eddie attended one of the seminars and significantly contributed to the cause through the Tulsa Gray Squad cold case concept. To me, their Gray Squad is an extremely innovative concept way ahead of its time and should be utilized more than it is in other jurisdictions. In addition to numerous conversations about the unit, Eddie provided the document in Appendix A that explains how the Gray Squad came about and is structured. Another success story.

Christopher L. Morano, J.D., presently practicing law in Essex, Connecticut, but formerly one of the state's attorneys that prosecuted Michael Skakel for the Martha Moxley murder. I have known Chris primarily through his legal considerations lectures he conducted at the Institute for the cold case seminars.

Carolyn Spence, CRC Press/Taylor & Francis, for her patience with me in writing my first book.

Melchor deGuzman, book editor, *Advances in Police Theory and Practice*.

James Tranium, detective, Violent Crime Case Review Project, Metropolitan Police Department (MPD), Washington, DC. Reputedly they have been one of the most successful cold case units in the country. Jim and I had many discussions about cold cases, the problems, DNA, and so forth, and he provided a copy of their SOP to serve as an example for others to see.

Stephen Wilson, Morris County Prosecutors Office, New Jersey. He represents another perspective of a cold case unit, one contained within a prosecutor's office. Stephen also discussed with me some of the problems encountered with cold case units and the investigations they evaluate.

Richard Walter, behavioral analyst and one of the original Vidocq Society founders, Philadelphia, Pennsylvania. Richard is a unique individual whom I have known over the past 25 years primarily through the meetings of the American Academy of Forensic Sciences. In addition to being the author of the chapter on suspect identification, Richard has taught me so much about the behavioral aspects of these crimes, and I thank him for this and his friendship.

Richard Walton, Ph.D. (not to be confused with the previous person, Richard Walter). Walton opened the door with the first-ever book on cold cases, and I am hopeful this book will augment his. Much of his research is mentioned in this book. Walton has been very supportive and helpful with my endeavor, and I greatly appreciate that effort and consideration.

Unnamed detectives who discussed cases at the HCL seminars whose information I used. Now this is very tricky, as I do not want to offend any of those who attended the seminars at the Institute. While I may not remember their names, I do vividly recall their true stories and tribulations. For 10 years, this was an experience of a lifetime with detectives from all over the country discussing their jurisdictional issues and problems regarding cold cases and the investigations. Again, without it, this book may not have ever been written. Therefore, the second part of my dedication is to the detectives who are charged with investigating these horrible crimes.

James M. Adcock, Ph.D.

Authors

James M. Adcock, Ph.D., served 20 years in the U.S. Army, primarily as a Special Agent Criminal Investigator conducting criminal investigations in Vietnam, Panama, Maryland, California, South Carolina, and in Germany. He progressed from a basic investigator to Special Agent in Charge and Operations Officer, supervising as many as 20 investigators. In 1976, he completed a one-year fellowship in Forensic Medicine at the U.S. Armed Forces Institute of Pathology, and in addition to attending numerous investigative seminars he also attended Scotland Yard's Advanced Detective Course at Hendon in London.

Soon after retirement, Dr. Adcock began working as the Chief Deputy Coroner for Investigations in Richland County, Columbia, South Carolina, while he returned to school to work on his doctorate at the University of South Carolina. During this time, he was certified in both Georgia and Florida (Institute of Police Technology and Management [IPTM]) to conduct training for law enforcement and coroners in their respective police academies, and he also lectured extensively in other states.

In 1997, prior to graduating, he accepted a tenure track position (he earned his Ph.D. in 2001 and tenure in 2004) at the University of New Haven (Connecticut) in its Criminal Justice and Forensic Science programs. He then became the director of the Investigative Services Program that went from 75 students in 1999 to over 425 in 2007. He designed an advanced investigative techniques course (undergraduate) and a death investigation course (graduate). He also taught the Advanced Investigation Courses for the Forensic Science Graduate Program.

In the spring of 2004, Dr. Adcock was a visiting professor at the Yale Law School. This was part of a joint venture between Yale and the University of New Haven to help design the mission statement and a case processing protocol for the newly created Connecticut Innocence Commission.

In August 2008, he accepted a position at Coppin State University, Baltimore, Maryland, to teach and design forensic-related programs at both the undergraduate and graduate levels in the Department of Criminal Justice. By the end of the academic year he had successfully designed five courses in forensic investigations at the undergraduate level and seven at the graduate level, both of which were awarded certificates by the State of Maryland Higher Educational System.

While teaching criminal justice courses online, Dr. Adcock is busy designing a book series titled "The Law Enforcement Guide to Investigations," and consults on death cases for police departments, attorneys, and families.

Outside academia, Dr. Adcock is a fellow with the Henry C. Lee Institute of Forensic Science, University of New Haven, where he designed a Cold Case Workshop and lectured for the institute on death investigation and managing the investigative process. For 2 years he supervised forensic science graduate students as they evaluated cold cases from police departments around the country. He has been and continues to be a very active fellow of the American Academy of Forensic Sciences (AAFS), serving on the Board of Directors from 2006 to 2008 and as a vice president for the term 2008 to 2009. He is also a member of the AAFS Ethics Committee. Dr. Adcock can be reached at jmadcock@jma-forensics.com.

Sarah L. Stein, Ph.D., received her doctorate in criminal justice from the University of Southern Mississippi. She received a master's degree in forensic science with a certificate in computer forensics from the University of New Haven in 2007. Dr. Stein attended and matriculated from American University in Washington, DC, in 2004 with a bachelor of arts in the victimology of pedophilia, a self-designed major comprised of criminal justice, psychology, and sociology courses.

During her attendance at the University of New Haven, Dr. Stein was a member of the cold case evaluation team for 2 years, where she conducted the review of numerous unsolved murders from police departments in Connecticut and one from Tennessee. Upon leaving the University of New Haven, she was hired as a cold case analyst for 6 months by a Connecticut police department.

Dr. Stein has extensive experience working with both families and law enforcement agencies in evaluating child abduction and cold case investigations. She continues her work in evaluating cold cases and child abduction investigations and hopes to help facilitate training for law enforcement officials in the arena of conducting efficient child abduction investigations.

Introduction

First Edition

I have had a fabulous career (over 30 years) in law enforcement where I started in Vietnam as a criminal investigator (Special Agent with the United States Army CID). After retiring from the Army I moved on to become a Chief Deputy Coroner of Investigations for 6½ years in Columbia, South Carolina, while I returned to school to get my Ph.D. at the University of South Carolina. It was 1983 when I first started conducting training for law enforcement at the Georgia Police Academy in Atlanta. I lectured on death investigation and contributed to the Georgia State Coroner's training program up until 1997. During much of that time I was also certified in Florida, where I lectured for the Institute of Police Technology and Management (IPTM). Then, in 1997, I went to the University of New Haven, Connecticut, and in addition to teaching at the undergraduate and graduate levels in the criminal justice and forensic science programs, I lectured for the Henry C. Lee Institute of Forensic Science to law enforcement officers from around the country.

It was at the institute that I designed a cold case seminar for law enforcement personnel that was conceptually similar to the one taught at IPTM in Jacksonville, Florida, by the leader of the Cold Case Investigations Unit, Sgt. David W. Rivers, retired Dade County, Florida detective. This 1-week seminar would start off with a couple of days of lectures, and then the attending detectives were encouraged to bring with them and discuss unresolved homicides that they had in their jurisdictions. These would be discussed in front of the entire class along with instructors, all looking for ideas and possible solutions or avenues for future investigative strategies.

Rivers'[1] initial concept and subsequent lectures focused on the development of cold case squads, paying particular attention to the selection process of cold case detectives, considerations regarding how the passage of time affects cold case investigations, and the advancement in technology (all of these will be discussed in detail later in this book). He then proposed a process for the initiation of cold case squads. These were:

1. Conduct a complete and thorough review of the case file and reorganize as needed.
2. Determine what evidence is presently available. Personally view each item.
3. Involve a district attorney to ensure all evidence and subsequent procedures will be prosecutable.
4. Determine who benefited the most from the death of the victim.
5. Recheck all background checks on suspects, subjects, witnesses, etc. It is here you look for arrests since the incident and for changes in relationships.
6. Make contact with medical examiner and review the autopsy file with him or her.
7. Make contact with the victim's family and see if they have any new information.
8. Initiate interviews with witnesses and associates of the victim.
9. Prior to interviewing major witnesses, determine if they have had any life changes that could affect their responses today.
10. Once you have gathered all the new information, obtain a warrant.

Remember that "control and direction" are essential. Consider investigative lead sheets, periodic meetings of the team including the prosecutor, and so on. Remember that not all cases are solvable. Using this as the foundation, and my own experiences plus those of others, I designed the previously mentioned cold case seminar for the Henry C. Lee Institute of Forensic Science. I ultimately ended up with the title "Cold Cases: Conceptualization and Investigative Strategies." One of the things I added was my concept of how all investigations can be broken down into three types of sources of information: physical evidence, informational evidence, and behavioral evidence. This then brought me to the point that the lecturers for the first 2 to 3 days should bring to the table all three aspects.

I would start the first day off with the concepts of how did we get here, investigative strategies, and so forth. Then at least one person would lecture on forensic science, new technology, and cold cases, while the third person would be one well versed on the behavioral aspects and analysis process. I also included a prosecuting attorney to discuss legal issues and concerns that may arise in a cold case investigation. The first person I used for the behavioral concerns was Gregg O. McCray, retired FBI Senior Special Agent in what was previously known as the FBI Behavioral Sciences Unit. I also asked Dr. Henry C. Lee to discuss crime scenes and forensic science and Dr. Heather Coyle to enlighten the group on DNA. This three-pronged approach balanced out the process, and after the lectures each detective who brought a case presented his or her cases for comments, strategies, and so on.

After about 7 years of directing and teaching these seminars, the institute received a National Institute of Justice grant for cold case training, and the number of seminars went from once a year to six times a year. Then, based on a suggestion of a forensic science graduate student (my coauthor Sarah L. Stein), I started a pro bono cold case team of specially selected forensic science graduate students to conduct a review and analysis of cold cases for law enforcement agencies in the State of Connecticut. Over the next 2 years, that spread to departments in Massachusetts, New York, and Tennessee.

Before I go any further with the description of how this all developed, I need to mention a couple of things that significantly contributed to my way of thinking. Soon after the U.S. Supreme Court Daubert decision regarding expert forensic testimony, I realized that as detectives we, too, need to be more scientific. It is no longer enough to imply that because I have over 30 years of experience you should believe that what I am saying is completely valid. True, experience is extremely important and we rely on it a lot, but why not make that testimony a little more acceptable and easier to believe? In other words, go beyond the experience factor and apply the principles of the scientific method by asking ourselves: How do we know that? What have others found in similar circumstances? Have we eliminated all other possibilities? And, as I lecture today, I emphasize the importance of this as an investigative step: Try to disprove your theory of the crime, and if you cannot disprove it, then it is probably valid. However, if you do disprove it, then more investigation is needed.

With this scientific approach toward investigations in mind, I created an atmosphere with these cold case teams of always asking themselves and each other if they can verify what they have observed and/or stated (i.e., How do you know that?). One way of doing this was to have them footnote everything they found so that the original source of that information could be readily identified and located for further analysis. Another approach was to convene several team meetings where I expected them to second-guess each other on a regular basis. This was not the time for egos or supposition; everything needed to be factually based on information in the case file and not just based on one's personal belief.

According to research conducted by Scripps News, nearly 185,000[*] homicides since 1980 remain unsolved. Keeping that figure in mind while you read further you will see that staffing in departments is low and that resources are frequently not available. Departments today have enough trouble keeping abreast of all the hot cases, much less the old cold ones in the basement. And if no one comes to their door knocking and asking why the murder of their family member has not been resolved, that case file will probably remain

[*] http://www.scrippsnews.com/projects/murder-mysteries/nearly-185000-homicides-1980-remain-unsolved, accessed June 18, 2010.

dormant and unresolved. It is with that problem in mind that some police departments have gone outside the department for personnel to assist them in the evaluation process of these unresolved homicides. This means going to the private sector for doctors, nurses, professors, salespersons, and, of course, graduate students, to help them evaluate their cases to see which ones have potential solvability factors and which ones do not, ultimately saving the department many hours and days of detective time and resources.

Over the years I have made another observation dealing with the review process of criminal incidents and especially those that fall into the cold case category, and that is: Not everyone is capable of reviewing a case file properly and accurately. Some detectives are really intuitive, and others are not so adept. That is not to say they are bad detectives, as they do bring other characteristics and needed value to the table, but rather they just do not have that special sense of seeing the case for what it is. In my opinion only a few select people have the capability that is needed to properly and accurately evaluate cases, especially with voluminous cold case files. However, if they were to follow the proposed cold case evaluation model that I designed, they would increase their chances of an accurate resolution or at least be able to say that everything has been done that can be done and barring further new information, the case will remain an unresolved investigation.

It is with this premise that I designed the cold case evaluation model. While initially designed to help non-police types such as the private sector or students in their process of evaluating cold cases under the supervision of a senior detective, the model can also be a valuable tool for police officers and detectives, especially those mentioned above. And for those department chiefs who are reluctant to allocate the manpower for a cold case squad, they can adopt this model and only have one detective part-time supervising the preselected private sector individuals reviewing their case files. As cases are identified as solvable, they can then be given to the detective unit with a comprehensive investigative plan for further investigation.

That being said, this book is divided into three sections. Section I: Getting Started: How Do We Prepare to Review and Conduct Cold Case Investigations provides a historical perspective of how we got to this point in helping us to understand the cold cases we review for further investigation. In this section I also provide a chapter on understanding the process of homicide and a few matters about those who kill. In Section II, the evaluation model is fully described. It demonstrates the key elements of organization, thoroughness, and the value of the scientific method. This section validates theories of the crime, provides evidentiary issues and concerns, addresses the informational and behavioral aspects relative to the crime and the participants in the crime, and documents investigative strategies for future efforts on the case. Section III goes beyond the actual model by discussing the investigation that follows the evaluation. What else do we look at beyond the case file itself?

Where has technology taken us since the date of the incident? Considering the personalities involved, which interview or interrogation techniques should be utilized in this particular case? Basically, what do we do next and how do we do it to maximize our efforts and obtain a conviction, not just an arrest? At the end, in the Appendixes, I have provided sample standard operating procedures from three agencies as a guide for those who may desire to set up a cold case unit. In this group I want the reader to pay particular attention to the Tulsa, Oklahoma, Police Department's Gray Case Squad, which uses the private sector to help them solve their cases. This is another innovative approach that saves time, money, and manpower. Last, I have included a sample victimology report and a list of additional resources a department may look to for assistance in their cases, hot or cold.

James M. Adcock, Ph.D.
Hattiesburg, Mississippi

Second Edition

Since we started this endeavor years ago many things have changed that have contributed to the need for a second edition. First and foremost, my coauthor Sarah L. Stein, completed her doctoral work and now has her Ph.D. and is teaching as an assistant professor at Western New England University, Springfield, Massachusetts. I am now semiretired, teaching part time, primarily online, and conduct cold case investigation seminars for police agencies in the United States and am a regular at the Dutch Police Academy in the Netherlands. The latter came about in 2010 when the leaders of the Dutch Police Academy contacted us for a consultation in the Netherlands regarding our book on cold cases. The end result is that they adopted our book for their detective master's training program for their detectives at the academy in Apeldoorn. Along with this came several trips to Holland where I lectured for 2 days on victimology and suspectology (the development of suspects). Needless to say, this experience and friendship has evolved where I have learned a lot from them and they in turn have written a chapter for this second edition called "Cold Case Investigation in an Educational Environment: The Dutch Experience."

In between those trips to Holland, we were involved in several lectures in the United States at various police agencies. These lectures, coupled with my experiences as a peer reviewer for National Institute of Justice (NIJ) Cold Case Grants, it became apparent that there is need for a second evaluation model that would not only be less labor intensive than our first model but more likely to satisfy grant requirements whether from NIJ or others, and provide the police agency with faster results. The goal is not to formulate the perfect model or process, but rather to provide something that agencies can use as a basis from which to work, especially dealing with the organizational structure.

Time has taught us many things with cold cases, not to mention that witnesses may be more willing to discuss the situation versus years ago, but also that agencies take different approaches searching for the same result. Some do not know where to turn or how to start and others just shoot for the DNA material without consideration that there may be other investigative leads with solvability possibilities. Not finding the silver bullet (DNA) they frequently do not return to the case file documents for other solvability issues that could be resolved with additional investigative work.

For these reasons, we need to assist wherever possible with our teachings and training. It was interesting to note that at a recent Vidocq Society meeting (January 2014), the society had just heard the particulars about a case from a relatively small department. Someone posed the question about larger versus smaller agencies asking why the society does not hear more from the big departments. Richard Walter responded that because the larger agencies have the manpower and funds, it is the smaller departments that truly need our help, as they are "our bread and butter."

With all that said we would like to introduce you to the second edition of this book by providing a brief chapter-by-chapter analysis. In Section I of this book, titled "Getting Started: How Do We Prepare to Review and Conduct Cold Case Investigations?" a cold case is defined and some of the reasons of how we got into this predicament are provided in Chapter 1. Then in Chapter 2 we thought it would be appropriate to help the reader understand a little about the process of homicide and those who kill. Chapter 3 then follows and provides concepts for creating a cold case team or unit, realizing that every agency is different. Issues regarding who should be on the team to procedural steps are reflected.

In Section II we start with the evaluation process and open with Chapter 4 where the different models and evaluation procedures are outlined. It is here that we also discuss the tedious steps necessary to conduct a thorough review of the case file documents. Then as we enter Chapter 5 the full comprehensive model is provided. This model is scientifically based and if followed completely, basically leaves no stone unturned, but over time we have found it to be labor intensive and more time consuming than most departments are willing to use. However, if an agency is willing to invest in the utilization of local citizens, graduate students, or the like, this is the best method to follow under the guidance of a trained and experienced detective.

In the next two chapters (6 and 7), two additional models are presented and described in detail. The first focuses on the physical evidence that may be present and how utilization of this procedure will expedite the resolution. The next model was put together as a possible tool to be used when investigating missing person's cases where you are confident the case involves a death but where the body of the victim has not been found. In the last chapter (8) of this section, my colleagues at the Dutch Police Academy have written about cold cases in Holland and how they address the problem through their educational system at the national police academy. You will find that they are extremely thorough in the way they investigate cases, far and above anything we have seen elsewhere.

As we enter Section III, the strategies for follow-up investigation are provided. This starts with an up-to-date chapter on the forensic sciences and what new technology is available. In the following chapter (10) we provide the "suspectology" or the procedures for identifying a suspect from a list of persons of interest. This edition provides two case studies, one in Chapter 10 and the other in Appendix C, "Suspectology," that illustrates the process. Then in Chapter 11, we address the investigative interviewing process reflecting on some of the theoretical premises others have proffered. Each case and each person you interview is going to be different and therefore the interviewer has to be flexible. Techniques around the world are different yet all have their successes.

As an addition to this second edition we decided to add a chapter (12) concerning staged crime scenes in cold cases. In many reviews of cold cases we have seen signs where the scene appears to have been staged to misdirect the investigative agency. That staging could very well be why the case is unresolved. Having more knowledge about the staging process and how to interpret it could be very helpful.

In Chapter 13 we discuss and provide examples of cold case evaluation reports where the information is frequently presented to a prosecutor. And, last, our conclusions and "where do we go from here?" Ultimately, our goal was not to establish a national standard but to provide the reader with different options, and while learning how and why others failed, provide the cold case investigators with the correct tools to obtain a conviction. As an old colleague, Detective Dan Goodwin, from the Rutherford County Sheriff's Office, Murfreesboro, Tennessee, once said: "Good bad guy hunting."

James M. Adcock, Ph.D.
Sarah L. Stein, Ph.D.

Endnote

1. All the information regarding Sgt. David W. Rivers' initial concept comes from two sources: One is an undated document titled "Metro-Dade County Police Department, Homicide Bureau, Cold Case Squad, Sgt. David W. Rivers." The other was from my personal communications with Rivers at the annual Markle Symposium, April 2004, sponsored by the Henry C. Lee Institute of Forensic Science. The theme for that year's symposium was cold case investigations.

List of Figures

List of Tables

Getting Started: How Do We Prepare to Review and Conduct Cold Case Investigations?

I

What Is a Cold Case and How Did We Get Here?

1

JAMES M. ADCOCK AND SARAH L. STEIN

For the purposes of this book we address the issue of cold cases as it relates only to unsolved homicides. However, the same protocols or evaluation models and subsequent investigative strategies could also be used for unsolved burglaries, rapes, and so forth.

A homicide is defined as a person taking the life of another. Other legal terms and laws may apply depending on the jurisdiction, and it is here that we find the following terms used depending on the legal statutes for the particular jurisdiction: murder (first degree, second degree, etc.), manslaughter (voluntary or involuntary), negligent homicide, and felony DUI.

What is a cold case? Walton[1] writes that because the definition of cold case varies from one jurisdiction to another, it is necessary to differentiate a "cold" case from a "hot" case. A hot case is one that is in the early stages of the investigation after just being reported. Walton[2] goes on to write that the most common events include finding a body where police and investigators have responded to the crime scene and witnesses are interviewed. He continues that the forensic unit responds, the victim is identified, cause and manner of death are determined, and the investigators seek to determine what happened and who did it. "Cause of death" is the medical reason for the death, whereas "manner of death" is the legal classification of the death (homicide, suicide, accident, natural, or undetermined).

The cold case is just that—cold, not hot. It could have occurred yesterday, last week, last month, or decades ago. The common thread we seem to see is that a case becomes cold when all the investigative leads have been exhausted and we know not where to turn. In the Introduction, we mentioned Sgt. David W. Rivers.[3] In the Dade County Sheriff's Office where Rivers worked, a case only became a cold case after the lead investigator for that particular investigation left the homicide bureau. It could have been unsolved for years, but as long as a detective was assigned to the investigation, the case remained open and was frequently investigated. When this lead investigator left the section, the case became classified as a cold case and was assigned to the cold case squad. It could be weeks to years old.

Other law enforcement agencies have their own definition of what a cold case should be. As mentioned earlier, the common thread is that all the investigative leads have been exhausted. Once investigators reach this point, many are filed away as "open," where detectives wait for someone to speak up, or for additional information or evidence to be brought to their attention. This brings to light one of the key elements regarding cold cases and that is the passage of time. As time passes, people change and relationships change, and many witnesses who in the past were not willing to talk to the police may now be willing and able to speak out. Why? Because the threat is gone; that is, the perpetrator has left the neighborhood or has been arrested and is no longer around to harm anyone. Or, the former partner wants revenge or wants alimony or child support from the suspect and now is willing to talk.

Another issue has to do with who the victim was. Unfortunately, prostitutes, the homeless, drug dealers, gang members, and so forth are not always given the same amount of attention by the police that might be given to a banker, a businessman, or some other more fortunate person in the community. Keel[4] writes that when studying police approaches to homicide investigations, demographics play a significant role. Chief among these is policing strategies relative to victim demographics and the notion that police "devalue" victims of certain demographics when investigating complaints. This goes hand in hand with our suggestion that the number of successes could very well be tied to the social or economic status of the victim. Further discussion by Keel will be presented in the next chapter concerning research on solvability issues and concerns.

A personal anecdote about this line of thinking came about during a luncheon I had with a police chief of a reasonably large police department[5] that had a very low clearance rate for homicides. When I asked the chief about this, he responded that the directions to his detectives were for them to give it all they have for the first 48 hours. If not solved by then, the file is left open but placed back in the filing cabinet with no investigative activity being performed unless someone came in and provided additional information. The detectives were no longer actively investigating these cases.

This police chief's philosophy was that most of these victims were prostitutes or drug dealers, and eventually someone would walk in or be arrested for drugs and tell them who killed this person in the hope of making a deal for themselves. His jurisdiction, in addition to these murders, experienced an extremely large number of burglaries and larcenies in the better neighborhoods, and he decided to spend more time and effort on these crimes. Granted, in our opinion, he was correct to a point because during the first few years he reduced these crimes by at least 50 percent, giving the citizenry in his jurisdiction an increased feeling of security and well-being. The murders did not occur in their neighborhoods, so they were less concerned. Meanwhile, the murders of drug dealers and prostitutes continued with few immediate resolutions.

Allow us to add another dimension to this dynamic situation of unresolved homicides. How have the media responded? The media, especially TV shows like *Dateline* and *48 Hours*, emphasize sensationalism, what they feel the public wants to hear or see. How many times have you seen them doggedly report the murder of prostitutes unless they suspect a serial killer? How about drug dealers? They will report the initial incident, but they rarely continue to push the police for more information because they are not felt to be newsworthy. However, let the victim be an upstanding citizen of the community whose house is invaded and who is killed. The media will not only report this up front but will continue to stay on top of the investigation until resolved. Does this contribute to the resolution of the incident? In some cases we are sure that it does because if no one is pushing the law enforcement agency for results, they may put the investigation to the side with no active leads, and instead pursue the "hot" cases that are coming in the door every day. This all goes to the issues of low resources and manpower in our law enforcement agencies, which are overworked and just physically not able to give every investigation the effort we might expect it to receive. It is a necessary measure of prioritization determined by the management within the police department.

There is also the issue of the survivors of homicides: families, loved ones, and friends. Do they not deserve to not only know what happened but see the investigation go to the fullest extent, so they might have some measure of closure? Of course they do. And for every homicide victim, many more survivors are added to the list. Again, like the media, if these survivors were to pursue this or put more pressure on the police department to solve the homicide of their loved one, more would be accomplished.

In Adcock's consultations where the investigation is classified as open but there is no activity being conducted, he has told the family members to stay on top of it, make regular trips to the department, and speak with the detectives involved, or visit the police chief. Let them know that you understand the dilemma they are in but that you are not going away. And, if possible, try to get the media involved to push as well; however, understand that if the victim was a prostitute or drug-addicted person, the media may not want to get involved. Bottom line, those who are persistent and push frequently get results that would not have otherwise occurred.

For decades, the United States has had more homicides than in any other country. Our society is plagued with this stigma, while at the same time mesmerized and fascinated by the mystique that surrounds the act of murder. News media and television play a significant role in the shaping of our views about homicide, and many suspense stories and thrillers have been written that we enjoy reading. We all love a good murder mystery, don't we? Why do we have this fascination with the act of murder? We believe a lot has to do with our desire to solve the unsolvable, to find out who did it and why. The opportunity to solve the ultimate of all crimes, the challenge it puts before us to sort through the information (physical, informational, and behavioral), and determine who did it intrigues us.

Regardless, hot or cold, the detectives tasked with investigating these cases search to answer the same questions:

- What happened?
- When did it happen?
- Where did it happen?
- Who did it?
- Who is the victim?
- Why this victim?
- Why did it happen?

These questions have been cited for years in every criminal investigation book as being the core to a proper criminal investigation. What we cannot move away from is the first question of what happened. The most important question that should be answered is what transpired that culminated in the death of this person, treating all deaths as a homicide until you can prove that it was something else (suicide, accident or natural, or maybe undetermined), thereby establishing that a crime has in fact occurred. Of course, the main thrust always seems to be to determine who did it. Catch the bad guy, make an arrest, and prosecute. As you will see later, understanding the question "why this victim?" becomes paramount, because knowing your victim and why he or she is a victim goes a long way toward understanding the perpetrator, which frequently helps determine who committed the act. And last but not least is "why did it happen?" This question will contribute to determining the motive of the act, "why did this suspect kill this person?"

Historical Perspective

There are many reasons why we are at this point in our history with hundreds, if not thousands, of unresolved homicides. Although no one can specifically explain the phenomenon, the reasons, as well as the types of homicides, vary from jurisdiction to jurisdiction. As we look back at our history, especially from the mid-1950s and 1960s on, we see trends emerging that are strong indicators of what is happening in our society with regard to homicides.

First, the method we utilize in the United States to collect our crime data and report related statistics comes primarily from the yearly Uniform Crime Reports (UCR) managed by the Federal Bureau of Investigation (FBI). As this is a voluntary system, some police departments do not supply their data. Therefore, be careful deducing too much from the results, except to say that it is the only data we have and is probably a good indicator as to what is going on with homicides in our country. The UCR also reports what is termed "clearance rates," which is the percentage of arrests made for the primary crime reported. This could also be labeled as "solved" based on an arrest but not on a conviction.

As stated, clearance rates are those percentages where an arrest has been made in a particular investigation. Over the years, homicides have always been the highest cleared (solved) crime of all the crimes committed or reported through the UCR, and it was not until after the 1960s that we began to see its decline from 93 percent in 1963 to 62 percent in 2007.

At the height of the Vietnam War, around 1967, the UCR began to report a slight rise in the number of homicides. By the 1970s the homicide rate rose above similarly developed countries. Contributing to this rise were the inner cities and the problems encountered by the police with drugs and poverty, making the inner city the most violent it had ever been.[6] Also during this decade, the unemployment rate reached an all-time high in the inner city. Local youth gangs became more powerful, and violent attacks broke out over turf and drugs. Attacks on strangers became more prominent than ever. Even with the new investigative/scientific technology, homicides became more difficult to resolve. Marvin Wolfgang, a criminologist, found that more and more homicides were committed with a decrease in clearance rates because "in comparison with the mid-20th century bottom, there were proportionately more killings of strangers, and in the same streets, fewer at home; more deadly brawls involving many contestants, fewer one-on-one domestic fatalities; more robbery murder; proportionately fewer women arrested; more interracial murder, fewer involving family, friends, or acquaintances."[7]

Add to these factors in the 1970s that in 1955 the homicide rate (per 100,000 population, not to be confused with clearance rate and percentages) was at a low 4.5 per 100,000. By 1974, that rate had more than doubled to 10.2 per 100,000. At the same time, the clearance rate (arrests made) in 1955 was about 90 percent (93 percent in 1963), but in 1974 it had dropped to 80 percent. So the number of homicides more than doubled, while the clearances decreased accordingly.[8]

Also in the 1970s, we began to see the term "serial killers" emerge. Our society was more mobile than ever before. It became clear that a new type of killer was out there committing "stranger-to-stranger" murders. In the 1960s, this type of homicide represented about 6 percent, but by the 1970s, that number had risen to 18 percent—over 4,000 cases a year.[9] However, prior to the 1980s, there was no reliable data about serial killers, which was probably due in part to the lack of coordination of police and their records from one jurisdiction to another.

In the 1980s, the homicide rate remained high, especially through 1982 when it reached 10 per 100,000. Then it declined one point between 1983 and 1990 to about 9 per 100,000, while the clearance rate continued to drop as well. During this decade the serial killer phenomenon continued to grow with a variety of victims, including prostitutes, alcoholics, the homeless, homosexual men, and children. Robert Keppel[10] writes about how he began his 25-year career of studying serial murder investigations in 1974, after being faced with investigating the murders of eight female coeds later attributed to Theodore Robert Bundy. He attributes part of the problem of not solving these cases at the time to "avoidance reaction." He writes, "People, and cops are no different from any other group of people, if given the choice tend to avoid those things which cause them pain, create anxiety, make them uncomfortable, or make them look anything less than successful."[11] Therefore, when they ultimately do succeed, they have to face the reality of what they did wrong.

It was during this decade that the FBI Behavioral Science Unit, designed to study serial killings, coined the phrase "serial murder," distinguishing it from mass and spree killings. Serial murders were characterized as being those homicides committed over a period of months or years. The FBI began developing classifications that would examine the characteristics of the different types of killers as a means of learning how to track them down. Their process of profiling, known today as criminal investigative analysis, has turned into an excellent investigative tool for all cases including unresolved or cold case homicides.

In 1993, the United States had the highest number of murders in its history, exceeding 24,530, while the clearance rate had dropped to 64 percent. In 1997, the number of murders dropped to less than 18,000. Yet the clearance rate had only risen 3 percentage points, to 67 percent. Let's look at that again: We had 28 percent fewer murders, while the clearance rate only increased by 3 percent. Furthermore, while serial murders continued to ravage our society, we also began to see more rage-driven killings than ever before—from road rage killers, to hits against business partners and lovers, to drive-by shootings.[12]

Ten years later, in 2007, the number of homicides dropped to less than 16,000, yet the clearance rate was less than 62 percent. As late as 2012, the number of homicides dropped to 13,092 with a clearance rate of approximately 62.5 percent. Contrast those figures to the ones in the 1960s when the number of homicides was significantly less yet the clearance rate was about 93 percent.[13] When we were at the height of murders in the United States (1993, more than 24,530), one can understand the lower clearance rate, but when the number of homicides significantly drops (approximately 36 percent), one would expect the clearance rate to increase, yet it did not. As a result, we now have thousands of cold case homicides in the country.

Statistics in the form of UCR data are only one part of the equation. What else has contributed to the declining resolution rate of homicides? Scientific technology has leaped forward in the form of computers, databases connecting not only police activity around the country but also databanks for DNA, fingerprints, firearms, and so on. So why haven't we been doing a better job of clearing these cases? First, science, especially DNA, is not the silver bullet that will solve all our cases, because such evidence may not have existed, we failed to recognize it, or we failed to collect the proper evidence. Furthermore, despite the use of DNA to exonerate individuals from our prison system, DNA only resolves approximately 30 percent of all criminal cases. In fact, DNA eliminates or exonerates far more than it identifies perpetrators of crimes. It is not the only answer to cold cases.

As of January 2014, the Innocence Project used DNA to exonerate 312 persons in confinement, all allegedly not guilty for the crimes they were convicted of (Table 1.1).[14] This table is based on information extracted from the Innocence Project Website. Note that the percentages overlap and exceed 100 percent because in many cases more than one reason existed for the wrongful conviction.

Table 1.1 Percentage of Exonerations

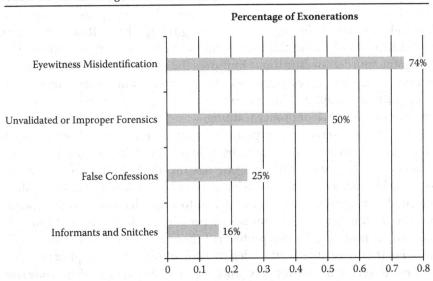

Source: Based on information extracted from the Innocence Project Website (www.innocenceproject.org).

So what happened? As you look at Table 1.1, you can see that in approximately 74 percent of the cases there was a misidentification; 50 percent of the cases had either nonvalidated or improper forensics; in 25 percent, a false confession was involved; and in 16 percent, problems with informants existed. The problem with this picture, however small it may seem compared with all the cases in this country, is that these issues are all related to those who either investigated these cases or served as experts through forensic laboratories.

Those charged with investigating the crimes of today, especially homicides, are challenged beyond belief. They are dedicated professionals who work long hours trying to solve crimes to arrest and convict the perpetrators of these crimes. So we need to look closer at how we have approached these cases. Have we been doing all the right things? Are the detectives adequately equipped to conduct proper and thorough investigations? Are they maximizing their use of the technology available to them today? Are they adequately trained? Are these detectives being properly supervised, and is the investigative process being properly managed?

These questions are very difficult to answer and no one, especially a detective, wants to hear that she or he made a mistake. And it would be safe to wager that there is not one detective out there who wants to put the wrong person in jail. But there are organizational traps that occur where the detective is caught up in the political environment, the forming of tunnel vision, media hype that applies pressure on the detectives, and the investigative process, which can sometimes cause a rush to judgment. Personally, from many years of experience of reviewing cases, we see where tunnel vision is formed, and the detectives can take the wrong direction primarily because they did not have a first-line supervisor guiding them. Research in the United Kingdom[15] and in the United States has proven that periodic review of ongoing murder investigations improves the clearance rate. When there is no case management, key witnesses may be missed and never interviewed. Inadequate and improper interviews or interrogations may be conducted that may indicate lack of proper training.

How did we arrive at the point of so many unresolved homicides? A multitude of reasons have already been highlighted. These have caused us great concern for years. Not everyone has the ability to review a case file, hot or cold, and see the file for what it is and what it tells us. The evaluation models presented here were designed to assist detectives to do a better job. The thoroughness of the models, especially the first model, if properly followed, almost negates the problems inherently seen in other investigations. Furthermore, it provides a department with a new concept of utilizing the private sector in one form or another to assist them in their endeavor to solve these cases for society and the victim's survivors, while saving the department time and money in resources.

Endnotes

1. Walton, Richard H. 2006. *Cold Case Homicides*. CRC Press: Boca Raton, FL.
2. Walton, Richard H. 2006. *Cold Case Homicides*. CRC Press: Boca Raton, FL, p. 3.
3. Rivers, David W. 2004. Personal communication at the Markle Symposium, Foxwood Resort Casinos, CT.
4. Keel, Timothy G., John P. Jarvis, and Yvonne E. Muirhead. February 2009. An exploratory analysis of factors affecting homicide investigations. *Homicide Studies*, 13(1), 50–68.
5. Sweeney, Thomas J. 1998. Police Chief, Bridgeport, Connecticut, personal communication.
6. Scott, Gini Graham. 2007. *American Murder*, Vol. 2, *Homicides in the Late 20th Century*. Praeger: Westport, CT, p. 39.
7. Lanes, Roger. 1997. *Murder in America*. Ohio State University Press: Columbus, OH, p. 303.
8. Scott, Gini Graham. 2007. *American Murder*, Vol. 2, *Homicides in the Late 20th Century*. Praeger: Westport, CT, p. 40.
9. Scott, Gini Graham. 2007. *American Murder*, Vol. 2, *Homicides in the Late 20th Century*. Praeger: Westport, CT, p. 41.
10. Keppel, Robert D., and William J. Birnes. 2003. *The Psychology of Serial Killer Investigations*. Academic Press: New York.
11. Keppel, Robert D., and William J. Birnes. 2003. *The Psychology of Serial Killer Investigations*. Academic Press: New York, p. xvii.
12. Scott, Gini Graham. 2007. *American Murder*, Vol. 2, *Homicide in the Late 20th Century*. Praeger: Westport, CT, p. 149.
13. Riedel, Marc. 1994. Homicide Clearances, Information and Informants: An Alternative View. Paper presented at: Homicide Research Working Group, Atlanta, Georgia, June 13, 1994.
14. Innocence Project. www.innocenceproject.org. Accessed January 8, 2014.
15. Dean, Jones, John Grieve, and Becky Milne. 2008. The case to review murder investigations. Policing advance access. *Policing*, 2, 470–480. doi 10.1093/police/pan053.

Understanding the Process of Homicide and Those Who Kill

2

JAMES M. ADCOCK AND SARAH L. STEIN

The purpose of this chapter is to create a framework of homicide that will help the reader have a better understanding of the homicide process and about those who kill. Besides addressing some of the social issues and theories of homicide, it will take the reader through the historical aspects, beginning with the 1960s as a lead-in to understanding homicides in the past and where we are today. Since most cold cases occurred during these decades, this information should be enlightening. The chapter will discuss some of the research regarding solvability of homicides and will end with a full discussion of the four phases of homicide. All of this will go a long way toward helping the reader understand the challenges faced by the detectives charged with investigating and solving these cases, "hot" or "cold."

Social Scientists' Research on Homicide

Over the years, social scientists have extensively researched the circumstances surrounding murder (homicides). Except for a few situations, they have severely neglected the detectives and the processes utilized to investigate this type of crime. Social scientists have evaluated demographic issues, relationships, location of the incident, types of weapons used as well as economic status of victims and perpetrators, all attempting to determine why these crimes are committed and to hopefully identify what society can do to reduce the number and prevent future episodes.[1]

One such researcher, Luckenbill,[2] describes homicide as a "situated transaction." He writes that the individual and social psychological processes that are a part of the murder event are anchored in volatile social situations: "Murder is conceptualized as an outcome of certain kinds of interactions between potential victims and offenders."[2]

Luckenbill goes on to describe the murder event as a six-stage process that begins with an opening move where the victim does something that is perceived by the offender as a threat. This could have been a verbal statement that the offender took exception to or maybe a refusal to cooperate with the offender. Or it could have been a verbal gesture of defiance. This all progresses into perceptions and involved responses that are encountered, and saving face becomes the issue where physical actions occur. The actors become committed to doing battle, and once the victim has fallen, the offender, more often than not, flees the scene. An interesting conclusion by Luckenbill was that in 70 percent of the cases, the incident occurred before witnesses.

Probably the core theoretical concept about murder comes from the subculture of violence theory proposed by Wolfgang and Ferracuti in 1967.[4] Corzine, Corzine, and Whitt as found in Smith and Zahn[5] explain "some subcultures among groups provide greater normative support than others for violence in upholding such values as honor, courage and manliness." A flaw found in some studies grounded in the Wolfgang and Ferracuti thesis is the implicit assumption that members of groups kill because of their subculture of violence in general.

Rice and Goldman[6] found that homicides in the United States are more likely to occur in the Southern states than in other regions, and arise from arguments rather than from other precipitating events. More often than not, they involve people who know each other instead of strangers, and these relationships between the actors are consistent across areas with different population sizes. Consequently, this suggests that the rural character of the South does not account for its regional homicide patterns.

What about homicide as "conflict resolution?" According to Simmel,[7] conflict is defined as a "resolution of divergent dualism," a way of achieving some kind of unity, even if it means that someone is killed. Further, as the study of homicide has progressed through the years, it mostly dealt with static features such as location of occurrence; type of weapon employed; or race, age, and gender of the actors involved, and later the issues of victim precipitation. Then, as mentioned earlier, Luckenbill described a theory of homicide as being a "situated transaction."

In 1980, Levi[8] managed to put together a study grounded in the theoretical premises of Simmel (conflict) and Luckenbill (situated transaction) to explain the act of homicide as a form of conflict resolution. He used Luckenbill's theory as his conceptual framework and integrated Simmel's theory on conflict. So we take the situated transaction and incorporate conflict, with the end result being conflict resolved with the killing of another human being.

In keeping with Luckenbill's premise, Levi adopted, with little alteration, the six-stage process seen in the situated transaction. These are designed like a game—the game of homicide—where six "pieces" are considered in the transaction: (1) the victim's opening move, (2) the offender's interpretation, (3) the offender's retaliation, (4) a "working agreement" to use violence, (5) combat, and (6) the killer's departure from the scene.

In stage four, contrary to Luckenbill, Levi determined that strangers will not always make a face-saving gesture and will in fact make every effort to run. Levi found that the killers felt trapped and were as fearful as the victim, and that they were going to be hurt by the victim with no immediate known avenue of escape. The objective of stage four, the working agreement, is to have the killer conceive of violence as a necessary and appropriate response.

What is the difference between normal conflict situations and those that involve homicide? Levi would suggest that the homicidal situation contains more "facilitators," such as weapons, concealment from the law or "an appropriate self image on the part of the offender."[9] But is this enough? He further posits that there is also probably a motive to kill that is suggested by the facilitators. He concludes his position by writing that with homicide one can be assured that a conflict resolution dynamic played a role, and that future research should attempt to determine when conflict resolutions lead to homicides and when they do not.

Collins[10] defines micro-sociology as dealing "with relatively small slices of space, time and numbers of persons with the individual and the interaction, with behavior and consciousness." In this concept, the ritual model proposes that different social groups can have different kinds and amounts of solidarity, and particular individuals can internalize certain strengths, all based on the ritual experience. This group comes together because they have common ideas and goals, like a detective unit in a police department. They have a focus of attention, a common emotional mood, and they have sacred objects or symbols (e.g., badge, gun) that represent their membership in the group. This all leads to an enhanced emotional energy and confidence for those in the group and creates anger and punishment for those who disrespect the sacred objects. The same could be said of street gangs.

Another interesting perspective comes from Abraham Maslow's hierarchy of needs theory. The case study:

In November 1966, an eighteen-year-old student, Robert Smith, walked into a hairdressing parlor, ordered four young women and a three-year-old girl to lie face down on the floor, and began blasting away with a shotgun, killing them all. Afterward, when he was led away by the police, he proclaimed to the press why he did it. "I wanted to get known, to get myself a name. ... I knew I had to kill a lot of people to get my name in the newspapers all over the world."[11]

The authors of the concept describe this as a crime of self-esteem that could correspond to Maslow's theory. They go on to state that at the bottom of the scale individuals are motivated by the need to survive, and any killings at this level would be motivated by this urge. Scott writes:

Once this need is satisfied, the individual looks for security; this could also include crimes with financial gain. On the next level is the need for sex, love and companionship, triggering the kinds of killings motivated by love triangles, jealousy, and romantic passion. Then, the need to be recognized and respected; in other words, the need for self-esteem. If this level is satisfied, a final level that sometimes emerges is the need for "self actualization," expressed through various creative means.[12]

Although this may be a stretch, we found it interesting enough to insert in this chapter.

Homicide During the 1960s to 1990s

As we look at homicide from a historical perspective beginning with the 1960s when the clearance rate in 1963 was at its peak of 93 percent, we see the act of homicide changing over the decades. According to murder historian Roger Lane as found in Scott,[13] following the assassination of President John F. Kennedy in November 1963, we moved into a more violent and angry decade. Lane points out that television became the major source of news, and horrible crimes of murder were publicized more "graphically" than ever before. Furthermore, the Civil Rights movement was in full force, where social unrest contributed to the rise of the homicide rate heretofore not seen in the United States.

The movement of African Americans to the inner cities coupled with the white middle class flight to the suburbs led to an impoverished inner city, which led in turn to an increase of urban homicides. At the same time, there was a growing mistrust of the police by African Americans due to their experiences with the "Southern justice system." All these issues fueled the growing number of conflicts and homicides throughout the nation, from the simply motivated personal killings to homicides for social reasons.

Over the next few years our city streets were filled with violent protests over our involvement in the Vietnam War. In Oakland, California, black activists such as the Black Panthers entered into an escalating war with the local police and the Federal Bureau of Investigation (FBI). Social unrest was the theme for many years, protesting not only the Vietnam War but also a general attitude of anti-authoritarian defiance against the government and illegal drug use that contributed to the clashes with authorities. Furthermore, there was disbelief of the Warren Commission's conclusion (1964) that Lee Harvey Oswald was alone in the assassination of John F. Kennedy. This was followed by the assassination of other prominent figures in our society: Malcolm X (February 1965), Dr. Martin Luther King, Jr. (April 1968), Robert F. Kennedy (June 1968), and Black Panthers leader Fred Hampton (December 1969).

While the theme of the hippie movement of the 1960s was "make love, not war," it turned ugly toward the end of the decade: from the euphoric concert at

Woodstock, New York, to the Altamont concert in northern California where the Hells Angels killed a concertgoer, to the murders of Sharon Tate and Rosemary La Bianca by the team assembled by Charles Manson, all in 1969. This apparent senselessness was the beginning of something new that came to increasingly characterize the homicides in the decades to follow.[14] The stage was set for the big explosion that came in the 1970s, 1980s, and 1990s, as growing social alienation and the breakdown of traditional social institutions led to a growth of homicides, including the Zodiac Killer in California, the Boston Strangler, and Richard Speck in Chicago, to name a few.

As mentioned in Chapter 1, around 1967, we started seeing a rise in the number of homicides. As we entered the 1970s the homicide rate significantly increased. Social scientists write that this rise was partly due to the problems in the inner cities where unemployment, drugs, and poverty expanded, making the cities more violent places than ever before. Local gangs became more important and powerful, starting the saga of turf wars and violent attacks on strangers. This all contributed to the inability of police to solve these cases as they had previously been able to do. The times had changed and so had the homicides.

The social environment proved to be fertile ground for new and different types of killers. Some, like Ted Kaczynski, who got his start in the 1970s as the Unabomber and for 17 years baffled the FBI with his manifestos and bombings of innocent people, were motivated by ideology and generalized anger against society. Along these same lines, the left-wing Weatherman group began its own bombing campaign. During this decade we also saw a growing trend of mass murders and serial killings. It is here that we believe new technology and advancements helped the serial killers carry out their crimes more easily due to the availability of cars and trucks used to kidnap their victims and take them far away from the kidnap site to be killed and later disposed of. According to Scott, "The anonymity of the city, coupled with the great openness and sensuality of the 1970s, contributed to their ability to attract victims and escape later."[15]

The media helped to keep the public eye on these murders as they tracked the actions of police and the story of the victims, as was seen in newscasts regarding John Wayne Gacy in Chicago; the Hillside Strangler in Los Angeles; and Ted Bundy's attacks on coeds in the Pacific Northwest, Colorado, and finally Florida. The serial killer phenomenon continued with killings in the Sacramento, California, area by Richard Chase, who was dubbed the "Dracula Killer" because he drank his victims' blood. And there was Ed Kemper killing coeds throughout the state of California to get back at his mother. All these cases caused psychologists, psychiatrists, and sociologists to conduct serious studies on the problem in an effort to understand the killers and what was happening.

The police were having a very difficult time resolving these cases. Today, after learning from our mistakes during the previous decades (1960s to 1990s), Keppel (one of the foremost authorities on serial murders) and Birnes[16] suggest the following to police departments:

> Consider the frequency of similar homicide cases throughout the region.
> Use modus operandi (M.O.), ritualistic and non-ritualistic behaviors to link cases.
> Determine the central theme among linked cases.
> For ritualistic behaviors, use the rarity of each factor as a step in using each behavior in the final signature determination.
> Combine ritualistic and nonritualistic features to determine the rarity of identifying a grouping of characteristics as a signature element.
> Heed the intent of the known words of the killer.
> Obtain the entire homicide file for each incident.
> State the final signature in terms of a summary that identifies a central theme to the series and those factors or constructs that make up that central theme.

In order to combat the increase in stranger-to-stranger serial murders, detectives started using the services of psychologists, psychiatrists, and profilers to help them understand and catch these killers. To add insult to injury, the media and public fascination with serial killers was starting to explode and it is believed this helped to inspire even more killers, attracted to the prospect of fame and notoriety. "In short, as the number of serial killers multiplied, so did the wide variety of killers, victims, motives, psychological dynamics, and methods, contributing to the difficulty of discovering the killers," writes Scott.[17]

As we entered the 1980s, the rate of homicides remained high through 1982 but declined slightly (to the rate of 9 per 100,000) through the next 8 years, while the serial killer phenomenon continued to grow. With this decade being the Reagan years, there was a shift in the social climate toward conservatism, resulting in a crackdown on all types of crimes. This drew more attention to the serial killers and the problems they presented to the society. We saw further fascination with murder from the media and new television cop shows and movies, for example, *Hill Street Blues, Beverly Hills Cop, Rambo: First Blood Part II*, and the *Die Hard* films. These tended to make police officers and crime fighters out to be heroes who were going to save our society from the evil in our midst.

There seemed to be a fear in society of the crime and the subsequent crackdowns inspired by the media exposure of serial killers. Specifically, the decade started seeing a change in serial killers moving from the classic victim of the past (primarily young, attractive women) to prostitutes, alcoholics, the homeless, homosexual men, and children. Americans began blaming the breakdown of the moral fabric of society with too much tolerance for divorce, abortion, homosexuality, drugs, and sexual promiscuity from the 1960s and 1970s as the reasons for the significant increase in murders and serial killers. Along these same lines it is interesting to note that the execution statistics reflected the attitude of the times: Between 1967 and 1976, there were no executions; between 1977 and 1981 there were 4; yet between 1984 and 1987 there were 82.[18]

Another example of the change in time for this decade was the Atlanta child murders that occurred during the early 1980s. These murders were different from other serial killings: The victims were young African American children, which was very unusual for serial killers as we knew them at the time, and the perpetrator himself was also black, which also did not fit the usual mold for a serial killer at that time. This case added to the fears about the safety of our children. It also was the beginning of a new era for the FBI, as its newly established Behavioral Science Unit played a significant role in bringing the Atlanta child murders case to a close with the conviction of Wayne Williams.[19]

In the next decade, specifically in 1993, the number of homicides rose to its highest number ever: 24,530. During the next 15 years, as mentioned in Chapter 1, this number steadily declined. And from the 1990s to today, our system has been marked with tremendous scientific advancements, yet the clearance rate has consistently been in the neighborhood of 62 percent. One would have thought that with these great advancements the clearance rate would have increased, which suggests that something else may be contributing to the number of unresolved homicides.

As time progressed, murder continued to receive front-page headlines in the 1990s; in fact, due to television shows like *Court TV* (later renamed *True TV*), *20/20*, *Dateline*, and others, murder has turned somewhat into a real-life soap opera of entertainment. One of the most captivating cases of all was *Court TV*'s coverage of the O. J. Simpson murder trial in Los Angeles. It was here that we saw DNA and forensic science take center stage. The debates about DNA that followed this trial significantly contributed to its acceptance in the legal community. Today we see it every day in the news, not to mention on television shows like *CSI* where it is glamorized and taunted as the silver bullet to solve all cases. The problem with that analogy is that DNA is not a cure-all because it only resolves about 27 percent of the cases.[20] In fact, it eliminates far more persons of interest than it identifies.

Scott, in her book *American Murder*, writes[21]:

> To some extent, homicide has continued to remain the most local of crimes, because it often results from conflicts within the family or intimate social networks, arising out of feelings of rage, jealousy, greed, revenge, and other

motivations. At the same time, some murders have become increasingly impersonal, as alienated, mobile individuals have turned their feelings against strangers or society as a whole. Such changes in the pattern of homicide have made the modern killer in the 1990s and today more difficult to catch in some ways—they are more alien and unknown, their reasons for killing more obscure, their motivations and ties to their victims less understood, all of which make their crimes that much more baffling.

Before we leave the 20th century that saw such a rise in homicides from the 1960s to the 1990s, peaking in 1993 and then significantly declining over the next 10 to 15 years, while the clearance rate also declined, we might want to count ourselves lucky, especially in light of a study conducted by Harris et al. regarding the subjects of murder and medicine.[22] They write "despite the proliferation of increasingly dangerous weapons and the very large increase in rates of serious criminal assault, since 1960 the lethality of such assault in the United States has dropped dramatically." Consider the premise that homicides are nothing more than aggravated assaults where the victim ended up dying. Therefore, the downward trend in lethality could parallel the developments in medical technology along with other medical support service.

Using the baseline from the 1960s, the authors state that "without this technology the U.S. would presently be experiencing 45,000 to 70,000 homicides a year instead of an actual 15,000 to 20,000." They conclude that their study showed there was a strong "relationship between lethality and a set of medical variables, including presence of a hospital, presence of a trauma center, and countywide membership within a coordinated regional trauma system." Without more research in this area we will never know for sure whether this is in fact accurate, but regardless, it makes sense and we probably need to be thankful for the developments in the medical sciences and their respective procedures.

Solvability Research

The research that exists has predominantly focused on demographic data, victim–offender relationships, location of the incident, types of weapons used, and so on, while very little has addressed the detectives or the investigative process and its relationship to solvability of a case. In 1994, Keppel[23] published research that described different time and distance factors as having a bearing on the solvability of homicides. These factors were:

1. Victim last seen site
2. Initial contact site
3. Initial assault site

4. Murder site
5. Body recovery site

In this research Keppel found six major implications in dealing with these data: (1) the more information that is known about times and distances among locations of a murder incident, the more likely the case will be solved; (2) knowing the dates of occurrence for the locations significantly improves the ability to identify the offender; (3) as time separating pairs of locations decreases, solvability increases; (4) the rate of solvability drastically increases when the investigators know more of the distances between pairs of the five locations; (5) "the shorter the actual distances between locations, particularly less than 200 feet, the greater the percentage of solved cases"; and (6) "solvability improves as both times and distances, together, decrease among pairs of locations, especially between Victim Last Seen and the Body Recovery Site."[24]

In 1999, Wellford and Cronin found that police response times and the number of detectives responding to the incident are important variables for understating clearances. Furthermore, the availability of witnesses and effective investigation of the information are of paramount concern in determining clearance issues.[25] In 2001, an Australian study found that unsolved homicides are more likely to occur in the course of another crime involving a single victim versus multiple victims and when they occur in a nonresidential setting.[26]

Keel[27] conducted a study on homicide investigations in which he reports that by utilizing the best practices standards of successful homicide units, supervisors of other units can in fact increase their clearances. He goes on to name the keys to a successful homicide investigation, followed by data results in each element.

No more than five cases per year as a primary for each detective. (Keel found that concerning caseloads, detectives who handled fewer than five per year as a primary had a 5.4 percent higher clearance rate.)

Minimum of two 2-person units responding initially to the crime scene.

Case review by all involved personnel within the first 24 to 72 hours.

Computerized case management system with relational capacity.

Standardized and computerized car-stop and neighborhood canvas forms.

Compstat-style format. (Those who used Compstat had a 3.3 percent higher clearance rate.)

Effective working relationships with medical examiners and prosecutors. (Those departments that have a good to excellent working relationship with their prosecutor had a 6.2 percent higher clearance rate than those with relationships rated at fair to poor.)

No rotation policy for homicide detectives.

Accessibility to work overtime when needed. (Those departments that did not require supervisory approval for overtime had a 9 percent higher clearance rate than those who did require the approval.)

Cold case squads.

Investigative tools, for example, polygraph, bloodstain pattern analysis, criminal investigative analysis, and statement analysis. (Those departments using investigative tools like bloodstain pattern analysis experienced a 4.8 percent higher clearance rate; those who used criminal investigative analysis experienced a 5.7 percent higher rate; and those that did utilize statement analysis had a 5.2 percent higher clearance rate.)

Homicide unit and other personnel work as a team.

The bottom line to all of these is that no single element will guarantee a higher clearance rate, but by assessing all of these and making the appropriate adjustments, commanders will increase the odds that their homicide clearance rates will be higher.

Keel, Jarvis, and Muirhead,[28] in their article, "An Exploratory Analysis of Factors Affecting Homicide Investigations," concluded that (1) the processes of management within a detective unit is a delicate balance between oversight and accountability that has to ensure latitude for the detectives to conduct their investigations; (2) homicide clearances can be increased with the utilization of analytical methods; and (3) formal training of the detectives significantly increases clearances, but the police cannot solve these crimes without the full assistance of the public and other agencies. Another important point they raised addresses a process called "devaluing" the victim based on his or her social status. Those cases involving victims from a higher status are much more likely to be solved than those from a lower economic position in society. This goes back to an earlier premise we made concerning the prostitute or drug addict victims not getting the same attention as those from the upper echelons of our society.

The Phases of Homicide

In a 2005 lecture on serial killers, Keppel[29] described how, with sexual serial killings, there are four phases of homicide: (1) the antecedent phase, (2) the homicide, (3) the body disposal, and (4) the post-offense behavior. Although his lecture focused on sexual serial killers, the same four phases could also apply to other homicides, particularly if they contained a sexual element, but were not necessarily serial killings. Phases 1, 2, and 4 are particularly interesting because they fall right in line with Chapter 10 of this book on pre-, peri-, and post-offense behavior issues of the perpetrator. When reviewing unresolved homicides be sure to keep these points in mind. In cold cases you have much more information before you than your colleague might have had the day the crime was reported, and in some ways that makes this easier. The following is a thumbnail sketch of the questions that need answering to establish the four phases.

In Phase 1, the perpetrator's behavior prior to the crime is what is important. As we look at the investigation, crime scene, evidence, the body site, and so forth, are there any indications of prior planning? What types of pre-crime stressors occurred in this person's life that were the catalyst for him moving into Phase 2 and the murder? For example, a change in his mental or emotional state, a conflict with a girlfriend, loss of job, an argument with family or parents, or financial problems.

In Phase 2, the actual murder takes place. Questions that need answering are: How was the victim selected? Why this victim over any other? What was the method of abduction and why that over any other method? What did he do to the victim and how did he do it? Where did he go to murder her? Did he leave his "signature" or calling card at the scene?[30] Were there any post-mortem injuries?

Phase 3 is related to the body disposal site. Here the investigators need to determine how the body was transported to this location; why this site over any other site; were there any attempts to conceal the body or was it open to public view; was the victim posed in a certain manner, sexually suggestive or not; state of dress or undress, and so on. Many of these could be important issues to the killer. He may want the victim discovered or he may want to shock society with his acts.

And finally, Phase 4, the post-offense behavior. What did he do after disposing of the body? Did he flee, get sick, overindulge in alcohol or drugs, not show up for work or school, or did he return to the disposal site?

All of these questions will become relevant as you progress through this book, especially when you reach the chapters dealing with the pre-, peri-, and post-offense behavior issues and as you develop your suspectology and the pros and cons for each particular person of interest in your case file. In the next chapter, you will be provided with information on how to create a cold case team, its concepts, and stumbling blocks.

Endnotes

1. Adcock, James M. 2001. Solving Murders South Carolina Style: Solvability Factors of Murders in Three South Carolina Counties, 1988–1992. Dissertation, University of South Carolina.
2. Luckenbill, D. 1977. Criminal Homicide as a Situated Transaction, *Social Problems, 25*. Society for the Study of Social Problems.

3. Keppel, Robert D. 1994. Time and Distance as Solvability Factors in Murder Cases, *Journal of Forensic Sciences*, *39*(2).

4. Wolfgang, M. E., and F. Ferracuti. 1967. *The Subculture of Violence*. Tavistock: London.

5. Smith, Dwayne M., and Margaret A. Zahn, Eds. 1999. *Homicide, A Sourcebook of Social Research*. Sage: Thousand Oaks, CA; p. 43.

6. Rice, T. W., and C. R. Goldman. 1994. Another Look at the Subculture of Violence Thesis: Who Murders Whom and Under What Circumstances, *Sociological Review*, *14*, 371–384.

7. Simmel, Georg. 1955. *Conflict and the Web of Group Affiliations*. K. H. Wolff and R. Bendix (trans.). Free Press: New York.

8. Levi, Ken. 1980. Homicide as Conflict Resolution, *Deviant Behavior: An Interdisciplinary Journal*, *1*, 281–307.

9. Levi, Ken. 1980. Homicide as Conflict Resolution, *Deviant Behavior: An Interdisciplinary Journal*, *1*, 304.

10. Collins, Randall. 1988. *Theoretical Sociology*. Harcourt Brace Jovanovich: FL; p. 3.

11. Wilson, Colin, and Damon Wilson. 1995. *The Killers Among Us, Book I: Motives Behind Their Madness*. Warner: New York; p. 11.

12. Scott, Gini Graham. 2007. *American Murder*, Vol. 2, *Homicide in the Late 20th Century*. Praeger: Westport, CT; p. 8.

13. Scott, Gini Graham. 2007. *American Murder*, Vol. 2, *Homicide in the Late 20th Century*. Praeger: Westport, CT; p. 8.

14. Scott, Gini Graham. 2007. *American Murder*, Vol. 2, *Homicide in the Late 20th Century*. Praeger: Westport, CT; p. 5.

15. Scott, Gini Graham. 2007. *American Murder*, Vol. 2, *Homicide in the Late 20th Century*. Praeger: Westport, CT; p. 43.

16. Keppel, Robert D., and William J. Birnes. 2009. *Serial Violence, Analysis of Modus Operandi and Signature Characteristics of Killers*. CRC Press: Boca Raton, FL; p. 223.

17. Scott, Gini Graham. 2007. *American Murder*, Vol. 2, *Homicide in the Late 20th Century*. Praeger: Westport, CT; p. 47.

18. Scott, Gini Graham. 2007. *American Murder*, Vol. 2, *Homicide in the Late 20th Century*. Praeger: Westport, CT; p. 88.

19. Scott, Gini Graham. 2007. *American Murder*, Vol. 2, *Homicide in the Late 20th Century*. Praeger: Westport, CT; p. 91.

20. Today@coloradoXState. www.today.colostate.edu/printstory.aspx?ID=1882. Accessed August 12, 2009.

21. Scott, Gini Graham. 2007. *American Murder*, Vol. 2, *Homicide in the Late 20th Century*. Praeger: Westport, CT; pp. 152–153.

22. Harris, Anthony R., Stephen H. Thomas, Gene A. Fisher, and David J. Hirsch. 2002. Murder and Medicine, the Lethality of Criminal Assault 1960–1999, *Homicide Studies*, *6*(2), 128–166, 2 (abstract).

23. Keppel, Robert D. 1994. Time and Distance as Solvability Factors in Murder Cases, *Journal of Forensic Sciences*, *39*(2).

24. Keppel, Robert D. 1994. Time and Distance as Solvability Factors in Murder Cases, *Journal of Forensic Sciences*, *39*(2), 400.

25. Wellford, C., and J. Cronin, 1999. *An Analysis of Variables Affecting the Clearance of Homicides: A Multistate Study.* Washington, DC: Justice Research and Statistics Association.
26. Mouzos, J., and D. Muller. 2001. Solvability Factors of Homicide in Australia: An Exploratory Analysis. *Trends and Issues in Crime and Criminal Justice,* 216. Australian Institute of Criminology, Canberra.
27. Keel, Timothy G. 2008. Homicide Investigations, Identifying Best Practices, *FBI Law Enforcement Bulletin, 77*(2). Federal Bureau of Investigation, Washington, DC.
28. Keel, Timothy G., John P. Jarvis, and Yvonne E. Muirhead. 2009. An Exploratory Analysis of Factors Affecting Homicide Investigations, *Homicide Studies, 13*(1), 50–68.
29. Keppel, Robert D. 2005. Lecture on Serial Killers at the West Haven Police Department, West Haven, CT.
30. Keppel, Robert D., and William J. Birnes. 2009. *Serial Violence, Analysis of Modus Operandi and Signature Characteristics of Killers.* CRC Press: Boca Raton, FL.

Creating a Cold Case Squad (Concepts for Initialization)

3

JAMES M. ADCOCK AND SARAH L. STEIN

Depending on the political climate, creating a cold case squad can be a very difficult and challenging task. In this chapter, while outlining the steps others have taken, we hope to provide the reader with some sound advice and approaches. There is no perfect way to do this because each department, jurisdiction, and crime and demographics in that jurisdiction are going to be different. What works in Baltimore, Maryland, may not work in Atlanta, Georgia. But the concepts and goals of the squad will remain the same regardless of the location. As these concepts are presented, keep in mind that your goal is to obtain a conviction, not just make an arrest.

For decades, detectives have been taught and worked under the premise that if you do not solve the homicide within 48 to 72 hours, then your chances of solving it significantly diminish, with a strong likelihood it will remain unresolved. To a certain extent we are confident this is true; however, with the advent of cold case squads we are seeing a different outcome. Those that seemed unsolvable 10, 20, or 30 years ago are now being successfully resolved. Although many of these have been resolved due to scientific advancements (e.g., DNA), only about 27 percent of all cases are actually resolved through the use of DNA. But what DNA has done is create a new and exciting environment with the hope that we can go back in time and solve these old cases for the sake of justice and the families that were left behind.

During the 1990s, before DNA really got a foothold in our criminal justice system, the emphasis was on crime scenes and physical evidence. Following the theory of the French forensic scientist Locard, "every contact leaves a trace," our system kept going back to the crime scene for that connection, however mystifying it might have seemed at the time. Remember that in 1993 we had 24,530 murders, the highest ever in our history, with a clearance rate of 67 percent. Since the scientific community was rapidly progressing, the distance between what was happening at the crime scene and at the crime laboratory was getting farther and farther apart. The emphasis was to find a way to bridge this gap between what the police departments were collecting at the crime scene and what the crime laboratory needed. Education and training had much to do with bridging the gap, but more and better crime scene techniques needed to be employed for maximum results.

As a possible response to this problem, the National Institute of Justice, after a thorough survey research project, published *Death Investigation: A Guide for the Crime Scene Investigator.*[1] This document was specifically designed to serve as a guide for detectives and medico-legal death investigators working with coroners and medical examiners to help bridge that gap between the crime scene and the crime laboratory. It also caused the creation of the American Board of Medico-Legal Death Investigators (AMBDI),[2] which subsequently designed death investigation standards whereby these death investigators could become certified in the field of death investigation through course attendance for training and periodic testing to maintain certification.

So why bother, or who cares about these cold cases? Why bother? Today, the detective is equipped with tremendous advancements in forensic science that she or he never had before, from DNA to a nationwide fingerprint database (for more forensic-related technology and possibilities, see Chapter 9). We are better equipped and we are doing a better job of communicating across the nation from one department to another, from local to state to federal agencies like never before. And who cares? All of us should care whether these cases are successfully resolved. Beyond the confines of the police department, the families and the survivors of these homicides deserve some closure. These relatives have constantly struggled to understand the death, maybe looking for forgiveness, possessing anger and even thoughts of retribution. As Cooper and King write, "To them the passage of time may soften the blow, but with each and every news story portraying events that are similar to the real-life experience they have endured, the emotions flood back. Each time this occurs, renewed concerns, questions and uncertainty arise."[3]

Contrary to the early belief that as time passes the case becomes less and less likely to be solved, with cold cases time can actually become our ally, not our enemy. All of this, of course, starts with the scientific advances that have already been mentioned and will be elaborated on in Chapter 9. Beyond science, time also has given all the witnesses time to reflect; for many, their relationships have changed to the point where today they may be willing to talk to police because the threat is no longer in their neighborhood or in their homes. Now they have gained new courage to step up, and relate facts and circumstances heretofore not known or not documented in the case file. Others may have become religious and want to get what they know off their chest. Or the perpetrator may actually think she or he has gotten away with murder and start bragging about it in bars, clubs, on the street, or in jail.

Then there are those who have been arrested by the police for a crime and may ask for leniency or a deal if they can tell the police about another's fate, helping the police solve a cold case of murder. A perpetrator may have been arrested and gone to jail for an unrelated offense, or die from a crime or natural causes. While in jail this person may have talked about his previous adventures to other inmates, again showing that the passage of time does help the cold case investigator. As time passes, evidence and witnesses may diminish but the resolve in our justice system should never die in the eyes of the law enforcers.

If nothing but good can come from revisiting these cold cases, why are some departments reluctant to venture in that direction? As stated earlier, a lot has to do with the political climate of the department at the time you are seeking to start a cold case squad. The political gain from solving one of these old cases will go a long way to helping you solve more, because the chief will love the opportunity to tell the press and his citizenry that we never forget. But departmental management is reluctant because resources are required in the form of personnel and sometimes money for training, equipment, and so forth. Why should the chief take two detectives off the road, so to speak, and put them on a cold case team? In our opinion the answer to that question is, it is the right thing to do; but as you read earlier police chiefs have differences of opinions as to how they should manage their departments and crime issues.

Ideally, the detectives selected to be on the cold case team must be separated from the other detectives. Their mission has to be nothing but cold cases. They cannot be on call like other detectives to respond to the everyday crime issues that come to the department's attention. They have to be able to focus entirely on the cold cases. The downside to this is that sometimes the other detectives become jealous and feel the cold case team members are special "pets" of management, and this can cause dissension in the ranks. When we say separated from the rest of the squad, we mean that they should have separate office space with administrative support that should include a crime analyst. The goal is to solve cases with a conviction, and for every one they solve, the department will gain in stature and in public opinion.

Understanding the drawbacks of the decision to create the cold case squad is the first hurdle. Beyond that, many other issues have to be addressed. What will be the format of the team? Which detectives do you select for this position? How much experience do you want them to have? What type of special expertise can they bring to the table that others do not have? The first thing mentioned is format. Across the country we see different structures relating to cold case teams. Some are just a couple of detectives put in a room to review and work the cases with no outside influences or duties.[4] Some departments have gone to their retired detectives and rehired them just to conduct cold case investigations. Others work for the local district attorney or prosecutor. And in a few, we have seen the departments go outside the law enforcement community and solicit the assistance of the private sector or college students, such as the Tulsa (Oklahoma) Police Department and its "Gray Squad" (Appendix A).

In addition to Tulsa's Gray Squad, similar formats have appeared in other parts of the country. The Charlotte-Mecklenburg, North Carolina, police department established its cold case team in 2003 with a blend of sworn officers and civilian volunteers consisting of a retired Duke Energy engineer and a professor from the University of North Carolina. As of late 2007, the team had reviewed 65 cases and cleared 17 of those. The Las Vegas Police Department had three part-time civilian volunteers. And in Chicago they use interns from local universities to assist with clerical tasks.[5]

As you will see by the end of this book, it is with this last format that the proposed cold case model is most advantageous. Police departments today are inundated with hot cases of all types. Most of the detectives in these departments are overworked and their caseloads are too high. So why not select one very seasoned detective and have that person select and supervise an evaluation team from the private sector to determine whether they should invest the investigative time and manpower in investigating certain cold cases? The Tulsa Police Department carefully chose certain citizens from various professions in the community and asked for their assistance in evaluating cold cases. After these people passed background checks, they were allowed access to the cold cases in the department under the supervision of a seasoned detective. This format and effort was very successful with many resolutions and convictions.

From a management standpoint, this format helps alleviate some of the potential dissension in the ranks because only one detective is being pulled from the division, even if it is part time. When it comes to the point of conducting the follow-up investigation of a cold case, they can solicit the help of the other detectives to accomplish this task. This way all detectives get a slice of the pie and it is a team effort from which everyone will benefit. The key element here is proper supervision of the evaluators and management of the evaluation process, and if you use a thorough system, such as the cold case evaluation model, then your chances of success will significantly increase.

The next question is, which detective or detectives do you select to conduct this effort of evaluating and investigating cold cases? Earlier I mentioned the "seasoned" detective, and while that is normally your choice, keep in mind that experience alone does not make a detective a good detective. This is a very important aspect, and the success or failure of your endeavors with the creating of the cold case squad may very well hinge on whom you select. When we look at the traits of those we want on such a team we see many attributes. As suggested by Walton[6] these could include:

Ability to think and act objectively
Ability to ask the right questions
A positive "can-do" attitude
Knowledge of modern investigative methods
Knowledge of advances in science and technology
Ability to work as a team member
Knowledge of the mechanics of homicide investigation

Knowledge of the variations in homicide law
Skill in interview techniques
Excellent oral and communication skills
Strong deductive and inductive reasoning skills
Good listening skills
Knowledge of crime scene reconstruction
Knowledge of behavioral types

Additionally, we suggest that departments consider hiring a crime analyst to conduct some of the mundane tasks like organizing the case file, running criminal record checks, locating witnesses, and notating the investigative plan. A colleague who used to be a state police detective in Mississippi used college students to organize cold case files, saving him a great deal of time before he reviewed them for solvability factors and potential investigative strategies. In 2007, the Milford Police Department in Connecticut hired (part time) a former graduate student who had had experience evaluating cold cases while a graduate student at the University of New Haven. She organized the files, verified that evidence was still in the evidence room, prepared an investigative plan based on what she thought was left to do in the investigation, and based on the behavioral aspects of the persons of interest, came up with interrogation strategies for each one. Her written report was subsequently given to the captain of detectives for disposition as he deemed appropriate.

If a department is willing to select detectives from its detective division and form a cold case squad, there should be a well-balanced team with regard to expertise. Every person must bring something to the table that will be beneficial to the team as a whole. Having one who is particularly good at interviews and interrogations would be a plus; having another who is a former crime scene technician would also be helpful; racial diversity might also be a consideration; analytical skills and intuitiveness help to create a well-balanced team. Also, remember, the goal is to convict, not just make an arrest. It is also suggested that you get a local prosecutor to obligate himself or herself to the team. You want your legal advice to be consistent, and you want to make sure that the prosecutor is confident in taking the case to court. Having a prosecutor involved from the beginning will satisfy that requirement and ensure better results.

Another issue that management should address is the training that the cold case team has or needs. The primary areas of concern would be a cold case training workshop or seminar, crime scene reconstruction, bloodstain pattern analysis, interviews and interrogations, advanced homicide investigation, and criminal investigative analysis (referred to in the past as psychological profiling) training for gauging the behavioral aspects of the actors involved in the murder. Of course, some of these might not be necessary if the personnel selection process ensured these training modules were already accounted for.

Then there is office space and equipment to consider. As stated earlier, the cold case squad should be in an office by itself away from the everyday activities of the detective division. The solitude and a quiet working area are paramount. The office must be equipped with computers, telephones, radios, and so on. These detectives may need photographic equipment for surveillance or other activities, and of course vehicles, to name a few of the staple items every detective needs to accomplish his or her job.

The biggest hurdle is getting the approval to form the team. In doing this make sure the ground rules are well established and understood by management, to include personnel selection, office space, equipment, training, funds, and administrative staff. Writing a standard operating procedure (SOP) (or policy and procedures) manual would be beneficial as well. A good example of this is one prepared in January 2004 by James M. Gannon, formerly of the Morris County Prosecutor's Office, Morristown, New Jersey.[7] It consists of the usual information such as purpose of the unit, personnel selection, solvability factors, case processing, the strategies of time, technology, and tenacity (taken from the Navy Criminal Investigative Service), investigative steps, exceptional clearance, and case management.

Another good example of how to organize and structure a cold case unit can be found in the Metropolitan Police Department (MPD) in Washington, DC. Rumor has it that it has one of the most successful programs in the country. Its processes of categorization and prioritization of information are reflective of what Walton[8] mentions as being appropriate procedures for such specialized units, which are described further in this chapter.

Once all this is accomplished, the next step is to locate the case files that have been closed in the files of the department pending the receipt of additional information that would warrant them to be reopened and investigated further. Prior to actually reviewing these cold cases keep in mind three important facts:

Regardless of the effort you put into an investigation, *not all cases are solvable.*

Since 1993, the clearance rate of homicides has been in the neighborhood of 62 percent. In 2007, it was slightly less.

In serial murder research conducted by Keppel, he found that "the police had the name of the suspect some place in their case file 95 percent of the time within the first 30 days of the investigation."[8]

In order to get the team off to a good start, pick the easiest case to solve first. You want to obtain positive results right up front, as this will fuel the media and bring positive attention to your chief and the police department, and the community and politicians will love you. Then you can start digging into the more difficult ones. The actual evaluation process that we recommend you use will be described in detail in subsequent chapters, but for the time being, certain general tasks need to be accomplished in all cases regardless of the process you adopt. The more organized this process is, the better you will become at evaluating cold cases. These will include case file organization, solvability factors, physical evidence evaluation, victimology, behavioral aspects of persons of interest, undeveloped investigative leads, and an investigative plan for all future actions. Another important element is to determine the *theory of the crime*: What actually occurred and why?

At the onset, case file organization is paramount. If you cannot track the information in an organized manner, then information will be lost and you could find yourself going in circles. The detailed process of organizing the file described in Chapter 5 will assist you greatly in this endeavor. For some, the next step is to determine what solvability factors exist. The ones most typically written about are (to name a few):

Can a suspect be named?
Is there a valid description of a suspect?
Can the suspect's vehicle be described?
Is there any physical evidence that will lead to a suspect?
Did anyone see what happened and are they willing to tell the police?

Gannon[9] designed a cold case solvability factors table that uses a point scale to determine whether the cold case he was reviewing had enough solvability factors to warrant further investigation (Table 3.1). He used a numbering system that placed a value for each factor, and the higher the number, the higher the priority the case received from the cold case unit.

Table 3.1 Solvability and Prioritization Factors

No.	Solvability Factor	If Yes, Add	If No, Add
1	Has the death been ruled a homicide?	+1	−9
2	Can the crime scene be located today and is it in our jurisdiction?	+1	−9
3	Has the victim been identified?	+5	−3
4	Is there significant physical evidence that can identify a suspect?	+5	0
5	Is the evidence still preserved and available?	+1	−5
6	Can any evidence be reprocessed to yield further clues?	+5	0
7	Are the critical witnesses still available?	+7	0
8	Are their leads documented in the last 6 months?	+2	0
9	Are there named suspects in the file?	+5	0

Source: James Gannon, formerly of the Morris County Prosecutor's Office, Morristown, New Jersey.

Along similar lines, Walton[10] describes prioritization schedules that are helpful when one is trying to sift through all these case files and determine which ones need immediate attention. He illustrates a five-part schedule, a four-part schedule, and a three-part schedule, as outlined next.

Five-Part Schedule
>   *Priority 1.* Those cases in which an offender has been identified and an arrest warrant has been issued.
>   *Priority 2.* There is a known suspect and physical evidence has been preserved.
>   *Priority 3.* There is no known suspect but physical evidence has been preserved. Here, as with Priority 2, modern technology may significantly assist.
>   *Priority 4.* There is no known suspect and insufficient evidence exists, but there are witnesses who were not previously available who may now provide material information.
>   *Priority 5.* There are no known witnesses and no physical evidence that can assist.

Four-Part Schedule
>   *Priority 1.* Suspect(s) have been previously identified. A warrant has been issued. A suspect has been identified by forensic methods. This must receive the highest priority for investigation.
>   *Priority 2.* There are witnesses that can assist in identifying suspect(s). Information and/or evidence have been developed that identifies possible suspect(s). Preliminary investigation indicates there are witnesses who were never located or need to be reinterviewed.
>   *Priority 3.* Evidence has been preserved and modern technology can be utilized to process and analyze this evidence.
>   *Priority 4.* There are no known witnesses who can assist in identifying suspect(s) and there is no physical evidence.

Walton writes that this system of high, medium, and low priorities comes from the Texas Rangers:

Three-Part Schedule
>   *High.* There exists viable investigative option(s) that can be expected to generate leads or suspects.
>   *Medium.* There exist reasonable investigative options that might generate leads and/or suspects.
>   *Low.* Remote investigative options exist and these are not expected to generate viable leads or suspects.

Cronin et al.[11] describe the Las Vegas Metropolitan Police Department Cold Case Solvability Criteria as being in five levels:

Level 1: A named suspect; forensic evidence (DNA, latent prints, firearms); witness identification of suspect and physical evidence that connects a suspect to the victim (photographs, writing, fibers, etc.).

Level 2: Unknown suspect; forensic evidence; witness identification of suspect or physical evidence that connects suspect to the victim.

Level 3: Unknown suspect; forensic evidence; physical evidence or witnesses unable to identify suspect.

Level 4: Unknown suspect; physical evidence; witnesses unable to identify a suspect and/or unidentified victim.

Level 5: Unknown suspect; little or no physical evidence; no witnesses and/or unidentified victim.

In Chapter 6 we provide you with another priority table (see Figure 6.3) that we think will significantly benefit the process; however, regardless of the system utilized, the goals are the same: Resolve the case and obtain a conviction.

The next major step in the process is to review and validate what physical evidence is or is not available. Here you need to conduct a full personal inspection/inventory of every item of evidence in your evidence depository. You must ensure that each item has a valid chain of custody, was properly packaged, was maintained properly over the years, and that there are no evidentiary issues that may cause a problem in court at a later date. Cross-reference each item with all those submitted to the crime laboratory and with any crime laboratory reports that might have been generated. Once this process is completed, go to your crime laboratory and speak with them in person to learn if there is anything they can do today that they were not able to do in years past. In doing this, I cannot overemphasize the importance of doing this face to face with your crime laboratory personnel and not over the telephone. If you want them to consider helping you in addition to their already backlogged workload, you must give them and this case the "personal touch" by taking the time to talk with them personally and show them what you have.

In the meantime, someone should be going through the file and running background checks on every significant person in the case, if not every name mentioned in the file. Why so much effort? You are looking for changes in relationships, changes in lifestyles, where are they now, and what have they been doing over the past 20 years. As an interesting sidelight, I was told in confidence about a cold case from the 1960s where the primary person of interest was the only person alive today and he was 98 years old, living in a home for the elderly. Now that begs the question, will the prosecutor want to take a 98-year-old person to trial? But the point remains, a thorough background check of all participants can reveal very valuable information.

Next in line for review should be the medical examiner's report on the autopsy. As with the crime laboratory, it is recommended that you make an appointment with the chief forensic pathologist, allowing him or her time to locate the file and related documents in the archives. Arrange for a sit-down briefing with the pathologist to ensure you have everything documented in the case file. Discuss possibilities where the pathologist may be able to assist in the investigation at this stage and have him or her review the material carefully for anything that might help or hurt the case in court. You do not want any surprises at the last minute.

The next major step in the process is to go see the surviving family members. Tell them that you are taking another look at the investigation and want to know if they have heard anything since the murder. What has transpired in the neighborhood over the years since the incident? Do they suspect anyone in particular for the homicide? Who would they suggest you interview regarding the incident? How have their relationships changed over the time that has passed? Where would they suggest you look for additional information or evidence? After this interview, the word will get out that the investigation has renewed interest, which may cause new information to surface. If the victimology was not completed during the hot investigation, use this time with the family to gather what you need to fulfill that requirement.

Then, as will be discussed in Chapter 11 on interviews and interrogations, it is suggested that you start your interviews first with those on the outside (outer circle), or peripheral edges, of the investigation. Gradually move closer in to your suspects, gathering the necessary information, until you complete the entire inner circle of people closest to your victim or suspects.

As with ongoing investigations, the cold cases and the cold case squad need appropriate supervision in which the entire investigative process is properly managed. As we saw in the previous chapter in the research on homicide clearance rates by Keel (2008) and Keel, Jarvis, and Muirhead (2009), a case review system needs to be in place. If this review process becomes excessive, it could be detrimental to the detectives and investigative process; therefore, although it should be performed, use it judiciously so as to not hinder the progress of the detectives or the investigation.

In further support of this premise and the necessity to conduct regular reviews of investigations, hot or cold, our counterparts in Great Britain have experienced investigative deficiencies with their homicides that, after much research, caused them to institute a more stringent review system. In this study, they found investigative weaknesses in response to incident and initial actions taken; information gathering to include witness and suspect management; exhibit management and submission problems with forensic evidence; lack of proper record keeping and storage of documentation; lack of proper staffing with experienced and well-trained personnel; and failure to have adequate communication internally, externally, and with the victim's family.[12,13]

As you will read later in this book, especially in Chapter 4, this review process is a very big concern and must be properly managed if we are to maintain the investigative standards we insist on having. And, if you do decide to utilize the private sector or graduate students, this becomes even more important. In the cold case evaluation model, Adcock instituted a very strict policy (protocol) about these reviews and reemphasized them every time the team met. It was imperative that all evaluators adhered to the requirements of the protocol (see Chapter 4 for more information on this protocol). At each meeting, everyone was afforded the opportunity to discuss what they had seen or read, and open themselves to criticism by the remaining team members, all moving toward the ultimate goal of being as thorough as we possibly could.

Endnotes

1. National Institute of Justice. 1999. *Death Investigation: A Guide for the Crime Scene Investigator*. NIJ # 167568. U.S. Government Printing Office: Washington, DC.
2. American Board of Medico-Legal Death Investigators (AMBDI), St. Louis University, St Louis, MO. www.slu.edu/organizations/abmdi. Accessed August 19, 2009.
3. Cooper, Greg, and Mike King. 2005. *Cold Case Methodology*. LawTech Custom Publishing: San Clemente, CA; pp. 2–3.
4. These formats were obtained from conversations with the many detectives who attended the cold case seminars at the Henry C. Lee Institute of Forensic Science, 1998 to 2009.
5. Cronin, James M., Gerard R. Murphy, Lisa L. Saphr, Jessica I. Toliver, and Richard E. Weger. 2007. Promoting Effective Homicide Investigations, *Police Executive Research Forum*, December 2007; pp.103–104.
6. Walton, Richard H. 2006. *Cold Case Homicides*. CRC Press: Boca Raton, FL; p. 29.
7. Gannon, James M. 2004. Standard Operating Procedures for the Cold Case Unit; Office of the Morris County Prosecutor, Morristown, NJ.
8. Keppel, Robert D., and William J. Birnes. 2003. *The Psychology of Serial Killer Investigations*. Academic Press: New York.
9. Gannon, James M. 2004. Standard Operating Procedures for the Cold Case Unit; Office of the Morris County Prosecutor, Morristown, NJ.
10. Walton, Richard H. 2006. *Cold Case Homicides*. CRC Press: Boca Raton, FL; pp. 56–57.
11. Cronin, James M., Gerard R. Murphy, Lisa L. Saphr, Jessica I. Toliver, Richard E. Weger, et al. 2007. Promoting Effective Homicide Investigations. *Police Executive Research Forum*, December 2007.

12. Nicol, Catherine, Martin Innes, David Gee, and Andy Feist. 2004. Reviewing Murder Investigations: An Analysis of Progress Reviews from Six Police Forces, Home Office Online Report, London, pp. 42–43.
13. Jones, Dean, John Grieve, and Becky Milne. 2008. The Case to Review Murder Investigations. *Policing, 2*, 470–480. Advance access January 1, 2008, DOI 10.1093/police/pan053.

The Evaluation Process

II

Introduction to Evaluation Models and Procedures

4

JAMES M. ADCOCK AND SARAH L. STEIN

As previously noted, from 1980 to 2008 the United States had accumulated nearly 185,000[1] unresolved murders. Based on the number of homicides and clearance rates for murders from 2009 to 2012 this figure is either closer to or well over 200,000. As of 2004 the United States also had approximately 14,000[2] unidentified sets of human remains, many of which could be homicides, further increasing our total number of unresolved cases.

The efforts to resolve some of these cases by law enforcement and others have been unrelenting. And while historically we can easily identify the early 1980s with the Dade County Sherriff's Office as the beginnings of the "cold case concept,"[3] a standard protocol for evaluating cold cases has not yet been identified and implemented, as noted by the Rand Corporation study for the National Institute of Justice (NIJ).[4]

This begs the question of how are we evaluating cold cases and does the process properly identify, not only solvable cases but ones that will withstand a prosecution for a conviction. The answer to that is probably yes and no depending on where you are located and how methodical and thorough is the review process. Most police agencies assign a seasoned detective to review case files to identify solvability factors and leads that may identify a person of interest. This is usually a one-person task and success relies heavily on the abilities of the detective to reach sound conclusions about the solvability of the investigation.

However, after many years of reviewing criminal investigations and seeing other reviews of investigative case files, Adcock's experiences tell us that not all detectives are effective case reviewers. That relying solely on the one reviewer, based on his or her experiences, is not enough nor is it sufficient. Let's face it, like anything else, some people are better than others at what they do and some detectives are more "intuitive" than others. In a British study[5] it was shown that sometimes the less experienced detectives, utilizing a carefully designed template, were better at case review than the more experienced ones. Although this study was not addressing cold cases but rather ongoing investigations, the results are interesting and do indicate that while experience is important it may not always be the answer.

In this British study, the carefully designed template for reviewers addressed many areas (31 to be exact) that they felt should be utilized during the review process. One big reason for the objective approach was to hopefully help eliminate any bias, thus making the review more thorough and more accurate. The template included the following areas of concern:

1. SIO (senior investigating officer) policy log
2. Initial response
3. Fast-track actions
4. Perennial actions
5. Identification of the inquiry team and key roles
6. Missing persons reports
7. Summary and aim of the investigation
8. Use of hypotheses
9. Standard analytical products
10. Identification as to links with other crimes
11. Evidence of review and management intervention
12. Multiagency partnership working
13. Investigative support
14. Identification of scene and scene parameters
15. Crime scene management
16. Forensic strategy
17. Pathology
18. Searches
19. Passive data generators
20. House-to-house inquiries
21. Witness management
22. Family liaison
23. Managing communications
24. Community involvement
25. Elimination inquiries
26. Suspect management
27. Surveillance strategy
28. Covert human intelligence
29. Reconstructions
30. Major incident and Holmes procedures
31. Postcharge maintenance

Granted, many of these actions are unique to the British system such as SIO policy, and major incident and Holmes procedures. The latter refers to their nationally computerized database of major incidents within the United Kingdom and is almost like artificial intelligence that will generate leads for the investigators based on the previously submitted data. The results of this study disclosed that the detectives with less experience who used the template did a more thorough job of case review than those with experience who gauged their evaluations solely on their experiences without a written guide. Again, a small study but with interesting results.

In reaction to this, Adcock and Chancellor[6] designed a template for case reviews of ongoing death investigations that both have utilized over the years and found to be quite helpful. Having this template does not mean the case reviewer is compelled to follow it exactly as described but can deviate as needed. This type of checklist is reflected next:

1. Initial response—Scene visited
   a. Identification of investigative team and their roles
   b. Proper assignment duties according to talent or capabilities
2. Victim/complainant interviewed
   a. Victim identified
   b. Statement evaluated and validated (does it make sense or is it probable?)
   c. Background and criminal history of victim
   d. Victimology completed
3. Scene and evidentiary issues
   a. Crime scene processed and documented (video, photo, sketch, notes)
   b. Staged scene, altered, or cleaned up
   c. Evidence collected
   d. Evidence evaluation (complete list and what does it all mean and what else is needed)
   e. Scene evaluation—organized or disorganized, control (offender behaviors)
   f. Evidence sent to lab
   g. Lab results
   h. Review of autopsy and cause of death with other forensic facts
   i. Other forensic experts needed or used
4. Canvas conducted
   a. Double checked for completeness
5. Significant witnesses interviewed and statements obtained
   a. Statement validated and corroborated each statement on their own
   b. Name checks and basic background on significant witnesses
   c. Look for changes in relationships
6. Hypotheses formulated
   a. Motive and type of crime
   b. Violent Criminal Apprehension Program (ViCAP) for similar offenses or suspects
   c. Local MO/signature check for similar offenses
   d. Criminal investigative analysis (CIA)
   e. Tested and validated or not

7. Suspect management
   a. Identified
   b. Arrested
   c. Background and criminal history
   d. Similar cases
   e. Family, friends, coworkers canvas
   f. Wives/girlfriends/parents/coconspirators
   g. Interviewed with statements: denials, admissions, confessions
   h. Admissions/confessions obtained
   i. Validated, confirmed, or discounted
   j. Motives
   k. Identification of other witnesses, victims, or other evidence
   l. Other potential information, for example, telephone toll records, financial documents, cell phone, texts, life insurance, ATM, checks, or time cards
8. Lead management
   a. Identified
   b. Followed-up on
9. Obtain written reports from all participants
10. Reconstruction (validate what you have)
    a. Physical evidence (bloodstain pattern and shooting reconstruction)
    b. Informational evidence (admissions/confessions, etc., all validated)
    c. Behavioral (pre-crime behavior, crime behavior, and post-crime behavior)
11. Prosecutor provided all the data
    a. Prosecution presentation
    b. Substantiated elements of proof
    c. List of witnesses and evidence
    d. Respond to DA questions and requests

If nothing else use it as a guide to follow that especially comes into play with younger less experienced investigators at the helm. Take what you can use from it and disregard the rest.

This now brings us back to the cold case problem and not only what is being done about it, but more important how do we go about resolving these unsolved murders. In the following two chapters three models are presented. The first one is very reflective of the methodology that Adcock used with his forensic science graduate students at the University of New Haven when they reviewed cases for surrounding police agencies. It is scientifically based that attempts to answer any and all questions that may arise that turn out to be especially helpful in answering questions and defense strategies. It is extremely thorough and all encompassing but labor and time intensive, which most police agencies are not willing to invest. However, like with the

Tulsa (Oklahoma) Cold Case Unit and the Charlotte-Mecklenburg (North Carolina) Police Department unit, the utilization of hand-selected civilians from the community to assist in the review process under the guidance of a seasoned detective have been very fruitful and produced resolutions with convictions.

After the first edition of this book was published, both Adcock and Stein made numerous presentations to law enforcement agencies around the country and it became clear from these police agencies that this model was too labor intensive and not something they wanted to deal with for the obvious reasons, such as lack of resources, funds, and the concern of allowing outsiders (civilians) to review unresolved murder cases. Therefore, the design of the second/alternative model that would address their immediate concerns of focusing more on whether physical evidence existed that would point toward a particular person of interest, for example, DNA or latent prints. For example, the NIJ DNA Cold Case Grants require that the only cases selected are those that have physical evidence where there is a potential for DNA material to exist. This second model goes beyond just DNA and includes other specific types of evidence such as latent prints that can, like DNA, point to a particular person of interest.

A major concern and potential problem is that agencies have become too reliant on DNA and if the material is too degraded or does not exist then the case is returned to the filing cabinet and not reviewed further for investigative leads that could identify a perpetrator. Nevertheless, a strong case can be built around DNA, even though sometimes fallible, but with other evidentiary items as well, such as latent prints, hairs, and fibers, the results can be encouraging. The emphasis should be to solve the case any way we can and if the physical evidence happens to be there then the resolution will be easier. Close to 70 percent of all cases are resolved through other evidentiary things like good witnesses, and a series of circumstantial evidence both physical and nonphysical, but our society expects to see DNA in our courts when the reality is it is not always there.

The third model found in Chapter 7 is a spinoff of one of the cases we reviewed while at the University of New Haven where there was no body (initially reported as a missing person). That, coupled with another "missing persons" (presumed murdered) case in Holland that we were thoroughly briefed on during our visits to the Netherlands, prompted the design of another approach toward resolving the case. In both situations all the efforts by police were to identify who "killed" the victim and while that is appropriate, we suggest that you also focus and give priority to finding the body. The chapter will elaborate on that suggestion.

One last point: In Dade County, Florida, where one of the first cold case units got its start, they found time and time again one of the biggest contributing factors to solvability of these cold cases was the fact that relationships had changed and people were now more willing to talk than they were 5 or 10 years earlier. This concept has continued to prove its value over the years and should be a predominant investigative lead in all unresolved murders. This book spends a considerable amount of space toward the nonphysical aspects of these investigations in hopes of creating an awareness that there are other ways to solve and convict without DNA. And, as the models illustrate, the key is organization with a methodical approach that will hopefully answer the questions and put the investigator into the position of substantiating all theories of the crime regardless of the position taken by the defense.

Endnotes

1. Hargrove, Thomas. June 2010. Nearly 185,000 murders since 1980 remain unresolved. Scripps News.
2. Willing, Richard. 2007. Report: Authorities have about 14,000 sets of human remains. *USA Today*, June 25.
3. Adcock, James M., and Sarah L. Stein. 2011. *Cold Cases: An Evaluation Model with Follow-Up Strategies for Investigators.* CRC Press: Boca Raton, FL.
4. Davis, Robert C., Carl J. Jensen, and Karin Kitchens. 2010. Cold case investigations: An analysis of current practices and factors associated with successful outcomes. A report submitted to The National Institute of Justice (NIJ) by the Rand Corporation. December 14.
5. Jones, Dean, John Grieve, and Becky Milne. 2010. Reviewing the reviewers: The review of homicides in the United Kingdom. *Investigative Sciences Journal, 2*(1).
6. Adcock, James M., and Arthur S. Chancellor. 2011. Managerial responsibilities in the homicide investigation process: Making a case for periodic reviews of all ongoing death investigations. Presented at the AAFS Annual Meeting, February.

A Comprehensive Cold Case Evaluation Model

5

JAMES M. ADCOCK AND SARAH L. STEIN

The premise of this text is the evaluation model we will describe in this chapter. The information in the earlier chapters was designed specifically to give the reader background information on cold cases, historical events, and an understanding of the times in relation to homicides and those who kill. In the chapters that follow, the presentation of the model and information regarding the follow-up investigation will be documented. After introducing the philosophy behind the cold case evaluation model and description of the regimented structure, this chapter will delve into Phase I to IV of the process.

Introduction

The actual design of the cold case evaluation model (Figure 5.1) came about as the direct result of two things: first, the Henry C. Lee Institute of Forensic Science at the University of New Haven, Connecticut, received a National Institute of Justice grant to conduct cold case training for law enforcement officers around the country. Over the years, the institute has trained detectives and police officers in cold case methodology from California, Washington, Arizona, Texas, Louisiana, Wisconsin, Tennessee, Alabama, Florida, Georgia, New Jersey, New York, Connecticut, Vermont, and Massachusetts. In 2006 we started a careful selection process of forensic science graduate students to serve as unpaid cold case evaluators, reviewing unresolved homicides as a service to the police under the direct supervision of a professor who had nearly 30 years of experience investigating cases and managing investigative processes. As previously mentioned, this process began with departments in Connecticut and blossomed to others in New York, Massachusetts, and Tennessee.

The thought was to create a system of review of these unresolved homicides that would ultimately produce a report for the department that would contain thorough, accurate, validated, and viable information for the detectives to consider for follow-up investigation. One of the many challenges was getting police departments to trust us enough for them to hand over their original case files. Although I fully understand the fear they have over letting this information out of their hands, the case is probably in a file cabinet

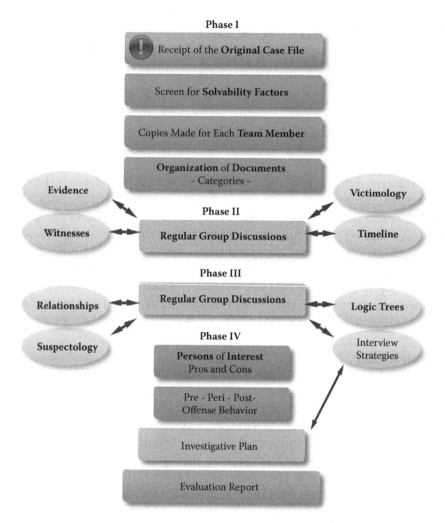

Figure 5.1 Cold case evaluation model.

drawer or box where it has not been touched for years. So in an effort to alleviate this fear, all evaluators, including myself as the team chief, signed "confidentiality" statements. Although this is no guarantee, it does make the process a little more palatable for the police department. As part of this confidentiality statement, each member was required to affirm he or she fully understood the cold case evaluation protocol and would follow it diligently.

Cold Case Evaluation Protocol

1. Confidentiality statement.
2. Do not find fault.
3. Organize file into logical categories.

4. Create evaluation categories.
   a. Victimology
   b. Timelines
   c. Logic trees
   d. Sequence of events
   e. Persons of interest (pros and cons)
   f. Psychological information on suspects (others?)
   g. Interview/interrogation strategies
   h. Investigative plan
5. Ensure that you identify and list every person mentioned in the file. Those who were not interviewed should be placed in the investigative plan (IP) for follow-up, as deemed necessary.
6. Make sure that you can answer the question, "How do you know that?" Footnote all written documents, citing where the information came from. It isn't something you made up or thought was interesting; you actually have a reason for making the statement.
7. If speculative, then say so. But be able to support your conclusions, regardless.
8. The investigative plan should include:
   a. Any interviews that need to be conducted.
   b. Any reinterviews that you feel are necessary.
   c. Issues regarding physical evidence.
   d. Other sources of information that may be helpful to the investigators.
   e. Anything that you find would be helpful toward the resolution of the case. Be able to support your reasoning.
   f. Bottom line, the investigative plan is your suggestion to the detectives of what you think should be done or considered in order to resolve the case.

Be practical and understand that not *all* cases are solvable. If a mistake was made, just move on. Move forward and try to get around any problems and assist the agency with information that will help it solve the case.

Next, rules and guidelines for the evaluators were firmly established, and as part of the confidentiality statements, the evaluators had to agree to these procedures as well. One of the critical concerns was that absolutely no one on the team would be allowed to conduct any type of investigation—no interviews, no phone calls to witnesses, no e-mails, absolutely nothing outside of reviewing the documents provided. And, as per the confidentiality statement, they were not allowed to discuss the contents of the case file with anyone outside the team, including spouses, friends, and fellow students. If someone outside the team needed to be contacted, all requests went through the team chief. These requests were never for any witnesses or actors found in the case file but rather for additional information that could be gleaned, for example, from a review of the autopsy protocol with the forensic pathologist or from asking the detectives to look at the physical evidence maintained in their evidence depository.

Anyone who ventures in this direction of utilizing outside evaluators must have a very specific standard operating procedure (SOP) in place where there is absolutely no question of what the evaluators can and cannot do. One must ensure that the process encompasses all possible theories of the crime that are supported by case file information and facts, not conjecture. Utilizing the scientific method as a backdrop to this, where you are constantly asking yourselves "How do I know that?" will help to solidify your conclusions and suggestions for the follow-up investigation. Furthermore, the team chief or squad leader needs to be an experienced seasoned detective who will serve as a sounding board for the evaluators, keeping them on track and following the SOP and confidentiality statement requirements.

The thoroughness of the cold case evaluation process, as depicted in the model, is due to the regimented structure of constant reviews and group discussions where evaluators are queried about their conclusions and how they came to those decisions. They are also required to create a footnote, fully citing their source for every piece of information provided and utilized to draw a conclusion. Everything must be fully supported by actual case file documents and the information contained therein; conjecture and supposition are not allowed. If in the end there are no conclusions that can be supported, then perhaps the case cannot be resolved. However, if the review produces different theories of the crime, then all of them have to be fully documented with suggestions of what else might be needed to either validate the theory or prove that it is no longer valid. Physical evidence is a great tool, but as previously stated it is not the *silver bullet* for resolving cold cases but only one process of many that can be accomplished by the detectives to resolve the investigation.

The concept of conducting and reviewing investigations hinges on three major aspects: (1) physical evidence, (2) behavioral evidence or actions by the actors involved; and (3) informational pieces consisting of interviews, media reports, record checks, and so forth. If one categorizes this information accordingly, the odds of resolving the investigation are increased. This process has to be organized so as to not lose pieces of valuable information that could be critical to determining who committed the crime—therefore, this evaluation model.

Phase I

Phase I of the evaluation model begins upon receipt of the original case file. Optimally, this file should include all original official reports relevant to the investigation filed by responding officers and detectives, the autopsy report, crime scene photographs, and any handwritten notes compiled by the original investigators. The importance of receiving the original case file in its entirety cannot be overstated; if the complete contents of the initial investigation are not made readily available, information or evidence may be overlooked that can have an impact on the final review. Thus, it may behoove a member of the reviewing team to approach the original lead investigator, if possible, and confirm with him or her that all pertinent information has been included in the file.

Once the team has acquired the original file, they must determine whether the case at face value reveals certain solvability factors that will significantly contribute to a successful analysis, follow-up investigation, and ultimately, resolution. Using Figure 5.2 as a guide, there are nine primary solvability factors that heavily influence whether a case will be successfully resolved.

Once it has been established that a case has merit and the potential for solvability, the order of the original case file should be maintained. Investigators should reproduce the case file in the exact order that it was presented to them,

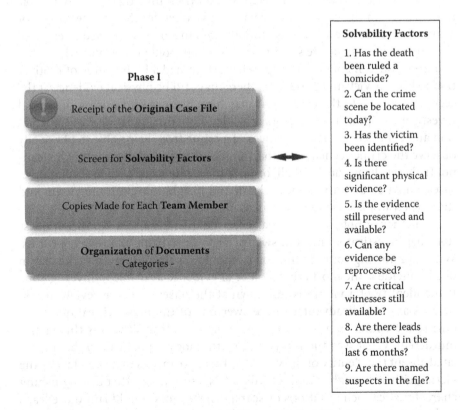

Figure 5.2 Cold case evaluation model, Phase I, solvability factors.

thereby maintaining the integrity of the file and demonstrating respect for the original investigating agency.

Let us now turn to the nine basic solvability factors to be considered by investigators at the onset of the review process.

Whether or not the death has been ruled a homicide represents the first solvability factor. It must be beyond doubt to investigators that the victim was indeed murdered and there is no question whatsoever of a natural death, accident, or suicide. If reviewers cannot definitively determine that a homicide has in fact occurred, it would be unwise to pursue the case, as resources, manpower, and valuable time may ultimately be squandered in pursuit of an equivocal circumstance.

The second consideration is whether the crime scene is still accessible to the current investigators. This question can be especially relevant for several reasons. First, for an investigator it is often helpful to visit the crime scene at the beginning of the review process to get a feel for the crime, the victim, and the perpetrator. For example, where the crime occurred (e.g., a house, a park, etc.) can tell the investigator a great deal about the circumstances surrounding the commission of the crime (e.g., crime of passion, premeditated, stranger versus intimate crime, etc.). In addition, investigators may be able to deduce from the crime scene what type of offender they are seeking. For example, if the crime scene was outdoors and in a highly traveled or exposed area, investigators may be seeking an extremely bold perpetrator who either had little concern about being apprehended or had a high degree of motivation to kill the victim. In addition, there may still be physical evidence at the scene pertaining to the crime that may have been missed during the initial investigation. Thus, investigators are able to obtain a great deal of information and experience certain nuances of a crime from being able to physically observe the crime scene rather than simply studying photographs. One cannot truly see, hear, touch, smell, or taste the elements of a scene through pictures, and a certain attention to detail and insight into both the victim and the perpetrator is lacking in pictures.

Whether or not the victim has been identified is also a significant question that investigators must answer prior to initializing the review process. Without knowing your victim, you cannot know the perpetrator. The victim of a homicide is the most critical piece of evidence available to investigators. If the identity of a victim is unknown at the onset of a case review, investigators are at a disadvantage to answer one of the most critical questions during the course of a homicide investigation: Why? Why was this victim murdered? What was the motive? A victimology report cannot be formulated absent the identity of the victim. If there are means that can identify the victim, either through dental records, a DNA profile, or other distinguishing characteristics such as tattoos or scars, investigators should run those leads and put the case aside until the victim has been identified.

Case Study

As a sidenote regarding the identification of victims, the following case is provided. During one of the cold case seminars in New Haven, Connecticut, a detective from California told a story regarding one of his cases that, besides being a phenomenal piece of investigative work and diligence, taught all of us a lesson to heed in future cases. His cold case unit had the unidentified body of a female found in a duffel bag in a desert-like environment. The cold case team of analysts and investigators worked through missing persons' reports, and so forth, for 2 years, managing to get the list from hundreds of possibilities down to nine. They had a forensic dentist examine the unidentified remains, hoping that he could make an identification based on the dental records. The detectives then went to the family and apprised them of their findings and requested a DNA sample to verify them. The DNA proved otherwise and they were back to square one. The family was devastated. However, the forensic dentist said another person on the list came close to the unidentified remains as well; and in the end, the DNA did confirm the findings and the second one was the unidentified victim. This should caution all investigators to not jump to conclusions without positive verification and in this case DNA.

In the same vein, does physical evidence exist, has it been properly preserved, and is it readily accessible by the current reviewers? This solvability factor carries perhaps more weight than the simple presence of physical evidence. If the evidence in question has not been properly preserved, new tests resulting from advanced technology cannot be performed, and confirmatory testing cannot be conducted to concretely identify a perpetrator.

The sixth primary solvability factor is also correlated with the presence and quality of preservation of physical evidence. That is, can any of the evidence be reprocessed? There have been significant advancements in technology pertaining to evidence processing within the last decade. One of the most relevant to cold case investigation is advancements pertaining to DNA replication and subsequent processing. Two new forms of DNA testing that have been identified by researchers are short tandem repeat (STR) testing and touch DNA. STR is a form of DNA testing whereby a minute sample of DNA can be replicated until the sample is of adequate size for analysis. Touch DNA is DNA that has been left behind by a perpetrator when his skin has come into contact with the victim or other items within the context of the immediate crime scene. Laboratory technicians can now retrieve DNA from epithelial (skin) cells that transfer from the perpetrator to evidence present at crime scenes. Thus with regard to solvability, it is important that investigators consider whether the evidence available to them is in a state where it can be reprocessed and reexamined for additional clues. For more information on the application of forensic science to cold cases, please read Chapter 9.

One of the most crucial elements to the development of a solid follow-up investigation and ultimate case resolution is the presence of credible witnesses. In determining if the case file demonstrates this element of solvability, it is suggested that investigators establish whether witnesses to any behavior (pre-, peri-, and post-crime elements) are still available for questioning. As seasoned investigators are well aware, relationships between perpetrators and their associates will inevitably shift with the passage of time. One of the distinct advantages that is applicable to a cold case investigation is that witnesses who were previously unable or unwilling to come forth during the initial investigation may now be free or willing to do so due to several reasons: The perpetrator may no longer pose a direct threat, may be in jail for another crime, or may have moved away. In addition, a significant other, such as a wife or a girlfriend, of a perpetrator may have ended the relationship and now may be more inclined to speak openly with investigators. Whatever the case, the existence and availability of material witnesses to the crime are among the most influential determinants in resolving a cold case homicide.

The next solvability factor investigators must take into consideration is whether there have been leads pursuant to the case documented within the previous 6 months. This is important, among other things, in determining the level of commitment shown by the community to resolve the homicide. In addition, the existence or absence of leads in the past 6 months demonstrates to investigators how cold the case has actually become. Is the case still fresh in the minds of community residents, or has it been completely forgotten due to either the socioeconomic status of the victim or perhaps other more important contemporary events? While this solvability factor does not weigh particularly heavily on the successful outcome of a cold case investigation, investigators have some options during the course of their evaluation to heat up their case. For example, if there have been no recently reported leads, it may benefit investigators to advertise a hotline, a reward, hold vigils for the victim, and promote media coverage to encourage the public to take an active interest in the investigation.

The final solvability factor is whether or not persons of interest or suspects are identified and named within the case file. Although it is of critical importance for investigators to maintain neutrality during the review process, the existence of named persons of interest within the file is nonetheless crucial in that reviewers have a starting point for their analysis. With named persons of interest being identified at the onset of the review process, investigators can construct the pre-, peri-, and post-behavioral matrix, as outlined in Chapter 10 on suspect identification. This will sufficiently aid the progress of the follow-up investigation, as persons of interest can be reinvestigated and reinterviewed according to their priority in the matrix. Regardless of the number of persons of interest who have been identified by the original investigators, the fact that they exist at least provides a modicum of direction for reviewers. If there are no named persons of interest within the case file, it is suggested that reviewers then formulate a behavioral profile of the perpetrator based on the crime and crime scene indicators, and perhaps also submit the case file for analysis to the Federal Bureau of Investigation's (FBI) Violent Criminal Apprehension Program. Following the development of a behavioral profile, the review team may or may not find individuals within the case file that are consistent with said profile. However, it is important for investigators to keep in mind that the facts of the case facilitate subsequent theories, and that facts must not be manipulated to fit theories formulated by reviewers.

The Case File

If the aforementioned solvability factors are found to exist within the case file, it is now appropriate for investigators to move to the next phase of our model, which is reproducing the original case file and organizing it into manageable categories. As stated earlier in this chapter, the original order of the case file from the requesting agency must be maintained. The reviewing team should reproduce the case file in the exact order in which it was received to facilitate its unaltered return to the original investigators or agency. In many departments, it is standard procedure to only have one case file available to investigators; this is done in an effort to centralize all pertinent information and minimize confusion and loss of information. One of the benefits in analyzing a cold case is the fact that all information related to the investigation is already centralized and investigators do not have the added pressure of maintaining order as numerous leads are coming in. It is acceptable, then, that a copy of the case file be made available to each analyst who is a member of the reviewing team.

We recommend that a copy of the case be distributed to each team member for many reasons. It is important to recognize that each analyst will approach his or her review in a different manner. Although each case file will be organized into identical categories, each analyst will elect to start his or her review at a different point in the case. It is therefore critical that each team member have the luxury of complete access to the file whenever they wish, so as to facilitate uninterrupted viewing and analysis. The second reason we recommend individual copies of the file is that each analyst is ideally bringing a different realm of expertise to the team. Each member of the review team will focus heavily on a particular section(s) of the file relative to the other categories (e.g., victimology, evidence, timelines, statements, etc.). Therefore, it is important that each team member have his or her own copy of the file in order to highlight passages, make notes, and so on, without the

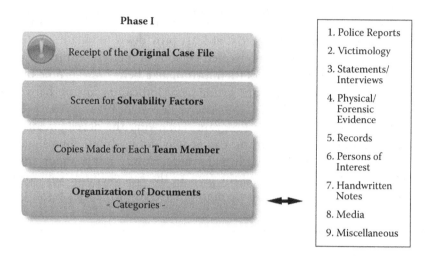

Figure 5.3 Cold case evaluation model, Phase I, organization of documents.

possibility of that information being compromised by another team member inadvertently disrupting the flow of the analysis.

Once the original case file has been reproduced and individual copies have been distributed to each team member, one of the most daunting yet crucial elements of a cold case analysis is undertaken: organization and categorization of the case file. It is of the utmost importance that each team member's copy of the case file be identical. This is because when information is cited and referenced in the investigative plan, detectives conducting the follow-up investigation must be able to turn to any of the copies made by the review team and find the location of that information easily.

Let us now identify and discuss the most common categories that are established during the course of a cold case analysis.

Although not all-inclusive, the most commonly identified categories can be seen in list format in Figure 5.3. It is important to discuss the content that should be found in each category.

Official Documents

We will begin with the official documents. This category is a compilation of communications between agencies, warrants, subpoenas, and various other legal documents. This category should be composed of any and all interdepartmental communication within the original investigating agency, and any communication between the original investigating agency and outside law enforcement entities. For example, if the investigating agency requested additional resources or records checks from a neighboring or federal agency, these communications would be found in the official documents section. Communication between the investigating agency and the district attorney's office would also be located in this category. A visual representation of the lines of communication will be helpful for the reviewing team in that it will demonstrate the openness, timeline, and extent of communication between agencies. Also, this category will provide the review team with an image of what further communications may be necessary within the context of the follow-up investigation and can include said observations and suggestions in the investigative plan. We recommend that this category be organized by type of document (e.g., interdepartmental communications, requests for assistance from other agencies, warrants, subpoenas, communication with the district attorney, etc.). The subcategories should then be organized chronologically, dating from the earliest to the most recent document.

Police Reports

The first category that should be compiled in the case file is police reports. This category should be comprised of all reports filed by responding officers, detectives, and supervisors of the original investigating agency during the course of the initial case investigation. The police reports that are generally filed will include a report from the initial response to the call of the crime, and all investigative measures taken during the course of the case. These reports are typically voluminous and contain a great deal of critical information to the review team. They provide the reviewing analysts with a general picture and scope of the original investigation. As many seasoned investigators know, hindsight is always 20/20 when one is reviewing the direction of an investigation. The following is not meant to be critical, but simply a reminder to reviewers as to what information is often displayed in police reports. Reviewers will be able to see in hindsight what direction the investigation went in: Did original investigators form tunnel vision or did they carry out a reasonably well-balanced investigation? What was done correctly and what may have been lacking in the original investigative efforts? Were there persons of interest who were not interviewed due to either lack of identification or lack of manpower during the course of the investigation? All of the above information is critical for a review team to examine, and other facts surrounding the initial investigation may become apparent during the analysis of the cumulative police reports category. We recommend that this category be organized alphabetically by the last name of the officer, detective, or supervisor; and within each individual's subcategory the documents should be arranged chronologically, from the earliest to the most recent date of investigative action.

As a final note regarding this category, we have observed that some law enforcement agencies elect to organize their cold case files in a strictly chronological manner. Although this is an acceptable technique, we feel that this methodology allows the potential for gaps in the flow of information being studied by a review panel. We recommend that the police reports section especially be organized alphabetically and *subsequently* chronologically for the following reason: When members of a review team have the luxury of reviewing police reports from each individual investigator, from their earliest to most recent action during the course of the investigation, certain information reveals itself. Team members can, in this manner, more accurately envision the original investigator's line of logic, why he or she pursued certain persons of interest or leads. At a later point in the review process, the team will be able to establish if the line of investigation by a particular detective or officer was legitimate and well founded, or whether it was a result of a red herring or tunnel vision. Unfortunately, as any member of the law enforcement community knows, tunnel vision does exist and has the potential to occur during the course of any investigation. It is important for the reviewing team to keep this fact in mind and be able to identify it; not only to refocus the investigation in the right track but also to preclude any further derailments due to faulty investigative foundations.

Victimology

The second and one of the most essential categories to a successful cold case review is that of victimology. This category should reflect all information that is directly applicable to the homicide victim. To know one's victim in the context of a criminal investigation is one of the most difficult and yet rewarding elements of a cold case analysis. If investigators do not have a keen, acute grasp of who their victim was in life, they cannot fully comprehend the motives or persons of interest related to the commission of the crime. Therefore, information contained in this category should be solely relevant to the victim's life and lifestyle choices.

Statements/Interviews

The next identified category within the case file is that of statements/interviews. This category will reflect all voluntary statements and interviews provided by witnesses to the crime, known associates of the victim, and potential persons of interest. It is vital that the statements and interviews relevant to the investigation be placed into a separate subcategory; this will allow the review panel to quickly identify any discrepancies or consistencies between statements, or statements given during the interview process. This can prove extremely useful when whittling down the list of persons of interest, in that the perpetrator(s) of the crime may have a tendency to alter their statement or timeline of events. The perpetrator(s) may also unwittingly reveal details of the crime as the interview process proceeds or a second interview is conducted. The authors recommend that this category within the case file be organized alphabetically by last name of the individual providing the statement, and then chronologically for each individual, from the statement given closest to the time of the crime to the statement given most recently to authorities.

Physical/Forensic Evidence

Physical/forensic evidence should be the next category compiled within the confines of the case file. This is why we focus so heavily on a rigid scientific model that provides review team members with the tools with which to analyze a cold case from the physical, behavioral, and informational aspects inherent to each individual case. The category of physical evidence should contain all information relevant to the physical evidence collected at the scene (including all crime scene reports), testing that was performed upon said evidence, and the results of those procedures. Depending on the volume of physical evidence, it is at the review panel's discretion as to how this category should be further organized. For example, if sparse physical evidence was recovered, it would be prudent for the review team to simply organize the category via alphabetizing the items recovered, followed by the tests performed on the items and the results. Conversely, if there is a large amount of physical evidence pertinent to the crime, organization of this category may be slightly more involved. The review team could, for example, break down the evidence into categories such as where the evidence was recovered, what type of evidence it was (e.g., fibers, fluids), and so forth. Whatever the approach, it is essential that all physical evidence relating to the crime be documented and organized in a fashion that enhances efficiency and ready accessibility to the review panel.

Records

The fifth category that the review panel should organize is records. The records category may include the following: phone records, criminal background checks, and NCIC (National Crime Information Center) documents. The documents contained in the records category often prove extremely valuable to the review panel. For example, in reviewing phone records, it may be revealed that an associate of the victim reported having no contact with the victim during the time immediately preceding his or her death, but in fact they did. Records have the ability to confirm or reject alibis, timelines, and versions of events given by witnesses, associates of the victim, and persons of interest. As such, they should be treated with respect and carefully studied by review members. It is recommended that these records be organized by type (e.g., phone, NCIC, etc.) and then chronologically based on when said records were obtained by authorities.

Persons of Interest

Persons of interest is the next category that should be compiled. This category is often fluid in nature and may be amended throughout the review process if individuals are excluded, and conversely, if reviewers have reason to believe that others *should* be included. The initial development of this category is contingent upon whether any persons of interest have been identified by the original investigators. If none have been identified, it is suggested that a category be made nonetheless, but left empty in the binder until such time in the review process when regular discussions between team members will possibly facilitate the development of persons of interest. The information contained in this category should be solely related to each individual person of interest and his or her connection with the victim. If a said person of interest has given a statement to or has been interviewed by authorities, a copy of said statement or interview should be made and inserted into this category. In addition to each person of interest's statement, other relevant information such as his or her place of employment, vocation, education level, place of residence, known associates, former intimate partners, and criminal history should be included. Constructing a person of interest category is much like that of a victimology category. The review panel should endeavor to discover as much as possible about the world in which the person of interest immerses himself, thereby constructing the likelihood of said individual committing a violent crime, and further, the particular crime in question.

Handwritten Notes

The category of handwritten notes should follow the persons of interest category in the case file. This category is often haphazard, as the writer of these notes often does not identify himself. This category should include all handwritten notes made by investigators during the course of the initial investigation. While this category at face value may seem superfluous, it is not. Handwritten notes often contain a wealth of information that is otherwise unavailable to the review team within the context of official documents and reports. It is here, in handwritten notes, that investigators will often reveal their true feelings, instincts, or hunches pursuant to a case. These theories and beliefs, though they should not be considered scientific or concrete, should not be excluded by the review panel. These notes may lend credence to a theory that has been formulated by the team at a later point in the review process or point the team in a legitimate direction that had not been previously considered. If possible, the team should attempt to further organize this category either alphabetically by the last name of the individual who composed the note; if this is not possible, perhaps it can be organized into subject categories such as theories, evidence-related questions, and so on.

Media

The eighth category within the case file should be the media. This category contains all media reports that are associated with the crime. This may include newspaper and magazine articles, transcripts of television segments, as well as tapes and DVDs of media coverage. The information contained in this category is vital to the successful review of a cold case. Depending on the notoriety of the case in question, media coverage may have been pervasive, or it may be little to nonexistent. Both high- and low-profile cold cases possess advantages and disadvantages. In a high-profile case, the primary advantage to investigators is a high degree of exposure and therefore a potentially increased chance for solvability as more people may come forward. The disadvantages inherent to a high-profile case are also directly correlated with a high degree of media exposure. Due to an intense volume of coverage, investigators may face additional challenges, such as leaks to the media regarding sensitive information that should have been kept private, and the possibility of red herrings and untruthful witnesses merely seeking publicity exists. In addition, as seen in the JonBenét Ramsey case with John Mark Karr, individuals seeking publicity may claim that they perpetrated the crime and may appear at face value to be legitimate due to the amount of sensitive information leaked to the press with which to corroborate their version of events. The review panel should keep in mind what type of case they are analyzing and quickly establish which facts of the case were presented in the media in order to exclude possible red herrings that will deter a successful review.

Miscellaneous

The final category that is often included in the case file will be labeled miscellaneous. This category, while it contains information that may not be otherwise categorized, may prove useful at a later point in the review process. There have been a couple instances when we were reviewing a case and at some juncture in the review process, a document from the miscellaneous section completes another report, statement, and so on, and is correctly identified and filed. No document that is included in the original case file should be approached lightly or discarded simply because it does not fit. Rather, file the document in the miscellaneous section and keep a look out during the review process for documents in other sections that may be relevant. This category may be further subcategorized by type of document, if necessary.

As the case file has now been appropriately divided, categorized, and subcategorized, the team may now begin Phase II of the review process.

Phase II

Introduction

This section provides the reader with a comprehensive and thorough discussion of Phase II of the cold case evaluation model. We identify and elaborate on the five components of Phase II, which are regular group discussions, evidentiary issues, witness lists, victimology, and timelines. Each of these components represents key initial phases of any cold case evaluation and must be undertaken in a vigorous, yet carefully considered and respectful manner. The review team must not rush to complete the compilation of evidence,

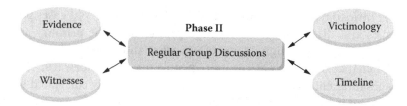

Figure 5.4 Cold case evaluation model, Phase II.

witness lists, victimology, or timelines, as they are indeed the core foundation of a successful evaluation (Figure 5.4).

The Evaluation Model

The crux upon which any successful cold case evaluation rests for the duration of the review is regular group meetings and discussions by team members. Although we suggest two meetings a week for a period of 2 to 3 hours each session, this may not be realistic, and adjustments should be made to accommodate all those on the team. As stated earlier, the evaluation team will ideally be composed of individuals representing various backgrounds and talents. The expertise of team members may range from a specialty in analyzing physical evidence to constructing behavioral profiles, to organizational skills, to shaping interview and interrogation strategies. Or it may include professionals from varying backgrounds and expertise. There is ample ground to cover during the course of regularly scheduled group meetings, and the process should never be rushed, allowing each individual to present his or her respective contributions to the group.

The review process officially begins following the distribution of the organized case file to each team member. It can be reasonably assumed that regardless of the physical size of the case file, there is a great deal of information to digest during the initial reading. A case file may be relatively sparse in physical size and yet rife with information and subtle nuances that must be considered by team members. We recommend a period of 1 week for reviewers to thoroughly read and absorb the material in the file. The week-long reading period is also suggested with respect to the individual talents of the team members. Each individual will normally read the case file once to get the general thrust of the investigation. Following this, they will often return to the file after a day or so to approach the case from their individual vantage point, whether it is analysis of the physical evidence, behavioral analysis, and so forth. The team supervisors should instruct evaluators to do just this. This process facilitates gaining an overview of the general information and then allows evaluators to begin to formulate their plan of attack, so to speak, for their individual assignment.

Once the week-long reading period has passed, the first group meeting should be scheduled. This first meeting often proves to be both energetic and chaotic. The high-energy environment is a direct result of information being exchanged, emerging theories coming forth, and so on. Supervisors should encourage this excitement at the first meeting and not try to stifle it.

At this first meeting, a team member should be designated to construct a complete name database of the case file, to include every person mentioned in the file. The master list will include both personnel relevant to the investigation (e.g., officers, detectives, supervisors) and those associated with the crime itself (e.g., the victim, associates, persons of interest, etc.). The master list should be subcategorized further in order to assist personnel ultimately responsible for conducting the follow-up investigation. The first manner in which the master list should be subcategorized is by the individual's association with the case; for example, law enforcement official, witness, associate of the victim, or person of interest. These broad categories should be identified and constructed, with the individuals organized alphabetically by last name. This can be a daunting task, as in one case we reviewed there were 1,757 names in the case file; meticulous attention to detail is a must.

The subcategories should include as much of the following information as possible (keeping within the confines of the case file, of course): the name of the individual, date of birth, address, phone number, social security number, whether they have been interviewed by law enforcement officials, the date of the interview, whether there was a follow-up interview conducted, and the date of that interview. To supplement these subcategories, as the review process progresses and evaluators get a more comprehensive feel of the case, it is suggested that motive, opportunity, and means (MOM) be added to the "persons of interest" category. Evaluators should list the motive that each person of interest may have had to commit the crime, which is established following the construction of a suspectology report. Once the timelines for the case are completed, reviewers will be able to insert opportunity for each person of interest, and finally, what means may have been available to said persons of interest to carry out the crime.

This master list must be completed in a timely fashion—preferably 1 to 2 weeks from the onset of the review process. It is important to complete the list quickly so the review team can have individual copies distributed to them for review. Also, this list can be prominently displayed in the meeting room for referral during the evaluation process. The primary value of the name database lies in its ability to reveal inconsistencies in investigative patterns and bring to light any investigative avenues that have not yet been fully explored. In one case we looked at, three persons of interest were named multiple times as being the perpetrators, yet they were never interviewed by the police, an oversight that could prove fruitful if they are interviewed later. During the course of a hot investigation, the flow and influx of information is sometimes completely overwhelming to investigators, either due to the media exposure of a case or simply lack of manpower. In addition, given the potentially chaotic nature of a hot investigation, there may be no central- ization of information. That is, investigators may not have known whether a witness was interviewed at all, let alone reinterviewed. This dysfunction may have caused a lack of fluid, reliable, and potentially critical information. The team evaluating a cold case having this master name database readily available provides a centralization of critical information relating to every- one listed in the case file. In the final investigative plan, evaluators will be able to definitively list, according to priority, which witnesses or persons of interest must be revisited and reinterviewed, or to identify those who were never interviewed.

Following the completion of the master name database, the group should now discuss evidentiary issues. We suggest the processing of evidentiary information prior to constructing victimology and timelines relevant to the case, as the latter two tasks tend to be much more labor intensive. The docu- mentation and exploration of evidentiary issues will logically begin with the crime scene report filed by investigators (Figure 5.5). The type of crime scene (e.g., outdoor location, apartment, house, warehouse, etc.) will assist investi- gators at a later point in the review process in narrowing the list of persons of interest based on their access to and affinity for the crime scene. However, at the primary juncture, evaluators should simply document and study all of the physical evidence that was observed and obtained at the initial crime scene processing. This may range from pattern evidence (e.g., blood spat- ter, tire tracks, shoe impressions, etc.), to fibers (e.g., foreign fibers found on the victim's clothing), to fluids (e.g., blood, saliva), to a murder weapon, and more. For example, in one case we reviewed, a piece of evidence located at a much later point in the investigation was the victim's vehicle that had been abandoned, presumably by whomever had murdered her. In an effort

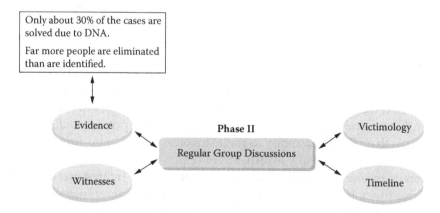

Figure 5.5 Cold case evaluation model, Phase II, evidence.

to determine whether or not the victim was capable of being the last individual to operate the vehicle based on the placement of the driver's side seat, the team had to conduct further experimentation. Therefore, we scoured local used car advertisements and contacted car dealerships to find the exact make, model, and color of the young lady's vehicle. Following that initiative, our team member who specialized in the analysis of physical evidence reconstructed the placement of the driver's side seat in the vehicle. From this reenactment, the team was able to determine that given the victim's height and stature at the time of her death, she would have been unable to operate the vehicle with the seat in that particular position. Consequently, it is critical that evaluators keep in mind during this phase that further action may be necessary to address evidentiary issues, as long as the action does not in any way interfere with an investigation.

The documentation of physical evidence relevant to the crime can be accomplished in several ways. We suggest two methodologies for documenting and displaying reports and findings from physical evidence: databases and visual flow charts and/or diagrams. To construct a database of physical evidence, the following categories must be named: type of evidence (e.g., fiber, fluid, pattern, ballistic), location of evidence (where at the crime scene the evidence was recovered), testing performed on each individual piece of evidence, date of testing, results of the forensic testing performed on each piece of evidence, the date those results were received by investigators, and finally, further forensic testing that can now be completed due to advancements in forensic technology. Many times during cold case reviews, evidence was not processed due to lack of technology, and evaluators should be up to date on current forensic literature that outlines new testing processes that may benefit their case. If evaluators choose to utilize flow charts and diagrams to visually display physical evidence relevant to their case (see Figure 5.6 for an example), a few suggestions are worth noting. Color coding is extremely beneficial when visually documenting physical evidence. For example, in one case we reviewed, a team member constructed a flow chart of fiber evidence recovered during the investigation. To better illustrate, the fiber evidence was color coded in whatever color the fiber that was recovered was—such was the color used to represent it in the flow chart.

The second issue that must be considered regarding flow chart and diagram construction is whether the team elects to construct these diagrams manually or with the assistance of a computer program, such as the i2 Analyst's Notebook program.[1] Although i2 has amazing organizational capabilities, the nuances of an individual's creative and organizational skills can supplement clarity and provide more impressive visual effects. If the team possesses a member with extraordinary skills in constructing these diagrams and an acute eye for detail, it is highly recommended that this individual be utilized.

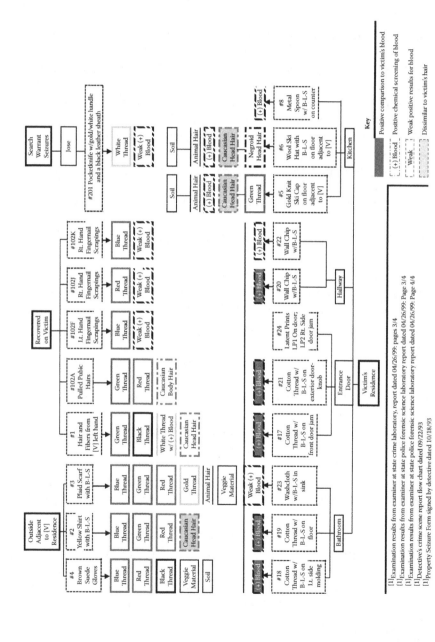

Figure 5.6 Cold case evaluation model, Phase II, victimology.

Having now completed the master name database and the thorough assessment of pertinent evidence, the team is now ready to begin undertaking the construction of a comprehensive victimology report. The primary purpose of a victimology report is to arm evaluators with a basic foundation of the victim's personality, lifestyle, and risk level for becoming a target of homicidal violence. The victimology report is one of the most daunting yet rewarding portions of a cold case review. The simple fact remains that if you do not know your victim, you cannot know your killer. Although compiling all information relevant to the victim and extensively documenting said information is an exhaustive process, there is a great deal to gain from this process, as it will narrow the field of persons of interest. The information within a completed victimology report should assist reviewers in the classification of the victim. For example, what was the risk level of the victim for being the target of homicidal violence? Was the victim at low, medium, or high risk? This classification can be determined by a myriad of factors. The primary factors that will assist reviewers in their classification of the victim's risk level can be broken down into four basic categories: professional life, education, personal life, and criminal history. Reviewers should look for information that is relevant to each of these four basic categories and file the information appropriately into subcategories of the victimology section of the case file.

Let us explore the information that should be contained in the four basic categories at a more detailed level. With regard to the victim's former professional life, the following information should be included: the victim's place and type of employment at the time of his or her death, the duration of the victim's employment at that particular establishment, any and all prior employment locations and job types, and any associated training the victim may have completed that was relevant to his or her occupation. This subcategory should be organized from the victim's most recent employment activity prior to death to the earliest time, location, and choice of occupation, thereby creating a stratum of relevancy with respect to the crime.

The subcategory pertaining to the victim's education should be organized from the highest degree obtained by the victim to the most primary education levels. The level of education achieved by the victim will assist reviewers in creating a clearer picture of the victim's reasoning and life skills. For example, someone with a higher degree of education may be more leery of forming relationships with questionable characters, or might be less likely to leave a party with a stranger he or she just met.

The third subcategory, that relating to the victim's personal life, is most often the most voluminous within the victimology report. This subcategory should contain all information that is relevant to the victim's personal life. This information may include, but is not limited to, marital status, friendships, dating habits, daily routines, exercise habits, any drug use, drinking habits, preferred clothing style, shopping locations, preferred music and television genres, what type of transportation the victim used most frequently (e.g., car, public transportation such as subway or bus, bicycle, etc.), preferred reading genres, and Internet habits (e.g., did they visit certain websites such as dating or auction websites on a regular basis; what type of e-mail, e.g., Hotmail or Yahoo, did they use; did the victim have more than one e-mail account; did they chat online; have a Facebook account). All of the information listed will assist reviewers greatly in creating an accurate portrait of the victim's lifestyle and further assist in the classification of the victim as a low-, medium-, or high-risk target for homicidal violence.

The final subcategory within the victimology report is that of criminal history. This subcategory should contain all information relevant to any illicit or illegal activities that the victim may have had direct or indirect involvement in during the course of their lifetime. The criminal history of the victim may or may not include police reports and convictions for their actions but, regardless, will further indicate the risk level of the victim for meeting a violent and untimely end.

The aforementioned categories are simply broad indicators for what type of information the evaluator assigned to this task should endeavor to uncover. A cold case review team should also consult the *Crime Classification Manual*[2] for further information regarding the compilation of a comprehensive victimology report. Table 5.1 shows a sample victimology report.

Upon completion of the victimology report, the evaluating team should possess a much clearer image of the victim, his life, and his respective risk level for being a target of violence. The team now has a great tool at their disposal to narrow the field of persons of interest relevant to the commission of the crime. Remember, if you do not know your victim, you cannot know your killer.

The last stage of Phase II is the construction of exhaustive and independent timelines pertaining to the case information. Several different timelines must be constructed by team members to ensure that all persons and elements of the crime are sequentially accounted for. We suggest that timelines related to the crime scene, the victim, the victim's associates, and persons of interest be developed by team members. As with evidentiary issues, there is a question of whether these timelines should be outlined manually or with the assistance of the i2 program. We almost exclusively recommend the use of i2 when completing this task, because the i2 program allows for a straightforward and complete visual representation of timelines that can be augmented or altered simply by clicking a button, as opposed to having to undertake the tedious task of manually adjusting the timeline. In addition, i2 provides graphics and illustrations (such as icons of homes, businesses, etc.) that can be extremely useful when evaluators are attempting to visualize the crime and the events surrounding the immediate timeframe.

Table 5.1   Victimology Report Format

Basic Information:

  Name: _____

  Date of Birth:_____

  SSN:_____

Descriptive Information:

  Gender: _____

  Height:_____

  Weight: _____

  Eye Color: _____

  Hair Color: _____

  Race: _____

Case Circumstances:

  Victim Last Seen at:_____

  Time: _____

  Date: _____

  Witnesses: _____

Residential History:

  Current Address: _____

  Length of Time at Current Address: _____

  List All Former Addresses: _____

Employment History:

  Current Employment: _____

  Position/Title: _____

  Job Description:_____

  Former Employment: _____

Education:

  Highest Degree Earned: _____

  Date: _____

  Name of Educational Institution: _____

  Other Degrees and/or Certificates: _____

Relationship(s) (Intimate):

  Current Boyfriend/Girlfriend/Spouse/Partner: _____

  Length of Relationship: _____

  Status of Relationship (Stable vs. Unstable): _____

  Criminal Histories (if any) _____

  Former Relationships: _____

Relationships(s) (Friends/Known Associates):

  Name(s): _____

  Address(es):_____

  Length of Time Known to the Victim: _____

  Type of Relationship:_____

  Criminal Histories (if any): _____

continued

Table 5.1 (continued)   Victimology Report Format

Weekly Schedule (Victim): _____
  Recreational Activities:
    Preferred Music (Style or Artist): _____
    Preferred Clothing Style:_____
    Preferred Television Shows/Movies: _____
  Locations Frequented:
    Restaurants:_____
    Parks/Jogging Trails: _____
    Gym: _____
    Movie Theaters: _____
    Shopping: _____
    Grocery Shopping: _____
    Other: _____
  Internet Activity:
    E-mail Server (Hotmail, Yahoo, etc.): _____
    Screen Name(s): _____
    Websites Frequented: _____
    Did the Victim Chat with or Meet People Online? _____
Criminal History (if any): _____
Mental Health Concerns/Issues (if any):_____
Anything Else That Might Be Relevant:_____

We will now address and examine the individual timelines that should be constructed by the team a bit more closely. The first timeline that we suggest is that of the victim. The timeline of the victim should begin at the earliest date of action made by the victim that is documented within the case file. This could be as early as a few hours before the victim was murdered, to as far back as a few days or weeks prior to the crime. The timeline of the victim should include the victim's work schedule during this time, any leisure or recreational activities the victim participated in during this timeframe, the contact that he or she made with other individuals (it is important that those individuals be named in the timeline, as well as the date, time, and reason for the contact), any significant emotional events the victim may have experienced during this timeframe and what they were, any drug and alcohol use, the victim's dating habits or marital status during this time, and any illicit activities the victim may have been involved with. Although this list of factors that comprise a timeline are extensive, they are by no means superfluous. Each element provides a greater degree of clarity for evaluators as to the physical movements, emotional status, and personal relations relevant to the victim during the timeframe immediately preceding his or her death.

The second timeline to be constructed, if necessary, is that which is relevant to the crime scene itself. The development of this particular timeline may only be imperative if the scene is either an outdoor location or a location that experiences heavy foot or vehicle traffic. A case example to further illustrate this point is that of a 16-year-old lifeguard who was abducted from her post at a local swimming hole in Massachusetts and subsequently murdered. The young woman's remains were found 3 years later on a wooded hillside 5 miles from the pond. To date, no one has been arrested in her case. In this instance, there are two crime scenes: the pond from which the young lady was abducted and the hillside where her remains were recovered. There is also the possibility of a third crime scene where the assault and/or murder occurred. In instances where there are multiple crime scenes, creating a timeline of each scene may prove especially helpful to evaluators, as the events surrounding the crime and access to each scene by particular persons of interest are clarified. In the case mentioned here, it is unknown whether investigators constructed timelines of either of these scenes, as this case is still active and records could not be obtained. However, we will nonetheless utilize the case as an example of constructing crime scene timelines.

In the 24 hours before the young lifeguard vanished, her mother had observed a man alone in a white vehicle in the parking lot of the pond. The man was acting suspiciously, smoking a cigarette, and paying close attention to the girl. In the weeks that followed, witnesses came forth to say that they too had seen this person and the white vehicle in the days preceding the abduction. Therefore, in this instance, a timeline of the crime scene itself proves to be quite important. Though it is unknown whether the man in the white car did commit the crime, his presence at the scene in the days preceding the crime is certainly important for investigators to note. The second crime scene, the wooded hillside, is an area that is frequented by hunters. In fact, it was ultimately a hunter who discovered the young lady's bathing suit on the hillside. It would be prudent in an instance such as this to interview all local hunters and members of the hunting club across the street from the hillside to determine whether they recalled anything suspicious during the timeframe of the crime. In addition, a timeline of the hunting seasons may have potentially been beneficial to investigators.

As stated earlier, evaluators need to determine whether the crime scene itself warrants a timeline. If a timeline of the scene is warranted, evaluators should look at traffic patterns (both pedestrian and vehicle) surrounding the scene, at what point in the day the population around the scene is most dense, what type of individuals visit the scene (e.g., soccer moms vs. drug dealers, as this may further indicate the type of perpetrator investigators are seeking), and, most important, the activity that took place at the scene itself during the immediate timeframe both before and after the commission of the crime.

The final series of timelines to be completed by the evaluating team are those regarding the various named persons of interest within the file. The production of additional timelines pertaining to persons of interest may become necessary at a later juncture of the review process, as the inclusion of additional persons of interest is often seen in cold case evaluations as further facts, circumstances, and motives surrounding the crime become more apparent as the evaluation process progresses. One of the primary core benefits of constructing timelines for each person of interest is that the finished timeline will better depict for evaluators the pre-, peri-, and post-crime behavior exhibited by each individual. That is, how each individual acted and what he or she did immediately preceding, during, and following the commission of the crime. A further discussion of the development of pre-, peri-, and post-crime behavior is presented in Chapter 10.

Keeping this in mind, evaluators should formulate timelines for persons of interest much in the same way that the timeline pertaining to the victim was fashioned. Therefore, the timeline for each person of interest should include the following: the person of interest's vocation and work schedule, leisure activities the individual engaged in, dating habits or marital status, location and type of residence, any drug and alcohol use, emotional status (any significant emotional events that occurred in their life, e.g., breakup, termination of employment), and any contact the individual may have had with the victim (including date, time, and reason for contact). These factors should also be considered, and are perhaps more indicative of the individual's guilt or innocence, in the timeframe following the commission of the crime. This is known as post-crime behavior. Timelines pertaining to each individual person of interest will also substantially assist evaluators in determining the MOM that an individual may have had to commit the homicide. Once the timelines have been completed, they should be prominently displayed in the meeting room utilized by investigators to provide visual representation of each individual's movements, as well as a quick reference point to spot-check the validity of alibis, statements, and so forth.

We will now briefly return to the issue of group discussions. The reader may be curious as to how the processes described earlier unfold within the context of a group dynamic. Throughout the course of a cold case review, one individual is often assigned to compile a victimology report, while another is assigned to analyze evidentiary issues, and yet another must complete timelines. The designation by a supervisor for a particular team member to complete these tasks is based exclusively on the background of the team member and their underlying expertise or interest. These decisions are not subjective. It is important to mention this due to the fact that some tasks within the context of a cold case analysis are viewed to be more "glamorous" than others. For example, constructing behavioral analyses of persons of interest, what some call "profiling," is often a desirable task in an evaluation, as criminal profiling has been so highly lauded by the media. However, the importance of each component of a cold case evaluation cannot be overstated. From establishing a master name database to developing interview and interrogation strategies, each task serves an integral role in the review process, and the efficacy and detail with which each assignment is carried out is paramount to a successful evaluation and subsequent follow-up investigation. So, although one individual is assigned to complete each element of the evaluation, the final product is a team effort.

Regular weekly meetings are essential in that within the context of a group dynamic, discussions will often lead to the discovery of nuances and details that an individual alone might not have previously detected. Therefore, at each iteration of analysis (name database, evidentiary issues, victimology, and timelines), the group should discuss the findings as a collective entity and attempt to draw out further information to augment the final report. As a supervisor, one should keep in mind that order must be maintained during these collaborations, and each individual should be allotted time to voice his or her opinions. Remember that team members serve as a sounding board for each other, and the supervisor is merely the referee to ensure that all theories and possible objections or suggestions are carefully considered and not dismissed frivolously.

As the team has now completed the master name database, analyzed the evidentiary issues, completed the victimology report, and constructed exhaustive timelines, they are now ready to proceed to Phases III and IV of the model.

Phases III and IV

Introduction

This section will effectively conclude the discussion of the first cold case model. The tasks required within the third and fourth phases are presented here. These two phases have been assimilated into one section due to the fact that the last two phases are more highly correlated with each other than Phase I and Phase II. First, we discuss Phase III, which includes the formulation of relationship charts, suspectology reports, logic trees, and interview strategies, all interspersed with group meetings and team collaboration (Figure 5.7). Phase IV of the evaluation model begins with the analysis of named persons of interest within the case file. The persons of interest are ranked from highest to lowest priority according to the correlating pros and cons identified by evaluators. This final phase of the evaluation model subsequently includes the development of pre-, peri-, and post-offense behavior as they relate to each person of interest. Following this, evaluators will shape an investigative plan pursuant to the follow-up investigation (Figure 5.8). Finally, an official evaluation report is compiled to present to investigators (Figure 5.9).

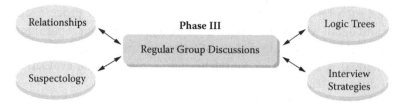

Figure 5.7 Cold case evaluation model, Phase III.

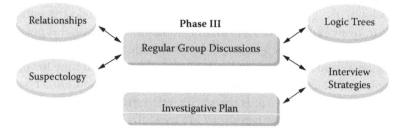

Figure 5.8 Cold case evaluation model, Phase III, expanded.

Figure 5.9 Cold case evaluation model, Phase IV.

Phase III

The first task to be accomplished by evaluators in this phase of the model is to construct relationship charts. These charts provide both evaluators and officials conducting the follow-up investigation with insights as to the scope, nature, and context of relationships among the victim and persons of interest and associates. These relationship charts can additionally shed some light on possible motives for the homicide and will contribute later in Phase IV to the construction of pre-, peri-, and post-offense behavior. The development of relationship charts is similar to the creation of evidence flow charts. The relationship charts should be fashioned in a simple, logical fashion so that, like the evidence flow charts, they are easy to follow visually and are broken down into manageable numbers. Several relationships will inevitably be identified during the evaluation process. However, it is the most central relationships, such as those between the victim and named persons of interest, that must be the most thoroughly scrutinized and flushed out by the review panel. To accomplish this, evaluators should document the following regarding each central relationship within the case file to the best of their ability with available information:

How and when the victim and person of interest met

What the context of their relationship was (e.g., were they friends, coworkers, family members)

Whether the duration of the relationship was constant or sporadic in nature (did they always maintain contact or was there a falling out that interrupted the relationship)

Whether any dynamic in the relationship shifted at any given point in time (was the relationship always platonic or did the two become intimate)

Any communications between the two parties (phone calls, text messages, letters, e-mails, face-to-face meetings)

The physical location of both parties for the duration of the relationship (address, place of employment, etc.)

Once this information has been compiled and documented by evaluators, the task of shaping these facts into a visual representation arises. Similar to evidence charts and timelines, evaluators have a choice as to the manner in which the relationship charts are visually represented. If there is no one available on the team who demonstrates an aptitude for constructing coherent, succinct, and aesthetically pleasing charts, the i2 program should be utilized. There can be several formats that a single relationship chart can take. We recommend that each chart be as exclusive and specific as possible. For example, if there is extensive communication via phone calls, letters, and so forth, between the victim and a person of interest, a separate relationship chart can be formulated to depict these communications, external to all other elements of the relationship. Whatever the content of the relationship chart, we recommend that the individual at the center of the relationship who is being analyzed should be named in the center of the document. A photograph of said individual should also be included, if possible. From there, a spider-web-like network of information should extend out from the individual relating to that person's relationship with the suspects, associates, and so on.

Each chart should also include at the bottom citations from where in the case file the information was gathered. This is to facilitate the process of cross-referencing by follow-up investigators when reviewing the material.

Following the creation of relationship charts, the team must also construct logic trees. These logic trees vary somewhat from evidence flow charts and relationship charts in that they are primarily used to put forth various scenarios of the crime. As the evaluation of a case file progresses, theories of the crime will inevitably be established by team members. Evaluators must keep in mind that the theory must align with the facts presented in the case. Evaluators must not allow themselves to twist the context of factual information to fit their own theory of the crime. This is where missteps in investigative processes often occur that can derail a legitimate avenue of investigation. The facts of a case must be used in the development of a theory and must be appropriately cited within the logic tree following completion. The logic trees developed regarding scenarios of the crime may be related to a sequence of events surrounding the crime or a particular person of interest. For example, in one case we reviewed, a team member constructed a logic tree of three separate scenarios. Although each scenario was unique and vastly different from the others, it was clearly shown through the layout of the logic tree that each scenario inevitably led back to a single person of interest who could not be ruled out. By visually depicting the scenarios in such a manner, this reflected to follow-up investigators that this particular person of interest had the highest level of priority. This logic tree was constructed with the person of interest at the center of the diagram, with the three scenarios surrounding said individual. At some future date, if this case goes to court, this logic tree of the scenarios could be a very valuable piece of demonstrative evidence. The final format could be similar to the one in Figure 5.10.

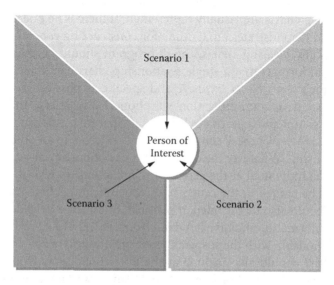

Figure 5.10 Person of interest model with multiple theories of the crime.

Creating suspectology reports is the third element of Phase III that must be undertaken by evaluators. The formulation of a suspectology report is quite similar to the process of developing a victimology report. The one critical difference between a suspectology and a victimology report is that when creating the suspectology report, particular attention must be paid to the person of interest's contact with the victim and the context of the relationship (if any) with the victim. The suspectology report should be a simply organized documentation of all relevant information pertaining to the person of interest, factual information both related to and not related to the victim of the crime. Information such as full name, date of birth, criminal history, education, employment, and marital status or dating habits should all be included in this report. Subcategories should be created within the suspectology report to break down a potentially colossal amount of information into manageable sections. This breakdown of information will also assist follow-up investigators. As you will see in Chapter 10, all the data you collect with the suspectology will help to fill in the blanks for the pre- and post-crime behaviors. Such data should also assist investigators in identifying the subtypes of perpetrators.

The final component of Phase III lies in the creation of interview strategies. We have observed that during various cold case analyses, the interview process is a central component of successful cold case evaluations and subsequent investigations. Given that in some instances physical evidence may be unavailable due to the passage of time or insufficient collection during the initial investigation, the resolution of a cold case may depend entirely on cogent, successful interviews. The importance of a properly and meticulously conducted interview can never be overstated. In addition, much like the collection of evidence, investigators only have one chance to get an interview right. If the process is sloppy or bungled in some manner, the person of interest may retain counsel and refuse to speak further, or a witness may clam up and refuse to talk. It is for this reason that the creation of well-organized, comprehensive, and individualized interview strategies is absolutely essential. The team member who is designated to construct the interview strategies for relevant persons of interest and witnesses should optimally have a background in behavioral analysis or psychology. In addition, this team member should possess a great deal of intuitive skill, as the nuances of interview strategies are created by gauging an individual's response to given lines of questioning, word phrasing, and physical environment. Because this is a cold case, the investigators have the advantage of having more information than before, such as more details regarding post-crime behavior. The topic of interviews and interrogations is detailed further in Chapter 11.

To begin creating an interview strategy for a person of interest, the typology of said person must be classified. That is, are they power-assertive, power-reassurance, anger-retaliatory, and so forth. Further descriptions of these typologies can be found in Chapter 10. The initial classification of a person of interest into one of these categories is paramount to a successful interview, as particular strategies are correlated with each typology. For example, with a power-assertive individual, it is important that he feels superior and his ego is stimulated. Therefore, statements such as "she had it coming" or "all women are horrible," and so forth, would prove effective. In addition, with power-assertive offenders, for example, the murder does not count, so to speak, unless someone knows. The offender wants to brag about his actions, and investigators should exploit this egotistical weakness by allowing him to boast about his exploits.

Once the typology classification has been designated, the team member constructing the strategy must accomplish several other tasks. The first is the suggested timeline of the interview (e.g., should the investigator accuse the person of interest outright or should they spend time simply conversing with him about his life, job, hobbies, etc.). Depending on the person of interest's typology, the progression of the interview is extremely important. The next element of the interview strategy is who should conduct the interview. Should the investigator be male or female? Should they be young or middle aged? Should there be one or two interviewers present? Should they be in uniform or plain clothes? If wearing street clothes, is there a particular style of dress that might appeal to the individual being interviewed or put him more at ease? All of these elements depend on the personality of the interview subject and should be considered carefully; if the subject does not feel at ease, does not trust, or is suspicious of the interviewer, all will be lost.

The third consideration that the evaluator constructing the interview strategy must approach is the appropriate physical arrangement of the interview room. That is, what type of environment would the subject respond best to, and what type of environment would then be most likely to assist in eliciting a confession. The factors involved in the physical arrangement of the interview room are as follows: Should the interview be conducted at the police station, at the subject's home, at the subject's place of employment, or elsewhere? In one case example, a subject told investigators he did not want to disappoint his father, who had passed away. So investigators took the subject to his father's grave and gave him the opportunity to confess his sins and apologize to his father for his indiscretion. Therefore, the location of the interview can prove extremely important. Following the decision regarding the location of the interview, the décor of the room must be addressed. If the interview is to be held at the police station, would it be more beneficial to place the subject in a stark interrogation room with simply a table and a chair, or in a more comfortable office space? Would it be more beneficial to the interview process to have something between the interviewer and the subject, such as a table, or have nothing separating the two, to convey a greater sense of intimacy and perhaps pressure? Is the subject the type of individual who would have a reaction to case paraphernalia being displayed in the room? This can range from a photo of the victim on the wall or table to a sealed evidence bag with perhaps a victim's belonging or the murder weapon inside. The temperature of the interview room must also be considered. Is the subject more likely to react to extreme hot or extreme cold?

Finally, the timing of the interview must be considered. By this, we do not simply mean the time of day, though this can also be relevant, but the timing within the context of the follow-up investigation. For example, if investigators will be soliciting media attention in assisting with the resolution of the case, would it be more beneficial to interview the subject before or after the blitz of media coverage?

All of the nuances of an interview as described may sound tedious to flesh out, and they are. However, each detail of the interview process must be carefully considered, for the omission or addition of one of the described factors could make or break an interview for investigators. All of this information regarding interview strategies dovetails with the information found in Chapter 11.

Phase IV

Phase IV is the final phase of the evaluation model where all previously created charts and documents are compiled into a cumulative evaluation report to guide the follow-up investigation. However, three tasks must be completed prior to the compilation of the evaluation report. These are: persons of interest (pros and cons); pre-, peri-, and post-offense behavior; and the investigative plan (Figure 5.11).

Let us begin with the development of the pros and cons pertaining to each person of interest. The reader might wonder why the authors chose to begin this phase with the development of pros and cons rather than with pre-, peri-, and post-offense behavior. In developing pros and cons for each

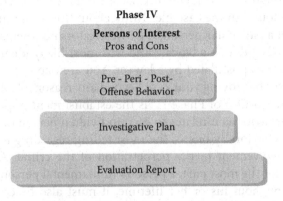

Figure 5.11 Cold case evaluation model, Phase IV.

particular person of interest, the elements within each list will greatly assist in the development of pre-, peri-, and post-offense behavior at the second iteration of Phase IV. For example, if on the pros list of a person of interest, an item listed is the fact that this person moved away from the immediate area directly following the commission of the crime, this action can then be inserted into the category of post-offense behavior for the person of interest during the next phase.

Let us examine the elements and facts within the case file that should be included in the pros and cons list for each person of interest. The list should primarily consist of elements related to motive, opportunity, and means (MOM) that pertain to each subject. The list for each individual should be visually represented by a large sheet of butcher paper on a wall in the team's designated workspace. Group discussion is a significant dynamic in the development of these lists, and all team members should be available and encouraged to participate in this process.

The "pro" portion of the list should include all facts that indicate that the individual may have perpetrated the crime. This information may include but is not limited to the motive of the individual, physical location at the time of the crime, connection to the victim, incriminating actions following the crime (e.g., moving away from the area in which the crime was committed, inserting himself into the investigation), opportunity the subject may have had to commit the crime, and the means available to the individual to commit the crime.

The "con" portion of the list should include all facts of the case that cast doubt on the individual's involvement, conflicting statements or circumstances, and so forth. This list may include, but is not limited to, issues such as a confirmed alibi, lack of means, lack of motive (or significant motive), and lack of opportunity. This is also the portion of the list where evaluators may note a lack of noticeable pre-, peri-, or post-crime behavior that speaks to the subject's possible innocence. A separate list should be created for each identified person of interest, with a reference list as to where each fact mentioned in the list can be found in the case file. Think about this for a minute—by listing the cons of a particular person, the investigators put themselves into the position of playing devil's advocate and will most likely identify for themselves any defenses postulated by a lawyer. You are one step ahead and are that much closer to proving your case beyond any reasonable doubt.

The second portion of Phase IV is the establishment of pre-, peri-, and post-offense behavior as it relates to each individual person of interest. This document is behaviorally one of the most telling regarding a given person of interest's involvement in the perpetration of the crime. Although it is accepted that, for the most part, a person's fundamental personality remains consistent throughout his or her lifetime, it must also be considered that situations involving extreme stress, anger, depression, elation, agitation, or any other extreme emotion may induce a sudden change in an individual personality and the actions that individual takes. This dynamic of extreme emotional experiences and how they come to affect an individual's behavior is precisely why the pre-, peri-, and post-offense diagram is essential to a successful cold case evaluation. The act of homicide is an extreme, primal, and emotion-laden/visceral event. The perpetrator of a homicide, as such, experiences a vast array of extreme emotional states before, during, and after the crime has been committed.

Prior to the crime being committed, the perpetrator may feel anything from rage to lust toward the victim. During the commission of the crime, the perpetrator may feel rage, exhilaration, fear, or achieve sexual gratification. Following the murder, the perpetrator may feel sexually satisfied, relief, fear, anger, or general relaxation and a sense of peace, depending on his or her psychological makeup. This range of emotions is inevitably transformed into a series of actions. These choices and actions made by the perpetrator before, during, and after the homicide are therefore directly correlated to his or her emotional state. This fact must be kept in mind by evaluators when constructing the pre-, peri-, and post-offense diagram for each person of interest. This correlation between a subject's emotional state and resulting actions is critical in that the degree to which patterns of behavior change from pre-offense to post-offense behavior is often indicative of guilt or innocence. That is, the greater the shift in emotional state and actions exhibited by a person of interest, the greater the likelihood of their involvement in the crime. Again, refer to Chapter 10 for details of how this suspect identification process works.

Let us now examine the factors that should be considered for inclusion in the pre-, peri-, and post-offense diagram. The elements included in the pre- and post-categories of the diagram are identical. These two categories should include the following: employment (if any), marital status and/or dating habits, physical address, physical appearance of the person of interest (for example, did they have a beard or mustache before the crime and then shave it afterward, perhaps attempting to disguise their identity), means of transportation used (did they have one vehicle before and then dump it after the crime), any drug and alcohol use (did the person not drink or use drugs prior to the crime but start afterward, or perhaps vice versa in order to better maintain his silence), criminal activity, and so forth. Once again, evaluators will eventually categorize each person of interest from highest to lowest in priority, and the degree to which each person of interest's behavior shifts from pre- to post-offense behavior is certainly a means by which to assign priority.

The peri-offense behavior is independent of each person of interest. That is, evaluators are not looking at the behavior of each person of interest, but rather the behavior that is evident within the crime itself. Therefore, prior to developing pre- and post-offense behavior lists for any person of interest, the evaluation team must carefully examine evidence from the crime scene (photographs, tapes, etc.) and determine what behaviors can be seen within the context of the scene. The first obvious thing to consider within the crime scene is the victim. Was he or she at low, medium, or high risk for falling prey to homicidal violence? For example, was she a married schoolteacher with three children and a stable home, or a prostitute? Defining this will assist evaluators somewhat in determining if the crime was personal in nature or random. The second element that must be considered regarding the scene is the physical location of the scene itself. Did the crime occur in a home, outdoors, in a condemned building, and so on? This will assist evaluators in determining both the personal nature of the crime as well as the exposure the perpetrator was willing to risk to carry out his crime. The third factor regarding the crime scene that must be examined is the time of day the crime was committed. Again, whether the homicide occurred on a busy street during broad daylight versus in the woods at night will tell evaluators about the risk level of the crime. For example, the reader may recall the case example given earlier about the young lifeguard from Massachusetts. In that particular scenario, the young lady was an athlete, and she was abducted from a public pond with a very narrow window of opportunity at 10 o'clock in the morning. All of these facts reveal that whoever abducted and subsequently murdered this young woman was willing to risk a great deal to abduct her, given the high visibility of the scene and the fact that the young woman was a strong, capable athlete. The fourth element of the crime scene that must be analyzed is the way in which the victim was murdered. Were they shot, stabbed, strangled (manually versus ligature), or drowned? The primary purpose of examining the manner in which the victim was killed is to further narrow the suspect typology that investigators seek. For example, if the victim was shot, this indicates that either the violence toward the victim was perhaps random or the perpetrator did not want to get too close to the victim to commit the crime. Conversely, if the victim was strangled (especially manually), this indicates a completely different typology to investigators. The perpetrator wanted to feel the life slipping from the victim. Manual strangulation is an intensely personal method of murder. In the same vein as how the victim was murdered, evaluators must also note whether overkill was involved. For example, if the victim was stabbed to death, were there 1 or 2 stab wounds, or upward of 20 or 30, far more than necessary to inflict fatal damage on the victim? The presence of overkill in a crime scene indicates a perpetrator who was in the throes of extreme rage at the time of the killing. This emotion can be correlated with pre- and post-offense behavior. All the subtle (and sometimes not so subtle) underlying psychological elements of a crime scene can be drawn out through the facts as they present themselves. Group discussions are highly important during this phase, as both intuitive and factual information are utilized and necessary; therefore, a group dynamic complements this element of analysis much more than a single individual being designated to complete the assignment.

As the elements of the pre-, peri-, and post-categories have now been laid out, let us examine how evaluators apply the knowledge from the three categories in order to designate persons of interest ranging from high to low priority. As stated earlier, in the majority of instances, in order to classify a person of interest as being a high priority to investigators, a noticeable and considerable shift in the pendulum between pre- and post-offense behavior must be evident. In addition to this, pre- and post-offense behavior must be correlated to the behavioral evidence contained in the peri-offense behavior category. That is, evaluators must determine whether the psychological evidence within the crime, and the crime scene itself, are consistent with the psychological makeup of a given person of interest. It is suggested that at this phase of the development of the pre-, peri-, and post-offense diagram, evaluators draw lines between correlating behaviors. A diagram depicting this process is shown in Figure 5.12. For the purposes of this diagram, the person of interest is the victim's ex-boyfriend. (This scenario does not reflect any actual case and is merely being used as a visual aid for the reader.) As shown by the diagram, it is apparent that the subject's behavior shifted drastically between the pre- and post-offense phases of the crime. For example, prior to the crime he was employed, did not abuse alcohol or drugs, and had a

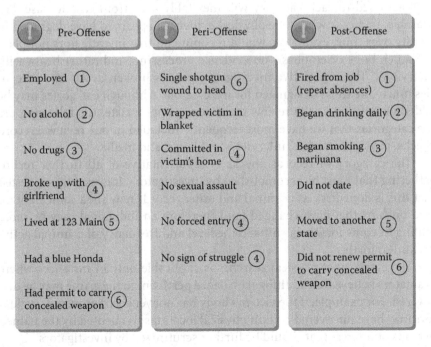

Figure 5.12 Pre-, peri-, and post-offense model.

permit to carry a concealed weapon. Following the commission of the crime, the subject was fired from his job, began abusing both drugs and alcohol, moved to another state, and did not renew his permit to carry a concealed weapon. These dramatic behavior modifications should indicate to investigators that the subject represents a priority for having committed the crime.

As the reader can observe, there are several high degrees of correlation among pre-, peri-, and post-offense behaviors. The amount and degree of correlation would indicate to officials responsible for the follow-up investigation that this person of interest is a high priority.

To reiterate, in closing, for the vast majority of cases, the higher the degree in shift of behaviors between the phases of the crime, the higher the likelihood that the person of interest was involved. Additionally, in serial investigations, detectives should also consider the consistency of pre- and post-offense behavior for persons of interest, in that, despite the interruption in their life due to committing the crime, does their pathology, and do their patterns of behavior remain consistent?

The final task to be completed by the cold case review panel prior to the compilation of the evaluation report is the development of a comprehensive investigative plan. The investigative plan serves to guide officials responsible for the follow-up investigation in an appropriate direction. The investigative plan is also designed to depict tasks that investigators should consider completing, ranked from highest to lowest priority. The priority level assigned to each category will inevitably vary from case to case. For example, in a case where the physical evidence appears to have degraded in quality over time, evaluators would recommend that investigators not place too much hope or emphasis on evidence processing, and rather begin with interviews. The cumulative investigative plan is broken down into categories much like those designated for the case file. Although categories may be added or omitted as the review team deems appropriate, the following are the categories that we have most frequently included in our reviews: record checks, physical searches, interviews, evidence, and media.

The category of records checks is representative of all further record gathering that must be accomplished by investigators. It is usually suggested that this is done first, as criminal and other records may shed some light on relationships that have changed (and therefore an individual may be more willing to come forward), shifts in the level and frequency of criminal activity, and so forth.

The category of physical searches is applicable only in instances where evaluators believe that additional evidence pertinent to the crime may be discovered. For example, if the victim's body has not yet been recovered, evaluators may have uncovered certain physical locations frequented by the named persons of interest that should be further scrutinized by investigators.

Interviews are the third category that should be included in the investigative plan. It is also important to note here for investigators what the order and timing of interviews are suggested to be. That is, what is the most effective strategy that will yield the best results? For example, if trying to put pressure on a person of interest, it may behoove investigators to begin interviewing associates of said person of interest, then move inward in concentric circles to his closest family and friends. This way the subject knows he is being investigated, and as investigators have not yet spoken with him, his degree of agitation may increase to the point that he makes a mistake and facilitates his own capture. Therefore, the order and timing of interviews and the designation of those factors to investigators is an important element of the investigative plan.

The fourth category to be included in the investigative plan is evidence. This category typically is concerned with retesting of original evidence and the capability of completing said testing due to advances in technology. The team member assigned to complete the analysis of the physical evidence mentioned within the case file must designate in the investigative plan the specific testing that is recommended. This way, when investigators approach the lab for additional testing, they can specify exactly what it is they need.

Media is the final category to be included in the investigative plan. Cold cases are often mercurial; that is, the attention given to them by the press can vacillate as the years go by or a hot tip comes in, and so forth. Given this fact, if investigators are at a dead end and are looking for ways to generate public interest in the case, the media is an excellent avenue. Therefore, if evaluators feel that this is relevant, they should include in the investigative plan specifically what media arrangements may be helpful (e.g., a press conference, a one-on-one interview with a detective). A good example of the way media sources can be used positively to assist in the resolution of a cold case is the case of Chandra Levy. In the summer of 2008, the *Washington Post* ran a 12-week-long series of articles to drum up publicity on Levy's case. The articles extensively covered the victim's life, her murder, the investigation, and the persons of interest. As such, the media can be an excellent resource for investigators and a great way to engender public interest in a cold case.[3]

Having completed the investigative plan, it is time for all of the documents created by the evaluation team to be compiled into a cumulative evaluation report. This report should be well organized and professional. The report should be professionally bound, preferably spiral binding so the booklet can lay flat when opened. The contents of the report should be categorized and labeled with numbered tabs that are then identified in a table of contents at the beginning of the report. The evaluation report will consist of every document that has been produced by the team's efforts during the evaluation process. It should include evidence; victimology; witness list; timelines;

relationship charts; logic trees; suspectology reports; interview strategies; pre-, peri-, post-offense behavior diagrams; persons of interest (pros and cons); and the investigative plan. When a meeting is scheduled to brief investigators, the evaluation team must ask how many people from the agency will be attending the meeting. The team must make a copy of the report for each individual attending as well as one for each member of the team, so information can be easily accessed during the briefing. To supplement the evaluation report, large reproductions of essential documents such as timelines, logic trees, relationship charts, and pre-, peri-, post-offense behaviors should be reproduced for the briefing. The creation of large, poster-sized documents is extremely effective during briefings, as investigators can then visually comprehend the material being presented to them and perhaps come away with a greater appreciation for the priority of certain persons of interest.

When the evaluation report is completed and a briefing is scheduled with the investigative agency, the team must conduct run-through rehearsals of who will speak when, what is to be said, and so on. Each team member responsible for the construction of essential documents pertaining to the case (e.g., evidence, interview strategies, victimology) must speak to how the document was created, the content of the document, and the significance of said document within the context of the investigation. Evaluators must dress professionally for the briefing and be punctual. This briefing is the primary reflection of the team's efforts and must be essentially flawless in order to convey professionalism and earn the trust and respect of investigators.

At the conclusion of the briefing by the evaluation team, the follow-up investigation optimally will ensue immediately.

Endnotes

1. i2 Analyst's Notebook, McLean, VA.
2. Douglas, John E., Ann W. Burgess, Allen G. Burgess, and Robert K. Ressler. 2004. *Crime Classification Manual*, 2nd ed. Jossey-Bass: Hoboken, NJ.
3. Since the first edition of this book a conviction in the Levy case was obtained. According to sources there was no physical evidence tying the suspect to the murder, but there was an alleged jailhouse confession. However, during the early part of 2013, secret meetings of the prosecution and defense have been rumored with a judge. Apparently they are now concerned about the reliability of the person who reported the jailhouse confession. You must be able to validate any and all confessions, regardless of the source.

An Alternative Model for Evaluating Cold Cases

6

JAMES M. ADCOCK AND SARAH L. STEIN

In the previous chapter we discussed the main, all encompassing and thorough model of evaluating cold cases but mentioned that we had learned from our lectures to police detectives that the model may be too labor intensive for most departments to employ. That in turn caused us to reevaluate it and design not one but two additional models that we believe will be more suitable to the needs of the majority of police agencies in the United States. Additionally, we were motivated by the requirements found in the announcements of the National Institute of Justice (NIJ) Cold Case DNA grants where they specifically require that only those cases where potential DNA material exist will be processed under the guidelines of the grant.

Another consideration worthwhile mentioning is that we have seen many agencies drawn immediately to the exactness (most of the time) and suitability of DNA, and who frequently do not pursue their cases any further unless they have DNA potential material or they have received a DNA match through the Combined DNA Index System (CODIS). In other words, they have become very reliant on DNA to help them solve their cases with the sad part being if DNA does not exist the investigation rarely gets a review for other solvability factors. This brings us to the point, how else can we solve these cases and how should we go about doing it. This will be explained in more detail as the chapter progresses and in other chapters as well.

Notice how the overall model is different from what was described in the previous chapter (Figure 6.1a,b). The emphasis has now been placed on the evidentiary issues of the physical evidence first, where detectives are asked to identify and eliminate those investigations that have such physical material because they have the largest potential to be solved with less effort.

Experience from seeing other cold case units work tells us, like mentioned earlier in Chapter 4, that frequently a detective starts the process off in a cold case unit by conducting a thorough review of the files looking for solvability factors, leads, evidence, and so forth. A lot of time is spent up front in this process, but many cases end up not being investigated further due to the lack of evidentiary information. This is not always wasted time, as some cases are resolved but many are not. As a result, we feel their time could be better utilized holding off this thorough review until a little later in the

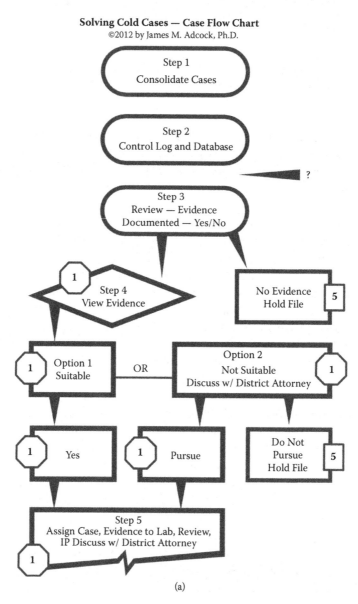

Figure 6.1 (a) Alternative cold case evaluation model, Part 1. (b) Alternative cold case evaluation model, Part 2. *(Continued)*

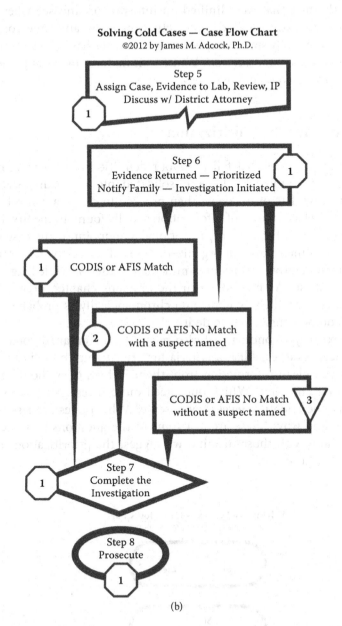

Solving Cold Cases — Case Flow Chart
©2012 by James M. Adcock, Ph.D.

(b)

Figure 6.1 (continued) (a) Alternative cold case evaluation model, Part 1. (b) Alternative cold case evaluation model, Part 2.

process where more and faster results could be received. Put your time and efforts first into those that you know have solvability possibilities. Then later, return to the files that were limited on information and see where investigative prowess can be applied. The actual thorough and time-consuming review does not really start in earnest until evidence has been identified and sent to the crime lab for analysis. While waiting for those results the detectives have time to conduct the review.

Step 1 and Step 2: Prioritization

At the onset, all cases that fall into your definition of cold or unresolved cases (murders or rapes) should be consolidated into one secure location and initially filed by date of incident. Then proceed to create a control log or a database of the basic pieces of information usually found in the first incident report (Figure 6.2). From an organizational standpoint, if the case file and associated documents are not organized, items of interest will be missed or lost, so it is imperative this is done immediately after or while logging them into the database. As mentioned in the previous chapter, organizing the file into categories, then by name and chronologically, is probably the best and most comprehensive way to do it.

The next major concern that also relates to the organizational aspects of this process is to establish a criteria for prioritizing these files that may change as you glean information from them. Which ones should get your attention first and why? Which ones need more investigative work before they rise to the attention level they deserve? Which ones are less likely to be resolved and why? These are just some of the questions that need to be considered and with those in mind we suggest the prioritization schedule described in Figure 6.3.

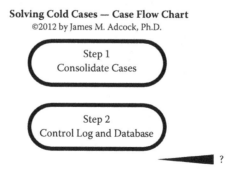

Solving Cold Cases — Case Flow Chart
©2012 by James M. Adcock, Ph.D.

Step 1
Consolidate Cases

Step 2
Control Log and Database

?

Figure 6.2 Alternative cold case evaluation model, Steps 1 and 2.

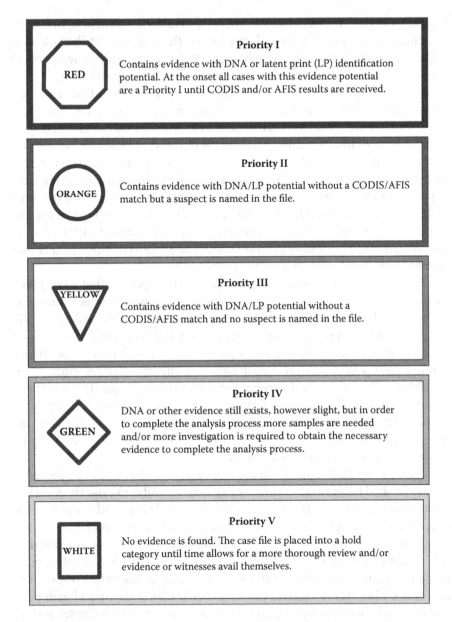

Figure 6.3 Alternative cold case evaluation model, prioritization.

These are quite simple and easy to follow, especially if you color code them as indicated. In the beginning assume that most cases will start off as being a Priority I and then as information is uncovered the prioritization changes. Following this process will help the agency spend its manpower and resources wisely as it will energetically go after those cases that present themselves as the most likely to solve. Those cases then become the best of the best, and besides creating public attention and interest will also significantly contribute to the political gain derived from the successes of the cold case team; a win-win for everyone including the surviving family members, all contributing to the issue of instilling trust in the police department.

Priority I—As one can see from Figure 6.3, Priority I (Red) cases are those that have the most likelihood of being solved sooner rather than later. These cases have evidence that contain DNA potential which meets the requirements of most granting agencies for processing. However, we feel this is not enough and have added evidence that may contain latent print material that is suitable for the identification of a specific person of interest, thus adding an additional important tool. Why stop with just DNA, as we have other tools that are also very effective? All cases that contain this type of specific evidence will remain a Priority I investigation until either CODIS or AFIS (automated fingerprint identification system) are received. These results may change the prioritization level of the investigation.

Priority II—Some cases may have physical properties that would lend themselves to an analysis and subsequent identification, but after submission to the crime lab no matches were received. The donor of this evidence is still out there but not yet in the system. The issue at hand here is whether a suspect is named in the file. If so, this investigation becomes a Priority II because it still has great potential for being solved with some investigative work.

Priority III—The only difference between Priority II and III is whether a suspect is named in the file. All other aspects are the same (i.e., evidence at the crime lab, results received but no match), however, the file does not reflect the name(s) of any suspects. As a result this investigation will require much more work to achieve solvability.

Priority IV—In Priority IV some evidence exists but it may be degraded or very limited in its value to the investigation. In order to raise the level to a higher priority, efforts need to be made that will identify and bring forward other physical samples from potential persons of interest listed in the file. There is no question that as we get further into these levels of prioritization that the cases become more difficult to resolve and progressively require much more time and effort. Therefore, the reason for the prioritization is to determine where the detectives can spend their efforts wisely and gain positive results. When time allows, go back to these lesser qualified cases and see what can be developed.

Priority V—Without a doubt, Priority V cases are at the bottom of the pile and most likely are not going to be solved. There is no evidence, no suspects are named, and information is very limited and may even be unreliable. Only when adequate time exists should these cases get your attention, because they will require an extensive amount of time, effort, conducting of interviews, and so forth, to raise the level of solvability expectation. Remember: Relationships change and those changes may be all you need to resolve it.

Step 3 and Step 4: Evidence

The first preliminary review of the case file begins here and the focus is on physical evidence. Do the case file documents reflect the presence of evidence that could lead to either a DNA or AFIS (latent print [LP]) match? At this point the reviewer has two choices that will indicate the level of interest and effort. If no evidence is found documented in the file, the case is relegated for the time being to the bottom, Priority V. Remember, the emphasis is to process those investigations that provide us with the highest probability of being resolved. Then, when time permits, return to the others (Figure 6.4).

Although Step 3 is relatively simple, as the answer is yes there is evidence or no there is not, Step 4 will require the actual viewing of the evidence where the detective or someone trained in crime scene investigation (CSI) or evidence concerns can physically eyeball the evidence to determine its suitability (chain of custody intact, maintained properly, not degraded, etc.). At this juncture in the model the evaluator has to make one of two decisions (Figure 6.5):

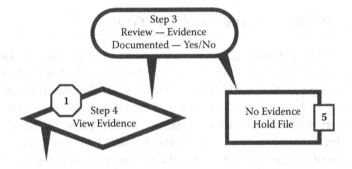

Figure 6.4 Alternative cold case evaluation model, Steps 3 and 4.

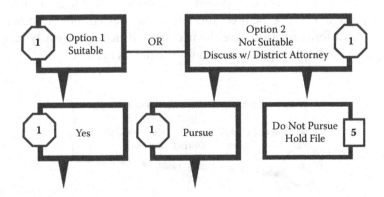

Figure 6.5 Alternative cold case evaluation model, Step 4 continued.

Option 1—The evidence is suitable for analysis.
Option 2—The evidence is not suitable for analysis.

If the evidence is suitable, the investigation remains a Priority I case and moves forward accordingly. If for whatever reason the evidence is not considered suitable for analysis, it does not stop there. The tendency at this point is to discard the case as not solvable and make it a much lower priority. However, prior to doing that we suggest the information thus far be provided to your district attorney (hopefully one is part of the cold case team) to find out if she or he may be willing to proceed with the case regardless of the potential problems. These problems could be overcome through additional testing of the evidence by the crime lab or other legal processes from the detectives or the district attorney. If the district attorney decides to not pursue the investigation further, then the case is relegated to either a Priority IV or V where it could get some attention later. But if the district attorney decides to take a chance (see Option 2 under Step 4) and move forward, then the evidence moves forward and the case remains a Priority I investigation.

Step 5: Case Review and Decision Time

In Step 5, the responsible detectives are going to spend most of their time reviewing a particular case (Figure 6.6). At this point the file has been identified as having physical evidence that may possess the material suitable for DNA testing or latent print items, both of which have the potential to positively identify a specific person of interest. The first phase of this step is for the detective to either arrange for or participate in the process needed to get the items of evidence to a crime laboratory for analysis. It is suggested that prior to the submission of any cold case evidence to a crime lab that coordination by the police department be conducted well in advance. Personally visiting or talking with the responsible lab personnel will go a long ways to getting the material expedited and quickly processed. Furthermore, this opportunity affords the detective the necessary time to personally view the evidence and have photographs taken for the file, as needed.

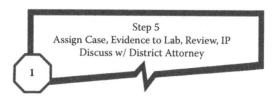

Figure 6.6 Alternative cold case evaluation model, Step 5.

We all know that the processing of the evidence by the crime lab may take some time, minimally 30 to 60 days. It is during this period that the thorough review of the file should begin. This will take time and the more methodical and organized the detective is, the odds of accurately resolving the investigation significantly increase. Searching for the "usual suspects" include solvability factors; naming of suspects in the file; looking for possible changes in relationships; linking people, places and things together; and so on. Ultimately developing, hopefully, the theory of the crime or at least identifying possible scenarios, all to be confirmed after the crime lab results are completed.

Part of this review should also include the formulating of a complete investigative plan where actions deemed necessary for proper completion of the investigation have been prioritized according to their importance, remembering to establish all the elements of the crime for the prosecutor. Along those same lines, as mentioned, having a district attorney as a member of the cold case unit is very helpful and will eliminate misinformation or misunderstandings of what each case is telling us. These discussions with the district attorney should keep the investigation (and investigative plan) on track acquiring all the necessary information.

One last comment regarding the case review process: while this could be, and frequently is, just one detective, we suggest that more than one person should review the information. And, if time and policy allow, the utilization of others (even outsiders) can be very beneficial as it brings an unbiased set of eyes to the table.

Step 6, Step 7, and Step 8

Utilizing the prioritization table provided, it is at this point in the process (Step 6) that the evidence gets returned to the department with laboratory reports of findings that will dictate the level of priority for each investigation (Figure 6.7). How much more time and effort will be placed in each investigation should be based on this priority level because it will indicate which cases have the highest probability of being successfully resolved.

Priority I—Those with positive CODIS or AFIS hits remain at the top.
Priority II—Those with no matches of either CODIS or AFIS but have a named suspect.
Priority III—Those with no matches and without a named suspect.

The Priority I cases should receive the dedication of the investigative team to validate the evidence and pursue the leads identified in the investigative plan. Every one of these investigations must receive the utmost attention from the

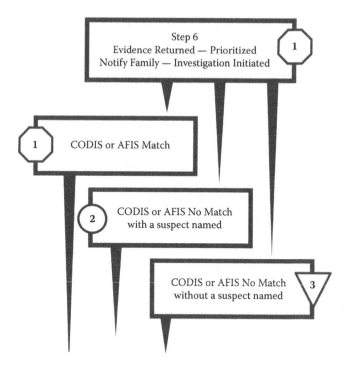

Figure 6.7 Alternative cold case evaluation model, Step 6.

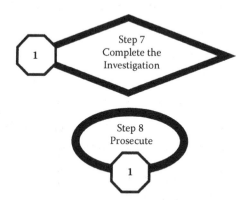

Figure 6.8 Alternative cold case evaluation model, Steps 7 and 8.

team until they are either completed or evidence to the contrary is uncovered that might indicate a theory of the crime other than what was developed during the major case review of Step 5. Therefore, completing the investigation, tying all loose ends together, and invalidating possible defenses becomes necessary all the way to court, which takes us to Steps 7 and 8 (Figure 6.8).

Once these investigations are completed, the detectives should then concentrate on Priority II and Priority III investigations. Each will present its own set of unique problems depending on whether a suspect is named in the case file. In Priority II cases you have evidence necessary to identify your person of interest but the suspect is a John or Jane Doe, or just a DNA profile. These types of cases tell us to concentrate first on the named suspects but then look closely at all other relationships both from the inner as well as the victim's outer circle of friends and associates. One important suggestion is to focus on the developed theory (or theories) of the crime, as this can point the investigation in a certain direction. As described later in Chapter 10, suspectology or suspect development may become necessary to narrow the focus of persons of interest, and this will have to go back to the theory of the crime.

Cold Case Evaluation Model III
Missing Persons

7

JAMES M. ADCOCK AND SARAH L. STEIN

Introduction

There are many advantages to reviewing a case that is "cold" rather than "hot": chief among them being that in most cases, a homicide has occurred and the body of the victim has been recovered and identified. Conversely, in cold cases involving missing persons, although the victim's identity is known, the body has not yet been recovered. The lack of a victim's body presents daunting challenges to investigators. First, without a body it is unclear if the victim is deceased. Second, without a victim's body investigators may not be able to determine where the individual originally disappeared from, thus they cannot make an accurate assessment of the crime scene and the risk level of the offender. Additionally, if the body of a victim is not recovered at the time a case review is commenced, it is impossible to narrow the field of suspects when considering who may have had access to the site where the victim disappeared from, the homicide site, and the dump site (if in fact all these locations are independent of one another). Last, without the recovery of a body, there is often a complete lack of physical, forensic evidence.

In those cases where it is suspected that the victim has been killed or seriously harmed, the investigative focus is on persons of interest who may have had a motive. As time passes, this effort becomes more difficult because there is no foundation of evidence or body containing at least a recovery crime scene to process and evaluate; ultimately a very difficult case to resolve. Therefore, when suspects are not immediately identified, the creation of a model that focuses on recovering the body is presented. This focuses not just on the individual persons of interest and their motives, but more on where would they have dumped or placed the body.

That being said, a cold case evaluation model specifically designed for missing person cases is comprised of only two phases with one goal in mind: to retrieve the body of the missing individual. In many ways, this model is the antithesis of the original cold case evaluation model featured in this text; however, it intuitively makes sense, as with missing person investigations, you must in many cases work backward from the end (the dump site of the victim) to the beginning (the disappearance of the victim).

The first phase of the evaluation model (Figure 7.1) is similar to that of the original model featured earlier: the team must receive the original case file and subsequently screen it for solvability factors. However, bear in mind that the solvability factors in a missing person case may be different than in a homicide or other type of investigation. For example, the following may be examples of solvability factors in relation to a missing person case: (1) is it possible the person left voluntarily, (2) can a "victim last seen" site be firmly established, (3) are there known enemies of this individual or is it more likely a random attack, (4) was there a sign of a struggle, (5) is it possible the victim is still alive, (6) were there witnesses to the disappearance, and (7) are there named suspects in the file or enemies of the missing person who might have a motive to bring harm to the victim? These solvability factors may help you determine whether to actively pursue the case.

The second phase of the model includes five primary categories of information to be developed: victimology, timelines, suspectology, relationships, and evidence. These five categories of information are designed for one purpose only: to help you recover the body of the missing individual. As to victimology, it is the general study of the victim; you will want to gather personal information regarding the victim from the following individuals: intimate partners, friends, and coworkers. Additionally, you will want to determine information about the victim's extracurricular activities (and whether they had begun new ones or abandoned old ones recently), the victim's daily routine (and whether they had altered it recently), and finally, whether the victim was involved in any deviant behavior that may have contributed to their disappearance (e.g., drugs, gambling, gang activity, organized crime activity, problems with intimate partners). Special consideration may be given to missing children under the age of 18; that is, there are additional factors to consider such as how they interacted with peers versus adults, were they introverted or extroverted, and whether they were instructed on how to react if confronted with a scenario of an abduction.

Timelines

As to the category of information labeled *timelines*, you may want to establish timelines regarding the following: first, the victim, as to what their habits had been over the last 6 months to a year, had they changed recently, their daily routine, and so forth. Second, if you have a definitive site where you know the victim was last seen, it is important to develop a timeline for that

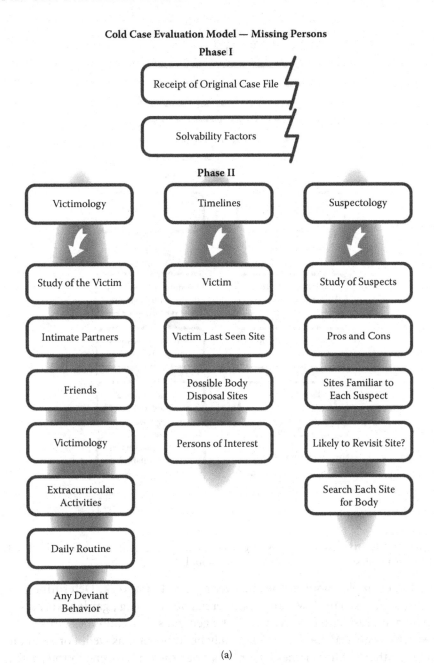

Figure 7.1 (a) Missing persons cold case evaluation model, Part 1. (b) Missing persons cold case evaluation model, Part 2. *(Continued)*

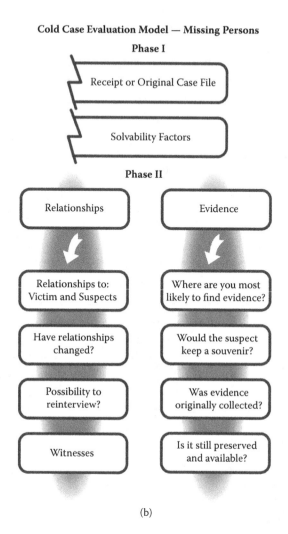

Cold Case Evaluation Model — Missing Persons

Phase I

Receipt or Original Case File

Solvability Factors

Phase II

Relationships

Evidence

Relationships to:
Victim and Suspects

Where are you most
likely to find evidence?

Have relationships
changed?

Would the suspect
keep a souvenir?

Possibility to
reinterview?

Was evidence
originally collected?

Witnesses

Is it still preserved
and available?

(b)

Figure 7.1 (continued) (a) Missing persons cold case evaluation model, Part 1. (b) Missing persons cold case evaluation model, Part 2.

site. For example, monitor the site over a period of a week. Determine traffic flows, pedestrian flows, any commercial activity (e.g., garden workers or repairmen), residential activity, and the general socioeconomic status of the area. The historical context of a site may be important as well. For example, did any other similar crimes occur at or near the crime scene in the past? If so, the perpetrator may have been revisiting his hunting ground. If the crime is fairly recent (and even if it is not this is still worth a try), set up a roadblock on the day of the week that the victim disappeared and ask individuals what usually happens on that day of the week and if they remembered seeing anything out of the ordinary on the date the victim disappeared.

Potential Body Disposal Sites

Possible body disposal sites can be developed by analyzing your persons of interest. You may want to develop timelines for each person and attempt to identify the sites each person of interest may have used. After locating such a site, determine what has happened at that site since your victim disappeared. Has there been construction or building of any kind, or has there been clearing if it is a forested region, and so on. People conducting business around the site may have stumbled across the crime scene and not even know it or thought they were looking at animal remains, so interviewing those individuals may be helpful. Additionally, in many areas where recreational hunting is permitted, it may be useful to advertise during the gaming season. That is, post flyers and announce to hunters what you may be looking for, whether it is remains, remnants of clothing, or other items related to the crime. Finally, timelines of your persons of interest are critical and self-explanatory, and can be very beneficial at time of prosecution.

Suspectology

In reference to the category of suspectology, or the study of your suspects, you can begin to narrow your pool once you complete your victimology. This is due to the fact that oftentimes, the possible motivation for the crime may be revealed in an individual's victimology (particularly if they were engaged in illicit behavior at the time or prior to their disappearance, or if they were having marital problems, etc.). That being said, as outlined in this book, determine to the best of your ability which type of offender you are dealing with: power-assertive, power-reassurance, anger-retaliatory, or anger-excitation (which will be discussed in Chapter 10). Depending on the subtype selected, the disposal sites will vary.

The power-assertive offender will leave his victim in place if the victim is killed in their home; however, if the victim is abducted, the disposal site will vary from the abduction site. The anger-retaliatory offender and anger-excitation offender will most likely dispose of their victims in secluded, wooded areas where the victim is unlikely to be found. However, each typology has one characteristic in common: the site where the body is left is a site familiar to the offender and one where he can return to check to see if the body has been discovered if he so chooses, which leads to the subcategory of "sites familiar to each suspect."

It is critical to discover the most remote, isolated sites that are familiar to each suspect. This may be discovered through interviews of intimate partners and friends (e.g., do they like to go camping, fishing, hunting, and if so, where). You may then wish to determine whether the suspect is likely to revisit those sites and set up surveillance equipment (e.g., weather-resistant tape recorders, video recorders, motion sensors) at said sites to monitor any activity. This may lead you to the body, or, if you are lucky enough to find it first, it may help to confirm the guilt of your suspect if he revisits the scene. Finally, it is critical to search each site for the victim's body.

In cases where the missing person may have been involved in organized crime, consider industrial areas or recently constructed residential areas as dump sites as well as wooded ones. In one case the authors reviewed, the primary person of interest was just such an actor. It is thought that the perpetrator (who was involved in organized crime) buried the victim under the foundation of a home built by a construction company that he owned as a front to launder his money. All indications supported that theory but the costs associated with tearing up a $1 million home were not exactly feasible at that point in time. However, in the meantime, while a grand jury was investigating the primary person of interest, he attempted to bribe an officer of the court and was subsequently convicted for that bribery. Since the subject is in his 80s, it is highly unlikely efforts and funds will be expended to pinpoint the location and unearth the remains of the victim from under the house. It is believed that by applying pressure to the suspect in searching for the victim's body in different areas caused him to take an action he might not have necessarily done under normal circumstances, thus exposing himself.

In another case, the victim was involved in a series of illegal activities that put him into contact with numerous undesirable criminal types. The victim was known for his shortcomings and suddenly disappeared from his home leaving a cell phone, wallet, and other personal effects including vehicles and keys at his residence to never be seen again. Like most detectives the police focused on the persons of interest who were criminal associates of the victim, which presented many plausible reasons for the disappearance and possible murder. Although this is a normal investigative approach, it becomes more difficult without the benefit of a body and physical evidence. The perpetrators are less likely to admit their involvement because you do not have a body that is linked to them. Therefore, we are suggesting again that while doing the investigative process be especially attuned to locations where the body may have been dumped and focus on those areas. Your efforts could either unearth the victim or place sufficient pressure on the perpetrator(s) to take revealing actions of their possible guilt, as in the case previously mentioned.

Cold Case Investigation in an Educational Environment
The Dutch Experience

8

R.A.M. HULSHOF, MCI, H.A.M. HEIJMERIKX, MSc.,
J.C. KNOTTER, Ph.D., AND Y.M. SPOORMANS, MSc.
Dutch Police Academy, Apeldoorn, Netherlands

Introduction

In the night hours of April 30 to May 1, 1999, a horrific crime takes place near the Frysian town of Veenklooster, a tiny hamlet in the countryside in the north of the Netherlands. After a night of partying, 16-year-old Marianne Vaatstra is found raped and murdered in a paddock just a few kilometers from her parent's home where she lived. For a long time all suspicions were directed to the asylum center located near Veenklooster but police were never able to close the case. The rape and murder remained unsolved for years and had a great impact on the Dutch society, especially since the perpetrator was never caught. Several investigative journalists performed elaborate analyses of the case and the investigation, and concluded that police had put all their efforts into solving the case in hopes of finding the killer, but to no avail.[1-3] The case turned cold.

The case was reopened in 2007 and the police performed (among other things) a major DNA investigation. In a radius around the crime location, men were asked to voluntarily submit their DNA for comparison with an unidentified DNA sample from the crime scene. Never before had there been a DNA comparison on such a scale.[4] Despite the impressive turnout for the DNA testing, a match was not found and the other investigative methods used by the police did not lead to a breakthrough in the case.

This kind of major event attracts attention from the media and the scientific community. It is not long before multiple articles and books are published on this case, but also on other cold cases, in which the authors pose critical questions and wonder why despite all the efforts of the police these cases are never solved and the killers never found.[5-10]

Not only are the media starting to be increasingly interested in cold cases, also within the police, the district attorney's office, and political circles cold cases (such as Marianne Vaatstra) have received growing attention[*] over the last few years.[11-13] One of the main reasons for this trend is probably the technical advances, such as the improved DNA techniques mentioned earlier, that can often lead to new insights and leads. There is also a call (mainly from the political arena) for better trained investigators that could assist on these difficult cases, who could on the one hand prevent judicial errors and cold cases, and on the other hand revive high-profile unsolved murders.

To fulfill this need, the Police Academy, commissioned by the political arena, developed the Master of Criminal Investigation (MCI), where students receive a degree in investigative skills and practice. From 2012, specific attention is paid to cold case investigation in one of the courses of this master, ACTESO. ACTESO is short for advising, coordinating, implementing, and evaluating the strategies used in major investigations. In this course, students learn how major cases are being investigated.[†] Classes focus on an actual cold case submitted for review by regional police units in the Netherlands. During this course, the goal is to combine scientific knowledge and expertise with investigative practice. This is done by teaching legal and behavioral theories, discussing different approaches to solving these cases, and asking students how they think the investigation should ideally take place.

In this chapter, we will describe the approach that is used during the ACTESO course. We do not pretend to have found the Holy Grail in cold case investigation. We merely wish to present this as a method that can help structure an investigation. We will begin with a description of the organization of the Dutch police system, after which some general statistics of homicide cases in the Netherlands are outlined in order to lay out the bigger context in which we operate. Next, we will focus on the history of cold case investigation in the Netherlands. The core of this chapter will be the presentation of our cold case review process (CCRP) as it is used in our educational program at the Police Academy.[14] A short summary and reflection is provided at the end of the chapter.

---

[*] An example of this growing attention from the political arena is the establishment of a program aimed at improving the quality of our investigations after a critical evaluative report on this topic was published (Commissie Posthumus, 2005). In this report the review of cold cases to come to new investigative leads (both tactical and forensic-technical) is named specifically (Commissie Posthumus, 2005, p. 21).

[†] The focus of ACTESO is not just cold cases. Other types of investigations that are highlighted during ACTESO include high-impact crime, high-volume crime, and organized crime.

The Dutch Police System

Since halfway through the 1990s, the Dutch police consisted of 26 regional police corps and one national police service. These corps worked according to national guidelines but were free to create their own protocols within those guidelines. This fragmentation led to each corps having its own protocol and it could therefore happen that no two corps had the same way of working on a certain topic. This meant collaboration between different corps was sometimes difficult.

On January 1, 2013, the Dutch police underwent a major reorganization, leaving just one national police corps, with the 26 former police corps restructured into 10 regional units, a national unit, and a national police service and support center (see Figures 8.1 and 8.2).

All units operate under the administrative responsibility of the Department of Safety and Justice, while the mayor of the municipality is the competent authority concerning criminal investigations. This means that the district attorney is the person who is formally in charge of and responsible

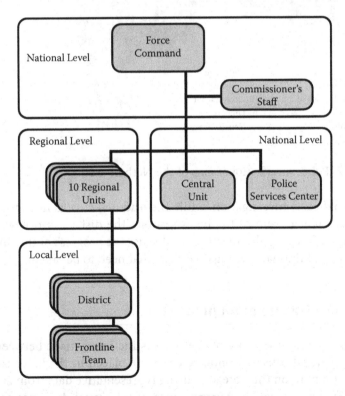

Figure 8.1 The Dutch police organizational chart.

1. Noord-Nederland
2. Oost-Nederland
3. Midden-Nederland
4. Noord-Holland
5. Amsterdam
6. Den haag

7. Rotterdam
8. Zeeland-West-Brabant
9. Oost-Brabant
10. Limburg
11. National Unit

Figure 8.2 Police jurisdictional map of the Netherlands.

for any (cold case) investigation, while the lead detective is in charge of the day-to-day management of the investigation. The district attorney and the lead detective have regular meetings to discuss the progress of the investigation and any additional investigative steps that need to be taken.

Homicides: Nature and Quantity

When determining the cause of death, a distinction is made between natural and unnatural causes. Homicide cases are placed in the latter category. When we zoom in on this category, using representative data from 2008 (see Figure 8.3), we see that the biggest cause of unnatural deaths is accidents (52.1 percent). Homicide is only a small part of this category (2.8 percent).

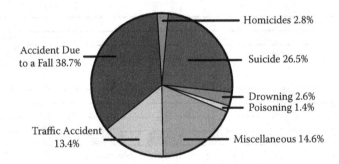

Figure 8.3 Distribution of deaths due to unnatural causes in 2008 (*N* = 5415).

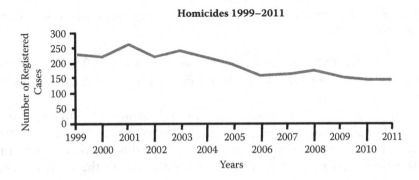

Figure 8.4 Number of homicides 1999–2011. The information in this graph is based on information from the Central Bureau of Statistics (CBS), and stems from the central administration of Dutch communities and judicial information.

When we look at the development of homicides from 1999 until 2011, we can see a clear trend. According to the official Central Bureau of Statistics (CBS) for 2014, the number of homicides in the Netherlands has been decreasing steadily since the turn of the century and seems to be holding steady for the last 6 years (see Figure 8.4).

This drop in homicide cases broke the trend of increasing homicides that had occurred since the 1960s. From the mid-1960s until the end of the 1990s, the number of homicides has been steadily increasing. In these 40 years, the number of homicides increased from around 40 cases a year to around 200 a year. Adjusting for the increase in population during these 40 years, this meant that the chance of becoming a homicide victim was almost three times higher at the end of the 1990s than it was in the mid-1960s.[15]

In the period of 1997 to 2005, there were on average 229 cases of homicide every year. With a population of a little under 17 million people, the homicide rate in these years was 1.36 per 100,000 inhabitants.

During the next 6 years (2006–2011) this number dropped. With an average of 167 homicides per year, the homicide rate dropped to 0.99 per 100,000

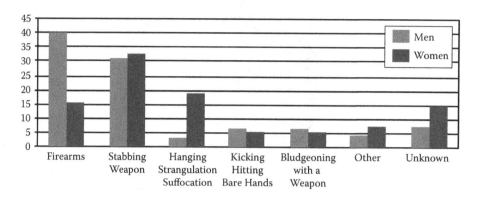

Figure 8.5 The distribution of the means of killing according to sex of the perpetrator.

inhabitants. In 2012, the homicide rate was even as low as 0.85 per 100,000 inhabitants, with just 142 homicides (see Figure 8.4). These current rates are comparable to other Western European countries.[16]

The downward trend in homicide cases is also similar to that seen in a number of other countries, especially in the United States. Although the relative number of homicides is higher in the United States than it is in the Netherlands, and the decline in cases started earlier in the United States, the development is similar.[17]

According to Smit and Nieuwbeerta (2006), the majority of homicides are committed by men, about 70 percent. Men are also more likely to fall victim to homicide, except in the case of homicides in the intimate circle where women are most likely to be the victim. Also, homicides committed by women are in the vast majority of cases committed among intimates. This intimate category accounts for 40 percent of all homicides, where stabbing weapons are by far the most common type of weapon used (see Figure 8.5).

Homicides committed in the criminal environment (where a victim and perpetrator are involved in criminal activities and there is a relation between their criminal activities and the homicide) account for 20 percent of all homicides. In this category, firearms are the preferred weapon. And, about half the victims are of foreign origin, or immigrants. More than half of the perpetrators are immigrants.

History of Cold Case Investigations

The structured reviewing and reopening of cold cases by so-called cold case teams is a relatively new development in the Netherlands. The first cold case team in the Netherlands was formed in 1999 in Groningen, a province in the north of the Netherlands. This team was given the name *onopgeloste ernstige delicten* (unsolved major crimes).[18] In March 2000, the units Amsterdam–Amstelland and Utrecht decided to start a joint cold case pilot. These two teams immediately had great success. While Groningen was investigating the murder of an 18-year-old woman in 1997, Amsterdam and Utrecht were investigating the murder of a 26-year-old woman in 1994. Using new technologies to reexamine DNA evidence, they connected the two cases and linked them to a single suspect, who was entered into the DNA database in 1998 for the abduction and rape of a 72-year-old woman.[19,20]

Politics got involved, with the Minister of Justice stating that all homicides and sex crimes should be reinvestigated. In 2000, a national team was formed that would focus exclusively on unsolved homicides of children, the *Landelijk Team Kindermoorden* (LTK, National Team Child Homicides). This team reviewed 13 cases of child homicides and disappearances. It reopened 11 of these cases because the team found new leads, and was able to solve two of them.[21,22]

These teams were able to solve some high-profile cases in the beginning of the 21st century, which also motivated other regions to also start reviewing their cold cases. This was not done in a structural way, and due to the lack of resources and manpower not every unit was able to actually investigate cold cases.

With the reorganization of the Dutch police, regional units are required to pay attention to their cold cases. Therefore, units are taking inventory on the number of cold cases they have. This however will not lead to an exact number of Dutch cold cases, since the definition of a cold case varies between regions. Some units only consider unsolved homicides to fit into this category, while other units use a broader definition, and thereby also label other unsolved major crimes such as sex crimes and disappearances as cold cases. For example, a unit that uses a more strict definition, reports having 22 cold cases (personal communication), while a unit using the broader definition reports having 158 cold cases to be investigated (personal communication). Because of this difference in definition, it is believed that the total number of cold cases across the units will range from several hundred to as many as 2,000 cases.

Cold Case Approaches

Research by Van Leiden and Ferwerda[23] shows that there are three general ways to organize cold case investigations: (1) temporary or ad hoc cold case teams, (2) permanent cold case teams, and (3) semipermanent cold case teams.

Forming temporary or ad hoc cold case teams is the most common way to organize cold case investigations. Here an investigative team is put together to investigate a specific cold case. There is no standard number of members or specialties that are assigned to the cold case team. Members can be derived from the district of the crime or from other major investigations in the region. When the investigation is completed the team is dissolved. Most of the cold cases mentioned earlier are being (or will be) investigated by these ad hoc teams.

Some Dutch police regions however have put into place permanent cold case teams. The members of these teams have been cleared of all other duties and only work on renewed investigations into major crimes. There are two ways in which these teams can be set up: some teams do both the preliminary investigation/review and also follow-up on any leads they find on the way, while other teams only review the case and hand over any leads they find to other investigative teams, although they are often involved in providing support for the actual investigative team.

In semipermanent cold case teams there is a core of permanent members who are complemented by ever-changing colleagues, depending on their need for certain specialists to assist the investigation, the stage of the investigation that requires more or less personnel, and the amount of hot case investigations that need to be staffed.[24]

Due to the relative independence of each police unit in the Netherlands, there is no standard way to work on cold cases (yet). Every unit that has started investigating cold cases has developed its own way of handling cold cases depending on the philosophy they adopt. With the reorganization mentioned before, units are now obligated to work on their cold cases. However, there is no mention in the reorganization plans about the way in which these cases need to be attended to, leaving every unit free to either structurally or more incidentally investigate cold cases.

The increasing need to investigate cold cases and to put into place investigative teams leads to a growing demand for knowledge and training in this field.[25] At a national level, people are working on a uniformly organized cold case approach incorporating best practices from both the organization of the teams and the investigative approach. The next section will outline the Police Academy's approach to cold case investigations, which has been tested and improved in our educational setting over the last 3 years.

ACTESO Cold Case Review Process

As mentioned earlier, the ACTESO course is centered around a real cold case from one of the regional units in the Netherlands as a form of integrated learning.[26,27] After completion of the course, the units are handed back their cold case (newly structured and completed) with a comprehensive analysis of the opportunities and (new) leads of the case as well as an evaluation of the initial investigation(s) with advice for future practice.

When we take on cold cases, we screen them for solvability factors, similar to the ones mentioned in earlier chapters. However, because we have not been reviewing cold cases for long, not all units have found their way to us. This means that we have a limited flow of cold cases, and we often do not have the luxury to discard a cold case when it does not meet certain solvability factors. Especially since two or three classes start every 3 months, and we need a new case for every class.

General Assumptions

Every investigation is centered around finding out what really happened, coming to the one and only true story of events. Our focus in the review process is coming to a story of the crime that describes what truly happened in the case as closely as possible. The way to get to these answers is through posing and answering research (or investigative) questions. The result is a written scenario of what most likely happened that is presented to the judges at trial accompanied by the evidence found. This search for the true story consists of determining the probability of several competing scenarios that explain the available data. The question is which scenario best explains the available evidence. The most likely scenario is the one that provides the simplest explanation of the available distinctive evidence.

Why do we want to come to such an elaborate description of what we believe happened according to the evidence? One reason is that while writing the story inconsistencies or missing or unknown facts become instantly clear and will lead to further investigative efforts to find these missing links. Another reason is that a clear-cut and well-based scenario is easier to understand by judges, and helps to convince them of the scenario. In fact, Crombach et al.[28] and Spong[29] report that 50 percent of the evidence in criminal legal cases is formed by the quality of the story, for example, the probability, believability, and completeness of the story. The other half of the evidence is how well it can account for supporting and falsifying evidence. This means that the eventual conviction is only partly based on factual evidence (for example, forensic and tactical evidence). How these pieces of evidence are put together to create a whole is of at least equal importance.

To create this story we formulate research questions about anything and everything that we need (and want) to know about the case. These research questions will cover the 7 W's: what, where, when, what with, in what way, who, and why. Following the hypothesis and scenario's model[30] as used in the Netherlands, which will be explained next, we start from very little information, and use research questions to guide us through the case file. This way we can avoid the danger of following the train of thought of the original investigation. Especially since this is a cold case and the original team's investigative lines have not been able to solve the case and the true story might not even be in the original case file, we believe it is essential to take a fresh perspective on the case. This way new lines of investigation have more of a chance of being identified, while promising existing lines will still pop up.[*]

We will now describe the different phases we distinguish in our cold case review process (Figure 8.6) in more detail.

Phase 1: Preparing

Before starting the work on the investigation, it is important to organize the formalities. This includes the selection of the team members and arranging a place to work from. With regard to the selection of the team it is important to have as colorful a team as possible. This includes people with different levels of expertise, background, knowledge, age, and sex. It is this variation that can lead to new insights in the case that may be important to solving it.

The next step is organizing the case file. This includes selecting the case file, making sure all documents are accounted for, and digitalizing the case file. Digitalizing the case file makes it easier to search through. Especially since our way of working requires searching for relevant information instead of reading the whole case file, digitalization is essential, because it enables one to use search engines to quickly search for answers in a sometimes very comprehensive case file.

Phase 2: Analyzing

In Figure 8.6, the analyzing phase is comprised of four columns.[†] We will discuss these columns from left to right. The basis for this phase is the hypotheses and scenario (H&S) column, which describes the different steps in the analyzing stage of the investigation. The other columns provide additional information or lead to products that can assist in the H&S steps. These columns should be read horizontally as well as vertically: these are parallel processes in the investigation.

Hypotheses and Scenarios

In reading the following section on hypotheses and scenarios one should carefully review Figure 8.6 and refer back to it as needed to fully comprehend the process.

---

[*] While the question-based approach has several advantages as stated in the text, there are also some dangers to be aware of. First, we realize that while asking questions ensures a broad view, it also limits what one will find. You will only find answers to the question you pose. When the question is not formulated accurately or the terms one uses to search the file are incomplete, critical information can be overlooked.

[†] The four columns are situated in a bigger square. The reason for incorporating this square is to keep in mind that every model has its limitations. Strictly following the steps of a model can lead to a false sense of security. It is essential to keep this in mind, and never forget to think outside the box.

Cold Case Review Process
R. Hulshof, J. Knotter, and H. Walles

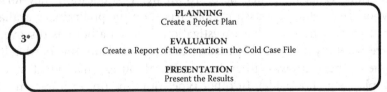

PREPARATION
Formalities
1. Put a Team Together
2. Organize a Workplace
3. Arrange the Formalities

STRUCTURING
Prepare the Cold Case File

1. Select a Cold Case File on the Basis of Solvability Factors
2. Organize and Complete the File
3. Digitize a Structure to the File
4. Determine and Select Starting Information

1

Formulate Hypotheses and Scenarios (H & Sc)	**Victimology**	**Suspectology**	**Registration/ Documentation**
1. Formulating hypotheses	1. Create a victim form (S.A.F.)	1. Identify and select traces of suspects	*Create a victim file
2. Formulating research questions	2. Classify the level of risk of the victim	2. Classify the peri-offense behavior by the use of typologies and identify the personality	*Create a decision and a working journal
3. Information gathering			*Create a name file
4. Qualifying pros and cons			*Create an H & Sc model
5. Eliminate hypotheses			*Create a timeline and relationship diagram
6. Formulation of scenarios based on prioritized hypothesis	3. Search for indications of a possible motive		*Create a media file
7. Formulate research questions	4. Identify possible suspects based on victimologic principles	3. Identify potential suspects	*Create a suspect file
8. Information gathering pros and cons		4. Create a list with pros and cons for every suspect	*Create a report of the literature review and the interviews held with experts
9. Prioritizing and eliminating scenarios		5. Prioritize suspects	*Create an evidence matrix
10. Completing the scenario description		6. Identify characteristics	
		7. Identify the pre and post-offense behavior	
Prioritize Scenario	**Prioritize Suspect**	**Prioritize Suspect**	**Identify Crime**

2*

PLANNING
Create a Project Plan

EVALUATION
Create a Report of the Scenarios in the Cold Case File

PRESENTATION
Present the Results

3*

*During these activities are regularly held group discussions in which it is important to think beyond existing frameworks.

Figure 8.6 The cold case review process.

Step 0: Preparation   In this phase, students do not have access to the complete case file. They are first instructed to search the literature for possible ways to work on a cold case file. Although we direct them to known and specific publications,[31-34] we also encourage them to seek out other sources for additional information.

The idea behind this is they might find useful insights from the literature that can add to our model. As mentioned before, we do not pretend to have found the best way to tackle these cases, and are continuously specifying and readjusting our model. Especially since no one case is the same, students may want or need to incorporate and focus on specific elements. We let them be inspired by the literature. Furthermore, this literature study gives them an idea of what they will be facing, while triggering them to make this their own investigation. It also makes sure they have not been contaminated with information from the case and can start the investigation with an open mind.

The elemental items students take away from the literature are usually also the items we already incorporate in our model: focus on the victim, keep a clear and thorough registration of the decisions made and the reasons for making them to ensure transparency of the investigative process.

Step 1: Formulating Hypotheses   After students have formed a plan to investigate the case, they can start working on the actual review. They are now provided with limited information to start with, similar to the information a detective has when he starts working on a hot case. It is limited to the most essential factual information that is needed to answer the central question of what happened. This usually involves the initial emergency information, where the date, time, and location of the crime scene are described. This is completed with some photographs of the crime scene and some demographics of the victim (for example, name, age, and address).

This initial information is kept very brief in order to prevent students from being influenced by information they might find in the case file that could (unintentionally) steer them in a certain direction. Everything is still possible at this point, as it is in a hot case.

After studying the initial information, students are asked the following question: What happened here? To answer this question they formulate hypotheses, which are assumptions based on the preliminary available information that need further investigation.[35] When a body is discovered, there are generally four possible answers to the general question of what happened here. The death was either due to natural causes, an accident, suicide, or foul play (e.g., homicide). In other types of crime (for example, missing persons cases) a fifth hypothesis is usually named: "unidentified causes" that can incorporate any information that does not fit the first four options and can be relabeled at any time to fit a more concrete description of what could have happened.

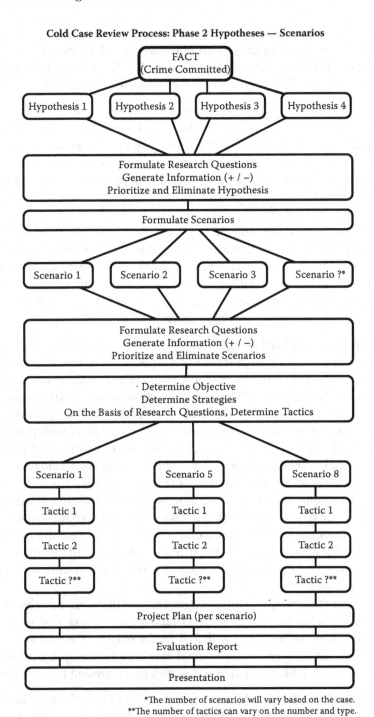

Figure 8.7 Hypotheses and scenarios.

Students are divided into smaller groups to discuss the what happened question. For every hypothesis (what question) they describe how the events could have led to this outcome (e.g., dead body). These descriptions of how did it happen are called (preliminary) scenarios (see Figure 8.7).

Step 2: Formulating Research Questions While thinking about what could have happened in the case, students will immediately start to formulate research questions about information they need in order to be able to rule out certain hypotheses or scenarios (for example, impossibility to self-inflict the wounds rules out suicide) or to find support for a certain hypothesis. The emphasis in this stage is on elimination, which will leave the most likely hypothesis standing.

Students discuss the different options they have identified (did they miss any options?) and their research questions (are they concrete and clear enough to lead to the answers that they seek?). All research questions are consequently gathered for each hypothesis and documented in a mind map that is being kept up to date throughout the entire review. All additional information and questions are noted down in this model.

Step 3: Information Gathering Once the group has incorporated options from as broad a spectrum as possible and are confident no crucial information had been missed, it is provided with the entire (digitalized) case file and can start searching for answers to the research questions in order to try to eliminate hypotheses. This is usually done by dividing the group into four smaller groups that each adopt one of the basic hypotheses, which they will try to disprove using the case file. They use keywords to search the digitalized case file with computer software to make the search more efficient than reading every affidavit.

There are three types of documents that provide the most information needed at this point: the forensic and autopsy reports, information about the victim, and any statement from the first witnesses at the crime scene.

When the case file does not (sufficiently) answer their questions, the groups have the option to interview experts and members of the initial investigative team. They are also encouraged to search the literature for answers to their questions.

Note that students perform a review and are therefore not able to perform any investigative actions such as talking to witnesses or requesting additional testing on evidence gathered in the original investigation. They look for their information in the original case file and any open source intelligence that is available to them or to the unit that provided the case file.

Step 4: Qualifying Pros and Cons The answers they find are quoted from the case file with the source specified. This is done to prevent (wrongful) interpretation on which further assumptions are being made and to retain the possibility of checking interpretations made earlier in the review. Next, these quotes are marked as either supporting (+) information or falsifying (–) information with an explanation of why this classification is being made and specifying the theory (scientific or common knowledge) that is the basis for this classification. By laying out these underlying theories, they become open to scrutiny from others and their truthfulness can be tested.

Step 5: Eliminating Hypotheses   When the research questions are answered as completely as possible, the findings of each group are discussed and hypotheses are eliminated if possible. The goal is to come to one hypothesis on which to do the further review. When it is not possible to eliminate a hypothesis, but it is found to be a less likely option, it can be put aside until any necessary additional information comes to light.

To guarantee a transparent review, these decisions and the arguments are recorded in an investigative journal that is also kept up to date with all decisions made throughout the review.[*]

Step 6: Formulating Scenarios   After the group has prioritized one hypothesis (usually crime) as the most likely cause of death, the procedure explained earlier is repeated for this hypothesis. Students will now think of as many realistic (preliminary) scenarios as possible in the broadest spectrum of possibilities.[36] They are encouraged to use the literature, as there have been studies into, for example, motives for committing homicides, which students can use to complement their scenarios or formulate new ones.[37]

The scenarios the students have formulated are preliminary scenarios, since they often consist of just one or two sentences and so do not yet give a complete explanation of events. These scenarios will generally consist of a description of why this crime was committed and by whom. The aim here is not to identify a specific suspect, but to have a more abstract idea of possible suspects. The who would consist of naming a group of persons such as "a friend" or "a relative," unless a specific person can be immediately identified.

Formulating these scenarios is also done in small groups to ensure a broad spectrum of scenarios. These are subsequently discussed in the group. Because students have started studying parts of the case file, they are able to redefine the scenario named by other groups on the basis of the available information. These scenarios are not based on an analysis of the entire case file, since students have not yet been able to take in all the information in the file at this stage. The stated scenarios are entered into the hypotheses and scenarios model and redistributed among the students. This process will normally lead to several dozen scenarios.

---

[*] This step will be completed at the end of week 2 of the ACTESO course.

Step 7: Formulating Research Questions   The next step is to formulate verifying and falsifying research questions for the different scenarios. Both types of questions need to be thought of to avoid tunnel vision and form a well-based opinion about the scenarios. These questions need to both supply additional information that is still missing in the scenario and describe the legal definition of the crime (for example, whether this was manslaughter or first-degree murder). Again, students are encouraged to also use the scientific literature and consult experts to answer their questions (and to come up with new questions).

Besides the who[*] and why that are covered in the separate scenarios, there are elements of the crime that will be the same independent of the scenario, namely, the other five of the seven W's:

1. What happened (legal definition)?
2. Where did it happen?
3. When did it happen?
4. In what way did it happen?
5. With what did it happen?

Since these five topics will be more or less the same in every scenario, they can be considered to be the backbone of the scenario. Furthermore, the answers to these topics can also be used to verify or falsify the scenarios: Could this perpetrator have committed this crime at this location at that time with that weapon in that way?

Because of the importance of these five W's and the relatively hard evidence they will lead to, compared to the softer evidence for the who and why, they need to be investigated first. The who and why have been formulated before establishing the facts of the crime, to ensure an open mind and prevent information from the case file influencing the scenario-building process. They have been named but are for now intentionally left aside to prevent a preliminary focus on possible suspects. Instead, by starting from the facts of the crime, we are using a crime-driven strategy (combined with a victim-driven strategy).[†]

Step 8: Information Gathering—Pros and Cons   Again, the research questions are leading in the gathering of information about the scenarios. Students search for answers in the case file, literature, and consult experts. Answers to the first 5 W's are critically discussed, complemented and documented in, for example, timelines, relationship diagrams, and lists of persons involved.

---

[*] In the Netherlands, the who stands for any person(s) involved in the crime. This includes the perpetrator or perpetrators, and also the victim. The gathering of information about the victim will be discussed in the "Victimology" section.

[†] Work on column 2, victimology, also starts at the beginning of the investigation. A description of this process is provided below in this chapter in the section "Victimology."

This part of the review process takes a lot of time, and it is essential that this receives enough attention since it is the backbone of the investigation.

When the concept scenario is established and written for the first 5 W's, it is time to investigate the formulated preliminary scenarios (who and why). Students search for evidence that can verify or falsify these scenarios. Important here is to start from the scenarios and the accompanying research questions and use these questions to determine what scenario best explains the evidence available in the case file (an important source here is the victimology report).

The first topic of investigation at this stage concerns the why question. The reason for focusing on the motive before focusing on a possible suspect is that there is a limited amount of possible motives, whereas the number of persons of interest (POIs) can be endless. Also, within one motive, there can be multiple POIs that could theoretically all be eliminated by falsifying the motive as a possibility. Furthermore, focusing on the motive again prevents focusing on one POI (or a group of POIs) too soon. When one motive is found to be the most likely motive, this immediately prioritizes possible POIs to be investigated first, thereby making the investigation more efficient.

In order to come to a complete description of the why question, all possible POIs are identified.

In the meantime, every piece of information discovered is entered into the hypotheses and scenarios model as either confirming information or as falsifying for certain scenarios (or part of scenarios). This adds to or is cause for adjustments in the scenarios.

Step 9: Prioritizing and Eliminating   All information gathered is now used to come to a selection of the most likely scenarios. The goal is to prioritize scenarios to end up with a manageable number of scenarios (usually five or six) for further in-depth investigation. This is a critical step in the process: On what basis can one choose one scenario over another? Are there certain indicators or other rational methods or grounds that can guide this process or do we have to be more subjective and use our own knowledge, experience, and intuition?

Usually, the selection is made based on a combination of factual information, experience, and intuition. The factual information consists of the information from the case file, the available literature, and the consulted experts. The literature, for example, can hold useful statistical information that can be used to assess the relative likelihood of different scenarios. This information is combined with knowledge about similar cases encountered previously, logical deductions, and some intuitive knowledge.

To minimize the downside of the necessary subjectivity in the process of elimination, first, students individually make their own selection of scenarios. The assumption is that if the majority of the group comes to the same conclusion about certain scenarios based on the same information; the choice for this scenario is legitimate.

Scenarios that do not make it through the elimination are retained in the hypotheses and scenarios model to be investigated further if the chosen scenarios do not lead to the solution of the case.

We are now left with a manageable amount of scenarios that are being investigated in depth for available information and opportunities for further investigation.*

The goal now is to gather enough information to come to a small number of scenarios that will be further outlined in separate investigative plans. The number of scenarios will be different across investigations, and depends on manpower, resources, and so forth. This is done by dividing the students into groups of three or four students, who are each assigned one scenario. They perform a comprehensive review on this scenario, as well as an evaluation on the investigation of this scenario in the original investigation. This evaluation can account for, for example, missing information in the case file but can also help in determining the reliability of the evidence collected and the interpretations made in the original investigation. If the evidence is not collected in a valid way, this can have implications for the value of that evidence. In extreme cases this could mean the evidence should not be used to base conclusions on.

Only now is the who question (seventh W) dealt with in depth. Who has not only (one of) the established most likely motive(s) to commit the crime, but also the means and opportunities to do so? For every identified POI, a separate file is made containing in addition to personal information the affidavits of any interviews or interrogations, timelines concerning this person, and their connection to the victim.

When the individual review and evaluation is complete, the groups come together to share results. This is important, since the selection needs to be done with all team members having the same information. This is done by presenting both the supporting and the falsifying information and the possibilities for further investigation.

Next the selection process is once again entered into. The Police Academy uses Group Support System (GSS) to assist this final selection process.[38] GSS is a sociotechnical system consisting of software and hardware, in which a team can work on the prioritization of the scenarios together. Students are asked to individually rate the probability of the scenarios discussed on a scale of 0–100. This ranking is based on the evidence found and the quality or reliability of that evidence. GSS then presents (in percentages) how the scenarios are ranked across team members, and which scenario is generally seen as the

---

* This step will be completed at the end of week 4 of the ACTESO course.

most likely scenario. It also shows the variation among individual rankings. A scenario that shows low variation is seen as equally likely (or unlikely) by everyone and therefore does not need to be discussed. Scenarios that show high variation in ranking, however, show a low level of agreement, and the reason for this variation should be discussed (for example, a different interpretation of certain facts can cause this variation). After discussing the origin, a re-poll can be implemented to reassess the ranking of this scenario.*

Step 10: Completing the Scenario Description   This will lead to a select number of scenarios (one to three scenarios) that is found to be the most likely explanation of what really happened in this case and therefore approaches the true course of events as closely as possible. The next step is completing the concept scenario (until now describing just the five W's) with the information of the who and why from the respective scenarios. With the comprehensive review that has been done, it now becomes possible to complete the description of the likely course of events in as much detail as possible. Because every scene has to be investigated and has to follow logically from the previous scene, this can lead to additional gaps in the story of the crime that need to be investigated further.

The importance of this elaborate description is twofold. On the one hand it forces one to describe different scenes in detail, thereby exposing weak spots and missing links in the evidence. By conducting additional investigative efforts, these weak spots can be (partially) eliminated leading to a complete and believable story of the crime. On the other hand, it is a way of accounting for all the available evidence. The most likely scenario is the one that gives a better explanation of the available evidence (both supporting and falsifying) than the other scenarios.

Victimology

As mentioned earlier, information about the victim will provide answers to a lot of questions students have in this phase but also throughout the rest of the review. Furthermore, starting from the facts at the crime scene and the information about the victim, one can prevent focusing on a particular suspect before this is warranted. Victimology ensures the broad view on the case.

Therefore, during the hypotheses selection at the start of the investigation, an attempt is also made at gathering fragmented information about the victim from the case file (see Figure 8.6). In the Netherlands, the SAF (Slachtoffer Assessment Formulier or victim assessment form) is used to gather and document information about the victim in a structured manner. It is similar, although more elaborate, to the victimology questionnaire that is mentioned earlier in this book and is preferably filled out by a behavioral

---

* This step will be completed at the end of week 11 of the ACTESO course.

expert. (A sample format of the SAF/victim assessment form can be found in Appendix B.)

When the SAF is completed, the victim's risk level is determined and possible motives are distinguished. The risk level gives information on possible suspects or suspect groups (e.g., is there likely a relation between perpetrator and victim). Next to the risk level, information about the victim in itself can provide motives for the crime, which can lead to a possible suspect or suspects. These topics are all input for the research questions formulated in the H&S process.

Suspectology

As shown in Figure 8.6, at the start of the investigation, while hypotheses are being formulated and work on the SAF is in progress, the crime scene is also investigated. The goal of this crime-based strategy is twofold: on the one hand reconstructing the actual crime, while on the other hand collecting evidence (DNA, trace, etc.) the perpetrator left behind.

The information gathered at the crime scene is then used to create a behavioral profile of the perpetrator. This profile can be used at a later stage in the investigation (i.e., Step 10 in the H&S process).

First, the POIs that have arisen from the H&S process and victimology research are listed, then pros and cons for each of these POIs are stated based on the evidence available. Based on this evidence, the first POIs are selected. Then, these POIs are compared to the behavioral profile based on the crime scene that has been written at the start of the investigation. Those POIs that fit this description best are investigated first and their behavior before and after the crime will be investigated. Important to look for here is behavioral changes that can indicate that the POI experienced a major life event (such as committing the crime) (Chapter 10). The POI that demonstrates the biggest behavioral changes is investigated first. This selection will be input for the selection and elimination process of the scenarios (Step 10 in the H&S process).

Registration–Documentation

The fourth column of Figure 8.6 shows a list of essential products that should be used in investigations. A number of the ones listed in this column are already discussed in the previous sections. We will outline only those that have not been discussed before.

We want to briefly point out the importance of documenting decisions made and the basis for making them during the review. Lack of proper documentation of actions is one of the most important difficulties encountered in reinvestigating a cold case. With the upcoming digital possibilities, case files become bigger and bigger. It is not uncommon for our cold cases to contain around 10 Gb (sometimes thousands of pages of documents) of information.

This staggering amount of information makes it more difficult to keep track of all the information and manage it in a structured way.* Several tools are developed to assist in information management, both analytical and instrumental in nature, for example, a list of names, timelines, and diagrams that show relationships between people involved but also (as mentioned earlier) formats for journals to keep track of every decision made, and the hypotheses and scenarios model to visualize the process of the investigation. This is also important to ensure the transparency of the investigation and the repeatability.

These timelines and relationship diagrams are essential in these types of investigation, but one should also create a so-called media file with a media timeline. This media file should contain every media coverage the story received around the time of the crime, but also afterward (possibly also after the case had been closed), and when this was covered. The reason for keeping track of the media coverage is knowing what is still inside information (knowledge only the perpetrator would have), which is helpful during possible future interrogations.

Finally, we want to mention the *bewijsmatrix* (matrix of evidence). This is a model of analysis that is complementary to the written crime story, in that it shows the extent to which the elements of the article of law have been proven by the evidence gathered. It quickly makes insightful how many elements have not been (sufficiently) proven and warrant further investigation before presenting the case to a judge.

Phase 3: Investigative Plan[†]

Since 2003 the Dutch police has used standardized models such as project proposals and the more detailed investigative plans. These models are designed to assist in making the investigative process more efficient and effective. They help steer the investigation and enable the chiefs to make decisions about which investigation to run and how based on valid and comparable arguments.

Investigative Goals

The investigative goal(s) is set based on the prioritized scenario. In every investigation, the goal is usually centered on reconstructing a plausible and believable story that best matches the evidence gathered. With the *waarheidsvinding* (finding out the truth), the goal can also stretch from

---

[*] These big case files are another reason why we take a question-based approach rather than reading the whole case file.

[†] This phase has to be completed within 2 weeks.

verifying and falsifying the scenario to looking for other persons involved, qualifying their role, and bringing them to court as well.

This goal (or goals) needs to be formulated according to the SMART rule: specific, measurable, acceptable, realistic, and time bound. A well-set goal demarcates the investigation and makes it easier for the investigative team to maintain focus.

Formulating a Strategy

A (investigative) strategy is the use of investigative methods at the certain point in time to attain a certain goal[39] and is therefore formulated in accordance with the investigative goal. It is the plan that states how the goals can best be achieved in the context of this specific investigation. With cold case investigations into homicides there are several basic strategies, including the crime-based strategy, the victim-based strategy, and the suspect-based strategy.

Formulating Investigative Methods

After selecting the strategy, one now determines which investigative methods will be implemented. It is the way in which one sets to work to attain the goal.[40] If the selected strategy is, for example, the victim-based approach, we want to work toward attaining our goals starting from the victim. What specific investigative methods should be used in order to get the most information about the victim and attain the goal in the most efficient and effective way?[41]

As becomes clear from the previous example, the choice of investigative methods is based on the research questions formulated before. These questions dictate what information is needed and now the most suitable methods need to be identified to deliver answers to these questions.

When all investigative methods are listed, there needs to be some thought on order and the timing of every method. The order and timing depend on the chosen strategy but also on the effect one method can have on the use of another.

Results and Presentation

All this information (goals, strategy, and investigative methods) is recorded in the investigative plan. This is a standardized format that also contains several administrative fields, such as the duration of the investigation, possible suspects, possible limitations, or barriers one might encounter during the investigation and possible partners from both inside and outside the police that may have information or can help the investigation in some way.

The results of the review and evaluation are presented to representatives of the unit. These could be former team members, managers, district attorney personnel, and any other persons that are interested in the case and the results. All documents used and created (journals, analyses persons, timelines, hypotheses and scenarios model, etc.) are also handed over to the unit that supplied the cold case.

Summary and Reflection

We have presented an approach to cold case investigation that we feel is very promising. However, our way of working with it in an educational setting brings with it some limitations that the reader should be aware of.

First, our experience with this model is based on a limited number of cold cases that we have been able to review in our educational program. Until now we have been able to complete nine cold case studies using this approach, which means that our experience is relatively limited. Furthermore, as of yet we do not have any results on our approach. Although several cases are being reopened or in the process of being reopened following our review, no cases have yet been completed by either being solved or being again closed.

This brings us to another limitation to our testing environment. As mentioned before, students are not allowed to perform any investigative actions, since the cases we review have not yet officially been reopened. This means that we must remain unsure whether our prioritized scenario is in fact the most likely scenario, since the verifying and falsifying of scenarios takes place on limited information. Ideally, according to our model these actions would be performed.

Also, the ACTESO course lasts for 13 weeks, in which time is divided between working on the cold case and lectures. Therefore, students only have a limited amount of time in which to perform the review. As a result, it is not possible to write an investigative plan on more than one scenario. Opportunities in the other scenarios are highlighted in the individual evaluative reports but not specified in an investigative plan.

Finally, our cold cases center on homicide cases, which limits the generalizability of our conclusions. We have, for example, no experience applying this model to sex crimes or kidnapping cases. Also, it remains unclear whether this approach could be used in hot cases as well. More experience and research are necessary to state our case more firmly.

What is clear however is that this way of working (question based and working with the hypotheses and scenarios) stimulates an investigative team to keep an open mind and look at the full scope of possibilities before coming to any conclusions, thereby avoiding dangers such as tunnel vision. We also find that this approach enables a team to get a thorough knowledge of the case file in a limited amount of time (3 months, divided between classes and working on the case), while getting a clear idea of possibilities for further investigation as well as pointing out critical moments in the original investigation that helped or hindered the investigation and can be food for thought for future investigations.

In closing, we want to look back at the Marianne Vaatstra case that started this chapter. As mentioned before, this had been a cold case for a long time. Throughout the years it became increasingly clear that the perpetrator was probably not an asylum seeker but someone belonging to the neighborhood of the Veenklooster area. In total, 12 different suspects were arrested at different points in time, first mainly asylum seekers, later also people from the neighborhood, but the killer could not be identified among them. In 2012, however, a breakthrough was created when it became clear that major DNA testing for blood relations could lead to solving the case. Pressure from the media and the public finally led to a change in legislation, which made this large-scale (voluntary) kinship DNA testing possible. Luckily, all these efforts were rewarded when a farmer from a nearby village confessed to the rape and murder in 2013, after his DNA was found to be a complete match to the sample found at the crime scene. He was convicted later that year. This is a great example of how a cold case can be solved by a combination of new forensic techniques and tactical investigative efforts.

Endnotes

1. Bakker, B. (2007). *Waarom is de moord op Marianne Vaatstra nooit opgelost?* Amsterdam: Gopher.
2. Vuyk, S. (2010). *De mysterieuze dood van Nicky Verstappen*. Het verhaal van zijn ouders. Utrecht: De Fontein.
3. Vuyk, S. (2013). *Marianne Vaatstra. Het verhaal van haar moord*. Amsterdam: Nieuw Amsterdam.
4. Bakker, 2007.
5. Ibid.
6. Derksen, T. (2011). *Leugens over Louwes. Deventer moordzaak*. Leusden: ISVW uitgevers.
7. Haan, B. (2009). *De Deventer moordzaak. Het complot ontrafeld*. Amsterdam: Nieuw Amsterdam.
8. Oomens, P. (2012). *De zaak Koos H. Dossier van een seriemoordenaar?* Voorburg: U2pi bv.
9. Van der Heuvel, J., and Huisjes, B. 2007. *Doden liegen niet. Spraakmakende misdaden in Nederland*. Kosmos Uitgevers.
10. Vuyk, 2010, 2013.
11. Pvov. (2005). *Programma Versterking Opsporing en Vervolging. Naar aanleiding van het evaluatierapport van de Schiedammer Parkmoord*. Ministerie van Justitie.
12. Pvov. (2010). *Eindrapportage programma PVOV. Deel Nederlands Forensisch Instituut*. Ministerie van Justitie.
13. Kaasjager, J. (2007). Coldcase onderzoek. Opnieuw spitten in oude zaken. *Blauw, 3*, 6–10.
14. Pvov, 2005.
15. Smit, P. R., and Nieuwbeerta, P. (2006). *Moord en doodslag in Nederland: 1998 en 2002–2004*. Den Haag: WODC.

16. Ibid.
17. Ibid.
18. Van der Wal, R. (2012). Cold case en review. In N. Kop, R. Van der Wal, and G. Snel, *Opsporing Belicht* (pp. 287–297). Den Haag: Boom Lemma.
19. Kaasjager, J. (2007). Coldcase onderzoek. Opnieuw spitten in oude zaken. *Blauw, 3*, 6–10.
20. Van Leiden, I., and Ferwerda, H. (2006). *Cold cases, een hot issue: Toepassingen en opbrengsten van hernieuwd onderzoek naar kapitale delicten.* Apeldoorn: Politie en Wetenschap.
21. Pvov, 2005.
22. Van Leiden and Ferwerda, 2006.
23. Ibid.
24. Ibid.
25. Pvov, 2005.
26. Coppoolse, R., and Vroegindeweij, D. (2010). *75 modellen van het onderwijs.* Groningen: Noordhoff Uitgevers bv.
27. Ploegman, M., and De Bie, D. (2008). *Aan de slag! Inspirerende opdrachten voor beroepsopleidingen.* Houten: Bohn Stafleu van Loghum.
28. Crombach, H., Van Koppen, P., and Wagenaar, W. (1992). *Dubieuze zaken: De psychologie van strafrechtelijk bewijs.* Amsterdam: Contact.
29. Spong, G. (2013). *De breuk. Een van mijn opmerkelijkste moordzaken.* Amsterdam: Uitgeverij Balans.
30. Snijders, K. (2011). *Hoe temmen we het zevenkoppige monster? Besluitvorming en straterieopbouw binnen rechercheonderzoeken.* Doetinchem: Reed Business.
31. Adcock, J. M., and Stein, Sarah L. (2011). *Cold Cases: An Evaluation Model with Follow-Up Strategies for Investigators.* CRC Press: Boca Raton, FL.
32. Davis, C. D., Jensen, C., and Kitchens, K. A. (2012). Cold-case investigations. An analysis of current practices and factors associated with successful outcomes. The RAND Corporation: Santa Monica, CA.
33. Jensen, C., and Nickels, W. (2011). Integrating intelligence methods into criminal investigations. The Mississippi approach to solving cases. *Laleia Journal, 20*, 58–75.
34. Lord, V. B. (2005). Implementing a cold case homicide unit: A challenging task. *FBI Law Enforcement Bulletin, 2*, 1–6.
35. Blonk, G. (2007). *De link in de veiligheidszorg.* Den Haag: Reed Business.
36. Heuer, R. (2005). Improving intelligence analysis with ACH. https://www.e-education.psu.edu/drupal6/files/sgam/Improving_intel_analysis.pdf.
37. Smit and Nieuwbeerta, 2006.
38. Snel, G., Mulder, H., and Van der Niet, A. (2012). Group Support System. Tactisch concept. In N. Kop, R. Van der Wal, and G. Snel, *Opsporing Belicht* (pp. 122–132). Den Haag: Boom Lemma uitgevers.
39. Snijders, K. (2012). Strategiedenken binnen rechercheonderzoeken. In N. Kop, R. Van der Wal, and G. Snel, *Opsporing Belicht* (pp. 253–262). Den Haag: Boom Lemma uitgevers.
40. Van der Sijs, N., Geeraerts, D., and Den Boon, T. (2008). *Dikke van Dale. Groot woordenboek van de Nederlandse taal.* Utrecht: Van Dale Lexicografie.
41. Snijders, K. (2011). *Hoe temmen we het zevenkoppige monster? Besluitvorming en straterieopbouw binnen rechercheonderzoeken.* Doetinchem: Reed Business.

Follow-up
Investigative
Strategies

III

Applying Science and Technology to Cold Cases

9

ALBERT B. HARPER

Science and the Scientific Method in Criminal Investigation

The role of science in criminal investigation has increased tremendously since the landmark decision in *Miranda v. Arizona* (1966), which limited the power of the police to interrogate suspects without a warning of the right against self-incrimination and the warning that any confession could be used against the suspect. *Miranda* so limited the ability of the police to solve cases by confession that new methods of providing the circumstantial link between the suspect and the victim or crime scene were needed. Certainly, science had been employed in crime solving for decades or even centuries, but only after *Miranda* was the true power of science to solve crimes recognized.

At the very time that police interrogation procedures were limited, the advance of information technology was beginning a revolution of analytic capacity unknown to mankind. Beginning with the need for highly sophisticated, miniaturized computer systems to monitor and control the multitude of complex parameters necessary for spaceflight, the NASA (National Aeronautics and Space Administration) science program spawned numerous inventions that led to the ability to investigate crime using objective methods.

Forensic science blossomed in the post-*Miranda*, post-NASA decades, growing into a high-profile, glamorous profession, as depicted by hit television programs such as *CSI* and others, where the authorities use science to solve crimes, arrest perpetrators, and see them convicted on a rocket-like timeline. The message of *CSI*, that crimes can be solved by science is a point well taken and applies to all criminal investigation, both current and cold.

What all criminal investigations that rely on science to solve crime have in common is that science is unbiased and objective. The objectivity of the scientific method creates fidelity in results that clearly demonstrate the linkage of suspect(s) to the crime. The scientific method, when correctly applied, solves cases.

The scientific method begins with a simple observation. Why is a particular piece of physical evidence present at a crime scene? The simple observation is then evaluated by objective testing in the form of a hypothetical question that posits a simple question: Does this evidence link the suspect to the crime scene? If the answer is positive, then additional questions and tests can be formulated to further refine the relationship between the evidence and the suspect, each objectively questioning and refining a hypothesis. If the answer is negative, then the inquiry can stop, as the hypothesis that the suspect is associated with the evidence is disproved and no further analyses would provide any new information. The power and economy of the scientific method are that it eliminates speculation as to dead-end investigative theories and directs the investigation to correct conclusions. Eventually, all competing hypotheses will be tested, proven to be false, and eliminated from the investigation. The remaining hypothesis is, by the process of elimination, the true hypothesis and the demonstration of the facts of the case.

Scientific Advances, Databases, and Linkage Possibilities

Application of physical evidence to scientific testing is, of course, much more complicated than simply sending whatever was collected at the time of the crime to the lab and having it tested. Analysis based on applying the logic of the scientific method as to how this piece of evidence would establish or disprove a hypothesis, that is, is the evidence probative, must be performed on each item of evidence collected at the scene. In addition to determining the probative value of the evidence, the investigator must determine whether the evidence has been stored in a condition that will permit the evidence to be tested or retested, that is, is the evidence contaminated? Last, the investigator must determine that even if the evidence is probative and uncontaminated, is the evidence competent or has the chain of custody (needed to establish that this evidence is the same evidence collected at the crime scene years ago) been broken? If any of these conditions are present, the value of the evidence is greatly diminished and it is likely to be a waste of resources to continue with an evaluation.

DNA and Biological Evidence

The forensic significance of the discovery that deoxyribonucleic acid (DNA) was the hereditary material of life in 1953 was not appreciated until Sir Alex Jeffrey's (1985) demonstration that certain areas in the DNA itself could be used to uniquely identify individuals. Until that time, forensic science had relied on red blood cell antigen markers such as ABO, RH, and others; white blood cell antigens of the HLA systems; and a host of serum proteins to include or eliminate a suspect from consideration as a perpetrator. The power to identify an individual using these genetically inherited markers was limited by the relatively small number of polymorphic alleles at each gene locus that produced the variant. For example, the ABO system comprised three distinct alleles, and the frequency of the most common allele was more than 40 percent. If a suspect was blood type B and the blood left on the victim was blood type A, then the suspect could be eliminated with absolute certainty. However, if the suspect's blood type was A, then the suspect was included in a pool of some 40 percent of the United States population, and no conclusion could be drawn other than that the suspect could be included as a possible perpetrator. Typing methods prior to the advent of modern DNA technology required large quantities of blood, but if a sufficient sample was available, it was theoretically possible to type other red cell antigens or examine serum protein polymorphisms to obtain additional discriminatory power.

Because these red cell and serum protein variants were inherited in accordance with Mendelian genetics, the probability that an individual was blood type B, Rh-negative, PGM (phosphoglucomutase) 2+ 1+, EsD (esterase D) 2-1, and GLO (glyoxalase) 1 could be calculated by simply multiplying the respective frequency of the alleles. In this example, if the frequency of blood type B is about 10 percent, Rh– about 15 percent, PGM 2+ 1+ about 20 percent, EsD 2-1 about 20 percent, and GLO 1 about 20 percent, the joint probability is 0.00012 ($0.1 \times 0.15 \times 0.2 \times 0.2 \times 0.2$) or 0.012 percent of the population, or 1.2 in 1000. This is a very small number of potential contributors, but in a city of a million people, some 1,200 persons would share this profile. Although this result is highly inclusive if the suspect is a match on all tested loci, the probability that another person could be the true perpetrator is significant. In most cases, the actual discriminatory power was more on the order of 1 in 100, and of limited value.

Forensic serology was replaced because of the recognition that DNA typing had the same advantage of being genetically inherited, one pair of the allele from the mother and the other from the father, but that in certain regions of the DNA, there were hypervariable areas where the DNA would be repeated numerous times and these areas could be identified, isolated, and analyzed. The power of DNA over serology was that instead of multiplying 3 or 4 genes with relatively limited variation at each locus, 7 or 9 or 13 or 16 separate, highly variable (i.e., rare) alleles could be multiplied, and match probabilities obtained on the order of one in a trillion or greater. The difference between one in a thousand versus one in a trillion is overwhelming and a clear reason why DNA technology so quickly supplanted serology.

What Is DNA?

With the exception of mature red blood cells, each of the 100 trillion cells in the adult human contains a nucleus that houses the genetic machinery to make and assemble the thousands of proteins and enzymes needed to keep the cell functioning, and the instruction set to make a duplicate copy of the cell. This incredible machine is deoxyribonucleic acid, or DNA, which consists of a backbone of ribose sugar molecules strung together with phosphate groups and containing one of four nucleotide bases: adenine (A), thymine (T), cytosine (C), or guanine (G). The exclusive pairing of the bases, A to T and C to G, creates the almost unlimited variation found in the 3 billion nucleotide positions of the human genome. The double-helix structure of DNA, with two complementary strands of repeating phosphate, sugar, and base molecules, was elegantly demonstrated by Watson, Crick, and Franklin in 1953. During replication of the double-helix strand of DNA prior to cell division, the DNA is opened at one end and the complementary base is added: G to C, C to G, A to T, and T to A. This complementary structure permits the creation of an exact duplicate strand of DNA. This important feature of replicating DNA will be taken advantage of when we seek to make multiple copies of certain regions of DNA.

The DNA itself is further organized in the nucleus into chromosomes, which are specific sequence segments of DNA and protective proteins called histones. In humans, there are 22 matched pairs of chromosomes, numbered 1 to 22. We receive one number 1 chromosome from our mother and one number 1 chromosome from our father, and independently one number 2 and number 3, and so on to number 22 from our mother and a similar matched pair from our father. Each person's mother contributes a 23rd chromosome, known as an X chromosome, and each person's father contributes a 23rd chromosome, which can be either a pair to the maternal X, in which case the person is female, or a Y chromosome, in which case the person is a male. With the exception of the 23rd chromosome, the pair of chromosomes has the same basic sequence of DNA base pairs in the same location on the chromosome. This does not mean that the paired chromosomes are absolutely identical; in fact, in most individuals there are small differences in either the letter sequence (ATCG) or variation in repeat sequences of each of the chromosomes that have arisen due to mutation or during chromosomal replication. These variations are known as polymorphisms and are the very factors that make DNA so useful in linking suspects to crime scenes and victims.

Forensic DNA

The opportunities to obtain DNA at a crime scene are almost endless. DNA can be obtained from any item of physical evidence that has come into contact with a suspect, or from any biological process associated with the suspect. If, for example, in a burglary, the suspect cut his hand on a shard of window pane glass, the suspect's blood would be an excellent source of DNA to link that individual to the crime scene, notwithstanding the fact that red blood cells do not have a nucleus and therefore no nuclear DNA. The white cells, or leukocytes, though much less common than red blood cells, have nuclear DNA and, in a single drop of blood, more than sufficient quantities of DNA to be analyzed. The value of serologic evidence is paramount in any investigation, as the significance of demonstrating a bloodshed linkage between the suspect and the victim is powerful evidence of guilt.

Skin cells are constantly shed whenever a person comes into contact with any surface. The investigator should be especially conscious of evidence that the suspect might have worn, touched, or handled. Clothing items, especially gloves, hats, shirts, underwear, and socks, that have close contact with the surface of the skin are excellent sources for potential transfer of DNA. Additionally, any surface that the suspect touched with bare hands may yield his DNA from his skin cells. Hair is frequently encountered in crime scenes. While most hair is hair that has died and is naturally shed, in some instances, hair may be forcefully pulled and the root contains nuclear DNA. Hair is also very important in the potential to obtain mitochondrial DNA, as discussed later. The ability to analyze minute amounts of DNA representing only a few cells worth of DNA is one of the most important advances in DNA technology in the past decade.

In sexual assault cases, the investigators should look for saliva from the suspect in any bite mark on the victim in addition, of course, to seminal fluid retrieved from the victim, her clothing, and bedding. Condoms are an especially excellent linkage tool, as the inner surface will contain the male suspect's semen and the outer surface the victim's epithelial cells from her vagina.

Other types of physical evidence that may yield sufficient quantities of DNA to permit analysis and identification include discarded objects such as cigarette butts, coffee cups, and beverage containers. With these kinds of objects, epithelial skin cells are transferred from the suspect's lips and saliva to the item and then discarded.

The investigator should not overlook other potential DNA sources, including urine, feces, and vomitus, which might be a possible link to the suspect.

Because of the tremendous sensitivity of DNA typing technology discussed in the next section, the potential for the investigator to contaminate the evidence with his or her DNA is extremely high. Just as suspects shed skin cells and hair in great numbers, investigators shed skins cells and hair in great numbers, thereby contributing an additional individual's DNA to the evidence. Contamination is a major problem in any case involving DNA evidence and must be prevented by the investigator wearing barrier clothing to prevent the transfer of biological material from the investigator to the evidence.

DNA Technology

The routine practical application of DNA in many case scenarios is in part due to the enormous statistical discrimination power of having 13 individual tests multiplied together to provide near astronomical probabilities of individual association of the suspect to the crime scene. Another factor that makes DNA so valuable is the fact that minute quantities of biological material are sufficient to make an accurate determination. The reason behind the ability to use minute amounts of evidentiary sample is the development of polymerase chain reaction (PCR) techniques by Dr. Kary Mullis in 1983. PCR permits the multiplication of each DNA sequence of interest countless times in a matter of hours. Without the ability to multiply to sequences of interest, often more than a million times, many forensic samples would not be possible to analyze. The PCR process works by identifying specific regions of polymorphic DNA by primer molecules that are complementary to one strand of the sequence of interest. The specific sequence is then heated, which opens the twin strands of DNA. When the strand is open, complementary bases pair with their counterparts, that is, A to T, T to A, G to C, C to G, to make two new exact copies of the original DNA. The solution is then cooled to allow the new strand to bind, the solution is reheated and two new strands open, and the new bases pair with their counterparts and are then cooled into four strands. Four strands become 8 strands, 8 become 16, 16 become 32; and after 30 cycles of the process, approximately a billion copies of the original DNA exist.

In actual practice, commercial kits permit the simultaneous multiplication of many selected areas of DNA of interest known as short tandem repeats (STRs). STRs are areas on the chromosome where non-gene coding DNA is repeated in four base pair units differential numbers of times. STRs are similar to repeat sequences of DNA known as minisatellites or microsatellites, depending on the length of the repeat sequence. STRs were selected for forensic analysis because the short length of the repeating unit makes PCR amplification simpler than with long base-pair repeating units. The fact that the number of times the repeating unit occurs is inherited and is highly variable and thus highly polymorphic makes STRs very effective for identification.

More important, STRs are extremely common in the genome, which makes finding an STR located on a particular chromosome relatively simple. The fact that an STR is on one chromosome and another STR is located on a separate chromosome means that their joint probability of co-occurrence is the product of the frequency of each allele. The Federal Bureau of Investigation (FBI) has identified 13 separate STRs located on 12 chromosomes that have become the basis for all forensic human identification. Forensic testing in laboratories is simplified by the manufacture of commercial kits that permit standardized testing and uniform reporting of DNA test results. Because the size of the STR is small, 100 to 400 base pairs, it is often possible to amplify the short sequence of STR DNA even when the larger strand of DNA is degraded by bacterial, ultraviolet exposure, or other factors that cause DNA to denature. Forensic samples often are less than pristine, and thus STRs make identification possible under marginal circumstances.

One of the more significant developments in DNA technology over the past decade is the refinement of analytical techniques that permit STR analysis in cases with extremely small amounts of DNA on the order of 0.1 ng. Most laboratories require 0.5 to 1.0 ng of DNA in order to amplify the sample in the PCR process. The advent of low copy number (LCN) DNA analysis permits analyses that would not have been possible only a few years ago. This increased ability to detect and amplify minute quantities of DNA is not without drawbacks as the methods are extremely sensitive to sources of contamination and random, stochastic variation that is inherent in amplifying such small amounts of DNA. The interpretation of DNA profiles is complicated and may result in legal challenges to the admissibility of LCN DNA profiles, however, as an investigative tool the method offers much promise in developing avenues of investigation in cold cases.

The Combined DNA Index System (CODIS)
Because of the extremely high individualization potential of STRs and the ability to amplify millions of copies of target DNA from minute or marginal samples, the FBI created CODIS in 1990, followed by congressional legislation that formally established the FBI's preeminent role in maintaining a DNA database. CODIS cross-references a database of DNA STR loci for convicted felons, DNA samples recovered from crime scenes, and DNA samples from unidentified persons. The linkage power of CODIS has resulted in many *hits* in cold cases and has led to solving many cases that would have otherwise remained cold. CODIS has become the cold case investigator's best resource in establishing the identity of unknown perpetrators.

CODIS's power is the ability to match or link DNA from multiple, disparate sources, including cases in which no suspect exists. Furthermore, the CODIS database links local, state, and federal law enforcement agencies, so that nationwide linkage is feasible. The CODIS system is based on a three-tiered system of ever-larger databases. First, the Local DNA Index System (LDIS) tests crime scene samples, which are processed, profiled, and entered into a local database. If the DNA matches a suspect file located in the LDIS, the case may be solved without further database searching.

If the sample does not generate a local hit, then the data are uploaded to the State DNA Index System (SDIS) for additional comparison to offender profiles of convicted felons and other persons who by virtue of that state's DNA sampling statute are part of the SDIS. The crime scene unknowns are also compared to other unsolved, hence unknown, samples in the database in an attempt to link multiple cases to a common DNA profile.

If the sample does not generate a state hit, the profile may be submitted for analytical comparison at the National DNA Index System (NDIS). Again, in state comparisons, the NDIS can make comparison of offender profiles from multiple jurisdictions and link remote crime scenes across state lines.

All database uploads and searches are limited to public forensic laboratories and operated and administered by the FBI, which maintains the secure network of authorized terminals in participating laboratories. If a hit is registered between the unknown sample and an offender in the database, the sample is retested and a report is generated to the local law enforcement agency. This report is the basis of probable cause to obtain a known DNA sample from the suspect, which would then be compared to the unknown DNA from the victim or crime scene. The importance of CODIS in cold case investigation cannot be overstated.

The significance of a database search hit is enormous in cold case investigations. Linkage of a suspect to a crime scene or victim by a DNA match is one of the most significant developments in cold case technology. However, there are many instances where the CODIS (and local) search fails to produce an exact 13 loci match but does provide a match on fewer loci than 13. In this circumstance, the investigator may wish to conduct an additional familial search based on the fact that siblings, parents, children, and other relatives share many chromosomes due to the biology of Mendelian inheritance. The search may reveal a person who is a relative of the perpetrator and thereby provide an important avenue of investigation. The availability and admissibility of familial searches differs among the states and the investigators should consult state law in their jurisdiction (Bieber et al. 2006).

Mitochondrial DNA, Y Chromosome, and Other DNA Analyses

Mitochondrial DNA   Despite the modern ability to amplify minute and otherwise marginal samples of DNA, the reality is that not all biological samples contain sufficient nuclear DNA to provide a complete STR profile that would permit a CODIS comparison. In many cold cases, the samples of biological evidence have been subjected to less than optimal storage in a warm, moist environment where fungal and bacterial action destroy often small biological samples. In these cases, there are other alternative methods of obtaining a DNA profile that can link a suspect to a victim or crime scene. The most useful of these techniques relies on the existence of mitochondrial DNA, which exists in quantities of hundreds to thousands of copies in every cell. The mitochondria are organelles in each cell responsible for the conversion of ATP into energy for the cell. They are similar to bacteria in structure and may have been incorporated into the eukaryotic cell hundreds of millions of years ago. The mitochondrion contains a single strand of circular DNA that is inherited through the maternal line. As with nuclear DNA, mitochondrial DNA (mtDNA) also breaks down, but because there are so many copies of the mtDNA in each cell, the probability of finding mtDNA after years of degradation is greater than finding nuclear DNA. Furthermore, mtDNA is found in hair of all types, even in hair where the root is not present. Hair is abundant at crime scenes, and mtDNA provides a unique way to obtain genetic information about a suspect when other methods fail.

Despite the many advantages of mtDNA for older forensic samples, the mode of inheritance presents a major limitation on the usefulness of mtDNA. Except in some very extremely limited cases, all mtDNA is inherited from one's mother only. The mitochondria located in the father's sperm cell flagella are destroyed by enzymes at the time of conception. The only source, then, is the mitochondria in the mother's ovum, which is fertilized. As the embryo divides and grows, the mitochondria from the mother's cell are multiplied and grow in the adult person. The forensic implication of this fact is that every person in the maternal lineage shares the same mtDNA; thus all siblings of the same mother, the mother's siblings, her mother, her grandmother, and all other maternal relatives will share the same mtDNA profile. Simply put, mtDNA cannot be used to identify an individual with the same level of confidence that nuclear STR DNA provides. Many persons may share a common maternal ancestor, and therefore may be included in possible sources of the sample. The ability of mtDNA to exclude a suspect is, however, absolute.

Nonetheless, the many thousands of different mtDNA profiles, though not unique, are still capable of being an important investigational tool. Mitochondrial DNA types are highly variable and have the power to exclude more than 99.9 percent of potential contributors. Additionally, in missing person and unknown victim cases, mtDNA may provide the only possible evidence of identity.

The analytical procedure for extracting and multiplying mtDNA is very similar to STR DNA; however, the analysis focuses on two hypervariable portions of the mtDNA molecule. The comparison analysis consists of identifying the actual sequence of some 780 nucleotides bases (A, T, G, C) in areas selected for analysis, and comparing the known sample to the questioned sample. In the event of a match, an mtDNA database, also maintained by the FBI, can be used to determine the frequency of the particular nucleotide sequence and then calculate the probability of a random chance match of the two samples. Again, it is imperative that the investigator remembers that a match only means that the suspect and his or her maternal relatives cannot be excluded as a donor to a questioned sample, as no mtDNA profile is ever unique.

Y Chromosome STRs   Just as we inherit all of our mtDNA from our mother, all males inherit their Y chromosome from their father. The Y chromosome contains regions of nuclear DNA that possess STRs exactly like the STRs on the other 22 chromosomes. These STRs are processed in the same manner as other STR sequences. The implication for forensic use of Y-STRs is exactly the same as in mtDNA. It is impossible to have a unique Y-STR profile, as the index subject, his male siblings of his father, his father, his paternal grandfather, and all paternal relatives share the same Y-STR profile. This does not diminish the investigative potential for using Y-STR to identify potential suspects but does limit the discriminatory power of identifying an individual to approximately 1 in 2,000.

In sexual assault cases wherein there is often a mixture of female epithelial cells from the female victim and a typically much smaller number of male sperm cells, the ratio of female cells to male cells may prevent the male component of the DNA mixture from being seen. Given the technical process for amplifying and analyzing all STRs in a common reaction, the presence of the male component of the DNA may simply be overwhelmed by the much more prevalent female DNA. A solution to this problem is to only amplify the STRs located on the Y chromosome. This permits the identification, subject to the limitation that more than one male has this profile, of possible sources of the Y chromosome. This can be especially valuable in three circumstances: (1) where the unknown evidence sample tests positive for semen but no STRs other than the victim's can be detected, (2) where the evidence shows signs of a male–female mixture, and (3) where more than one semen donor is suspected.

Single Nucleotide Polymorphisms In addition to mtDNA and Y-STR analysis, the investigator should consider the potential of single nucleotide polymorphism (SNP) testing in those cases where the evidentiary sample is so degraded that the CODIS STR loci cannot be identified. SNPs are single-base sequence variants that are also extremely common throughout the genome. SNPs were first developed as a useful medical procedure to identify human genetic diseases. Only recently has SPN technology been applied to forensic questions, as SNP sequences are usually very short in length and therefore more apt to be present in highly degraded DNA. Because SNP loci normally have only two possible alleles, the discriminatory power is much lower than STRs. It is estimated that some 50 SNP loci would need to be tested to reach the discrimination power of STRs.

More recent studies involving SNPs include the demonstration that SNPs are nonrandomly distributed in different human populations, and therefore can be used to establish the racial ancestry of the source of the sample. The association of a particular complex of SNPs and the racial ancestry of the source is of course limited because individuals with admixed ancestral backgrounds may not show the phenotypic or physical characteristics that would be expected. Predicting the physical appearance of the source of the evidence sample is under study in numerous laboratories with promising results. It is now possible to identify individuals with red hair based on a SNP assay for a gene associated with red hair. Likewise, studies on SNPs and eye color, fingerprint patterns, and other physical characteristics may provide investigators with some information about the physical identity of the source of biological evidence.

Nonhuman DNA   In a limited number of cases, the association of nonhuman biological evidence to a suspect or victim may provide the necessary evidentiary linkage to resolve a case. Humans frequently live in close association with either a dog or cat, and dogs and cats tend to shed large quantities of hair, so it is nearly impossible to be in an environment with a dog or cat and not have transfer of the animal hair to the suspect. Forensic researchers have developed batteries of STR and mtDNA testing for both dogs and cats that create the potential to link suspect and victim through the hair of the animal present in the environment.

In other cases, the transfer of plant material may provide the necessary linkage. If the particular species of plant is rare in the location of the crime scene, then the association of plant evidence found on the suspect or victim can be a powerful association that links the evidence to the crime scene.

Fingerprint Evidence

The forensic application of friction ridge morphology variation is not new. Fingerprints have been used as a means of personal identification for centuries in China. Sir William Herschel made handprints of native Indian workers to identify them in 1858, but the first recognition that fingerprints could be used to identify or exclude criminal suspects was made by Dr. Henry Faulds in 1880. By the turn of the 20th century, fingerprints were known to exhibit extraordinary individual discrimination power, and by the early 1920s had all but totally eclipsed the Bertillon anthropometric classification scheme for identifying individuals.

The biology of fingerprints is well established. Friction ridge skin of the finger digits, the palms, the toes, and the plantar surface of the feet develop in utero at about the 16th week. Basal cells in the underside of the epidermis grow rapidly and create the unique ridge features that persist in an individual until the death and decomposition of the skin. The inner layer of skin, the dermis, contains blood vessels, nerves, and sweat glands that are responsible for wet and oily secretions that are deposited on smooth surfaces to create an impression of the ridge pattern and morphology. Fingerprints are considered to be unique to an individual; no person, including genetically identical twins, who possess identical DNA, has ever been found to possess an identical pattern of fingerprints.

Classification of Fingerprints

Fingerprints are especially valuable as a means of identification because they are easily classified into characteristics that permit both manual and computer-aided identification. The first level of classification consists of the basic determination of existence of an arch, loop, or whorl pattern. Within these three basic patterns, subpatterns exist, so that an arch may be plain or tented, a loop may be ulnar or radial depending on the direction of the slope, and a whorl may be described as central pocket, double loop, or accidental. The primary fingerprint classification system developed in the early 1900s by Sir Edward Henry relies on the variation in ridge count among the different pattern types on different fingers. The 10-print card system permitted law enforcement agencies to collect, categorize, and search millions of fingerprint records by hand.

Level II morphology consists of the detailed pattern variation in the friction ridges. A ridge may come to an end. It may bifurcate into two ridges, or two ridges may converge to form a single ridge. Ridges may form islands or dots. Additional discrimination potential is found in the pattern of minute detail of the pore shape, number, and relative location one to another, and in the variation of morphology of the edge of the ridge. This variation is known as Level III, and taken with consistent concurrence with Level I and II variations permits the examiner to make an identification. Any unexplained difference in any of the three levels between two fingers results in the conclusion that the questioned and known prints are from different persons, and the suspect is excluded. Only if every feature examined is consistent with both fingerprints can the examiner conclude that the same person made the prints.

Advances in Fingerprint Recognition

There are usually two types of fingerprints encountered at a crime scene, or on physical evidence. The first type is either visible to the naked eye or is found impressed into a soft material where it is readily identifiable as a fingerprint without additional processing, while the second type of fingerprint, which is not visible to the eye and requires additional processing to be made visible, is known as a latent print. The advances in development and enhancement to make otherwise invisible fingerprints visible have progressed enormously in the last several decades.

Traditionally, latent prints were discovered by dusting surfaces on physical evidence or areas at the crime scene that held promise by virtue of proximity to physical evidence that might be associated with the crime. Black powder (or white powder, depending on the color of the background surface) dusting has been supplanted by the use of powders that fluoresce under ultraviolent light, cyanoacrylate (superglue) fuming, powerful forensic and alternate light sources, and new enhancement reagents. Depending on the surface, different analytical sequences can be applied to increase the probability of discovering latent prints. The wide array of possible approaches requires that the investigator carefully consult with the crime laboratory to determine the most appropriate method to use in each case.

Unfortunately for cold case investigators, the chemistry of fingerprints leaves diminishing hope that any previously undetected fingerprint will be discovered years after it was deposited. Latent fingerprints are primarily the product of eccrine sweat glands, which is a watery mixture of inorganic salts and various organic lipids, amino acids, proteins, and other organic compounds. If left undisturbed, a latent print may persist for lengthy periods of time; with time, the print dries and can be easily damaged or wiped off during the original processing or by careless handling after the evidence is collected.

Analysis of Previously Developed Prints and the Automated Fingerprint Identification System (AFIS)

Just as new technology may permit the cold case investigator to reexamine physical evidence for previously undetected prints, old prints may also shed new light on the identity of the suspect. One of the more important techniques to be developed in the past 20 years is the use of digital enhancement techniques to either remove background interference or improve the visible resolution of an existing latent print. While these types of enhancement techniques could in some cases be accomplished by the use of filters in film photography, digital enhancement software is commonly available, relatively easy to use, and highly effective in improving the quality of the appearance of existing prints. The enhancement routines are found in most commercial photographic manipulation software packages such as Photoshop and CorelDRAW, and through various programs available at no charge on the Internet.

The importance of image enhancing becomes clear when it is combined with an automated fingerprint identification system (AFIS). AFISs are a critical tool for cold case investigators because with the older 10-print card an examiner could review a limited set of records using the Henry system. With AFIS, a computer can review millions of records and provide the fingerprint examiner with a set of ranked candidate prints for examination and elimination in a matter of minutes or hours. The actual comparison of known to questioned fingerprint has not changed. The examiner reviews each print looking for a sufficient number of common Level II and Level III features in exact relation to one another with no unexplainable differences in order to conclude that the two prints came from the same source. What is different is that with AFIS the process of selecting which prints to compare is enormously increased.

The Integrated Automated Fingerprint Identification System (IAFIS) is the national fingerprint and criminal history system maintained by the FBI. The FBI maintains the largest digital fingerprint database in the world, containing the fingerprints and corresponding criminal history information for more than 55 million subjects in the Criminal Master File. The IAFIS provides automated fingerprint search capabilities, latent searching capability, electronic image storage, and electronic exchange of fingerprints and responses to law enforcement agencies across the country. The response to an agency submitting fingerprints electronically may be as little as 2 hours. The fingerprints acquired by arrest and the corresponding criminal history information may be submitted by state, local, and federal law enforcement. The fingerprints are processed locally and then electronically forwarded to a state or other federal agency system for processing. The fingerprints are then electronically forwarded through the FBI's Criminal Justice Information Services (CJIS) computer network to the IAFIS for processing. Ten-print fingerprint cards may be mailed to the FBI and are then converted to an electronic format for processing by IAFIS.

AFIS provides the cold case investigator with three possible search scenarios. First, the unknown print can be compared to 10-print images from known persons stored in the database. If no match is made, the unknown can be stored in an unsolved database for future searching. Second, new 10-print images may be searched against previously unmatched unknown prints. Last, unsolved unknowns may be compared with other unsolved unknowns to link a single suspect to multiple crime scenes.

In addition to IAFIS, a number of agencies maintain local AFIS databases. The question raised for the cold case investigator is whether the unknown print has been previously searched by an AFIS system and not identified. If so, the print should be resubmitted, as the capacity to enhance the digital image submitted to AFIS has increased enormously, new algorithms for selecting potential matches have been developed, and local AFIS and national IAFIS databases have constantly expanded to include more arrestees. These factors, when combined, require a cold case investigator to resubmit any unidentified print for additional search by an AFIS.

Ballistics Evidence

A third major advance in linking suspects to crime scenes comes with the development of comparison databases for cartridge casings and bullets. All firearms have individualized characteristics that are idiosyncratic and therefore unique to an individual gun. When a gun is fired, the mechanical forces of metal on metal create distinctive imprints from the harder metals of the gun onto the softer metal of the cartridge case and bullet. The use of breech face marks, firing pin impressions, ejector markings on the cartridge case and land impressions, and other random striations on the fire bullet have been used for nearly a century to associate cartridge cases and bullets to a particular gun. The matching process of the fired cartridge case and bullet to the gun is done with a comparison microscope, where the firearms examiner views both known and unknown specimens simultaneously. As with fingerprint identification, a match is based on the experience of the examiner, who decides whether the known and unknown specimens share a sufficient number of identical characteristics with no unexplainable discordances to be considered, in his opinion, to have been fired from the same weapon.

The relevant comparisons include the linking of cartridge cases and bullets recovered at a crime scene to a suspect's gun. If a gun is recovered from a crime scene, then known test firings can be used to link this particular gun to other crime scenes or preserved for future comparisons. It is also possible to link spent cartridge cases and bullets from multiple crime scenes, thereby showing an association among multiple crimes, which may provide useful information about the identity of an unknown suspect by association to more than one scene. These comparisons have been the extremely time-consuming and laborious work of individual examiners, working most often in a single agency. The ability to associate multiple events was limited to the memory of the particular examiner, and multiagency comparisons were nearly impossible.

The advent of computerized databases in the early 1990s created the ability to search for linkage between gun and cartridge case, and later between gun and bullet, across agency jurisdiction. Just as in the case of fingerprints, the cold case investigator now has the possibility of using computer databases to provide linkage associations between a weapon and a suspect, which was once all but impossible. The Bureau of Alcohol, Tobacco and Firearms (ATF) created the initial comparison system, known as CEASEFIRE, and almost immediately the FBI created a competing and completely incompatible system known as DRUGFIRE. By 1999, the two agencies combined efforts into the current system, NIBIN (National Integrated Ballistic Information Network), which has the capacity to associate both fired cartridge cases and fired bullets to a particular weapon in regional and national databases.

The NIBIN network is managed by the ATF, which provides equipment and training. ATF administers automated ballistic imaging technology for federal, state, and local law enforcement, forensic science laboratories, and attorney agencies that are permitted to enter ballistic information into NIBIN. The agencies use integrated ballistic identification systems (IBIS) to acquire digital images of the imprint markings made on cartridge casings and bullets recovered from a crime scene or a known crime gun test fire, and compare those images against earlier NIBIN entries via electronic image comparison. If a high probability match between known and unknown emerges, then firearms examiners compare the original evidence to confirm the match or

NIBIN hit. The automated search provides either local, regional, or national comparisons that are able to provide links between crimes, including links that would never have been identified absent the technology.

For the cold case investigator, NIBIN opens linkage possibilities that may have never been explored. The ability to reexamine existing ballistics evidence for association of crime scene cartridge casings and bullets to a suspect's gun, or associate multiple crimes that may have been committed by the perpetrator, provides valuable information for solving cold crimes. As with the IAFIS database, new ballistics data are constantly being entered into the NIBIN database, which makes resubmitting ballistic evidence for new searches against the database especially critical in cold case investigations. New linkage associations are always possible and should be made in every case where ballistics evidence exists.

Evolving technology promises an even greater capacity to associate fired projectiles and cartridge cases with guns and link multiple crime scenes. Forensic technology's development of 3D automated IBIS systems for both bullets and casings provides additional linkage capacity that was not available with traditional database comparisons. The potential exists to renew inquiries into previously unmatched bullets and casings using 3D imaging.

Other Database and Analytical Tools

In addition to the three major national databases that provide the cold case investigator with the ability to link DNA, fingerprints, and ballistics evidence, there are several smaller, more limited databases for other types of physical evidence that may be useful in certain cases. Cases that involve automotive paint chips, typically from hit-and-run incidents, may find assistance in the International Forensic Automotive Paint Data Query (PDQ), which contains chemical and color information pertaining to original automotive paints. The FBI and the Royal Canadian Mounted Police (RCMP) have collaborated to create and support a current, validated, and searchable automotive paint database that can be used to identify make(s), model(s), and year(s) of questioned paint samples in hit-and-run fatalities and other investigations involving automotive paint. This is an extremely valuable investigative tool in this limited class of unsolved cases where paint chip evidence exists.

Other potentially important databases include databases for shoe print comparisons. TreadMark and SoleMate provide comparisons of manufacturer, size, pattern, and wear of shoe prints found at a crime scene. TreadMate is a database of more than 5,000 vehicle tire tread marks, which in some cases may be an invaluable link of a suspect's automobile to a crime scene. Physical characteristics of automotive glass may be searched in the Glass Evidence Reference Database. Handwriting may be searched in the Forensic Information System for Handwriting (FISH) maintained by the Secret Service, which also maintains the International Ink Library of more than 9,500 inks. Though limited in application, the nature of the evidence available may make the obscure database a particularly valuable resource for the investigator. As with all database inquiries, it is imperative to repeatedly search, as databases are continuously updated.

In addition to physical evidence databases, analytical tools may be of great assistance in reopening an investigation. Many cold cases have no one to guide a new investigator through what is typically a mass of paper documentation. The Cold Case Analytical Toolkit (CCAT) helps organize massive paper files of information to create a basis for informed decisions and effectively planning a new course of action. Developed by Ingersoll Consulting, Inc., CCAT is a multifaceted analytical tool designed to assist law enforcement with managing large amounts of previously captured documents (via OCR) and case facts, allowing comprehensive management of data while providing a fresh analytical perspective to all related evidence. CCAT can search and organize unlimited volumes of electronic records and databases as well as Web-based resource sites. It permits the cold case investigator to use the full extent of previously investigated and researched material to help prepare and conduct new investigative initiatives.

Conclusion

Cold case investigators face the daunting task of solving the ever-increasing number of unsolved homicides and serious assaults. Although the reasons cases are unsolved are highly variable, there exist cases wherein physical evidence is available and may now be tested or retested using highly sophisticated forensic science methods that may not have existed at the time the evidence was first collected. In some cases, the evidence may have never been submitted because the evidentiary value was not appreciated or the sample was too small to be analyzed by then-contemporary technologies. In some cases, the evidence may have been analyzed but would benefit from retesting with modern techniques. In most cases involving physical evidence, new scientific developments permit the reevaluation of the evidence, especially because of the development of comprehensive evidence linkage programs such as CODIS, IAFIS, and NIBIN, which are capable of providing linkage of unknown, unidentified specimens from the crime scene or victim to known specimens associated with a suspect. The recent establishment of these databases provides an opportunity to solve cold cases that has never before existed. The challenge to the cold case investigator is to recognize the potential of the physical evidence in the case and conduct the necessary forensic analysis to establish the associative link of physical evidence to suspect, victim, and crime scene.

Endnotes

Bieber, F. R., C. H. Brenner, and D. Lazer. 2006. Finding criminals through DNA of their relatives. *Science, 312*(5778), 1315–1316.

Bowen, R., and J. Schneider. October 2007. Forensic databases: Paint, shoe prints, and beyond. *NIJ Journal, 258.*

Butler, J. M. 2005. *Forensic DNA Typing.* Elsevier Academic Press: Burlington, MA.

Coyle, H. M. 2008. *Nonhuman DNA Typing: Theory and Casework Applications.* CRC Press: Boca Raton, FL.

Forensic DNA Databases: Linking Criminals to Crimes. http://www.dna.gov/dna-databases.

Gaensslen, R. E., and K. R. Young. 2005. Fingerprints, in *Forensic Science,* 2nd ed., S. H. James and J. J. Nordby, Eds. Taylor & Francis: Boca Raton, FL.

Integrated Automated Fingerprint Identification System (IAFIS). http://www.fbi.gov/hq/cjisd/iafis.htm.

Jeffreys, A. J., V. Wilson, and S. L. Thein. 1985. Individual-specific "fingerprints" of human DNA. *Nature, 322,* 290.

Komarinski, P. D. 2006. Automated fingerprint identification systems, in *Cold Case Homicides,* R. H. Walton, Ed. CRC Press: Boca Raton, FL.

Lee, H. C., T. M. Palmbach, and M. T. Miller. 2003. *Henry Lee's Crime Scene Handbook.* Academic Press: San Diego, CA.

Melton, T. 2004. Mitochondrial DNA heteroplasty. *Forensic Science Review, 16,* 1–20.

Melton, T., and K. Nelson. 2001. Forensic mitochondrial DNA analysis. *Croatian Medical Journal, 42,* 298–303.

Miranda v. Arizona. 1966. 384 U.S. 436.

National Integrated Ballistic Information Network (NIBIN). http://www.atf.gov/publications/factsheets/factsheet-nibin.html.

Saferstein, R. 2007. *Criminalistics.* Prentice Hall: Upper Saddle River, NJ.

Spalding, R. P. 2005. The identification and characterization of blood and bloodstains, in *Forensic Science,* 2nd ed., S. H. James and J. J. Nordby, Eds. Taylor & Francis: Boca Raton, FL.

Watson, J. D., and F. H. C. Crick. 1953. Genetical implications of the structure of deoxyribonucleic acid, *Nature, 171,* 964.

Walton, R. H. 2006a. *Cold Case Homicides.* CRC Press: Boca Raton, FL.

Walton, R. H. 2006b. National Integrated Ballistics Information Network (NIBIN), in *Cold Case Homicides,* R. H. Walton, Ed. CRC Press: Boca Raton, FL.

Suspectology
The Development of Suspects Using Pre-, Peri-, and Post-Offense Behaviors

10

RICHARD WALTER, SARAH L. STEIN,
AND JAMES M. ADCOCK

This chapter addresses a method for identifying the primary suspect in a murder investigation, which has proven to be especially beneficial when undertaking a cold case evaluation. This method requires evaluating the information pertaining to pre-crime events, the facts of the crime, and post-crime behaviors, and is wholly comprehensive. As such, the primary benefit to cold case evaluators is this: At the onset of a cold case evaluation, investigators have the advantage of having all relevant case information available, whereas during a hot case they must rely on a trickle of incoming information. This process is started by first examining the core elements of the crime where a subtype is identified and subsequently moves outward from a working premise toward identifying like characteristics in identified persons of interest.

Although the rule of thumb of working from the inside of the case outward is generally adhered to, this method does have the potential to go awry when leads or tips have been presented that shift the focus away from the thrust of the investigation into a new direction. As a consequence, independent of whether the information provided was relevant to the investigation, the pursuance of these leads can quickly build a number of *persons of interest* that cannot be affirmed or dismissed. Often, when the potential suspect list exceeds 4, 11, or 50 people, it becomes a major concern when weighing the importance and value of the evidence. Here, a method is offered to resolve this dilemma and is accomplished by using the primary suspect's own behavior to aid the investigation.

Two case studies (one in this chapter and the second in Appendix C) will be presented to illustrate the process of identifying the suspect through the behavioral actions of the perpetrator before, during, and after the crime. However, it is important to understand this is not "profiling" but rather an assessment of the actions found within the crime itself looking for indicators that will assist in the identification of the perpetrator(s). With that being said we offer the following explanation by Richard Walter.

Crime Assessment versus Profiling

In order to fully comprehend the concepts and functions of crime assessment versus profiling, it is important to understand the linkage and differences between criminology and psychology. For the purposes of this we will define criminology as the study of crime and criminals in a social setting. Specifically, this is directed toward crime patterns, interview strategies, methods of operation, police work, and probabilities for crime subtypes. It is important that, unlike psychology, the language and conceptual thought of crime is in the deviancy continuum. Alternatively, psychology is concerned with the individual with interest in the person's interaction and thinking processes. Here, by discipline limitations, the interest in the individual is restricted to diagnosis and treatment of the patient. The language of psychology uses specific definitions related to mental disorders and paraphilia. Again, psychology is the study of the behavior and the processes of the *mind*. Once the relationship between criminology and psychology are understood, the groundwork has been established for discussing the conceptual framework between crime assessment and profiling.

Crime assessment is defined as an evaluation of the crime scene for the presence or absence of probative evidence. This evidence may be physical, direct, or circumstantial. The presence of a stick in the eye, taped arms, or handcuffs would be identifying the presence of evidence. Alternatively, the absence of evidence might be lack of victim clothing, body parts, or money. Given the collection of evidence, the evaluator can reconcile the information with a recognized criminal pattern of crime; be it homicide, suicide, accident, sexual misadventure, and so forth. Dependent upon the quality of the evidence and crime prototype, the evaluator may determine the probabilities related to motivational structures, and the complexity of the crime acts. Once accomplished, the data can result in refined probability factors relative to who, what, where, when, why, and how. Here, the investigator may capitalize upon the dimensional information and formulate a refined investigative strategy. Inasmuch as the process of crime assessment is predicated exclusively within the criminological continuum, the methodology is reflective and subject to examination and validation. As a consequence, some courts have allowed this type of evidence to be introduced into the court proceedings.

A profile is defined as a projective process of looking for probabilities related to the type of unknown individual who may commit this type of offense. Here, the focus is upon the offender's implied and probable behaviors, mental health status, character issues, motivations, and sexual paraphilia. Within this paradigm, the acquired data may infer information about the perpetrator's age, race, work, education, hobbies, and so on.

Again, the profiler is concentrated upon the individual through the psychological continuum seeking individualized identity factors.

In the application of a case, when the bedrock of the crime assessment is insufficient to assist the investigation, a psychological profile can create an outline sketch of the offender to assist in developing potential leads. Given this scenario, the psychological profile, though projective and speculative, can be of some valuable insights and clues for the investigator. However, the investigator must understand the questionable reliability of this information. Again, although the crime assessment is the primary foundation for an opinion, the psychological profile can be a secondary enhancement to the original work. Given the inherent projective nature of the psychological profile, this process does not meet the standards of the courts.

Following the conceptual differentiation between crime assessment and profiling, it can be stated that, although separate, they are not mutually exclusive. That is, when crime assessment and profiling are used within appropriate continuums for the purpose intended, the psychological profile can become a valuable accent articulation to the primary crime assessment. Accordingly, this means that the expert in crime assessment may or may not be a psychologist. The critical difference would be that the expert must understand crime, not just the offender's probable behaviors. Likewise, the profiler may or may not be a psychologist. Here, the expert must understand not only crime but behavior probabilities. True, given the expertise, both can be done at the same time. However, it is critical for the evaluator to ask the right question of the appropriate discipline.

In a murder investigation, the pursuit of *who, what, when, where,* and *how* can be difficult, elusive, and problematic due to criminal sophistication, lack of evidence, or victim selection. Furthermore, to avoid detection, the perpetrator may have *staged* the crime scene to resemble an accident or suicide. Again, many complexities can offer misdirection and red herring searches to no avail. During this time, investigators may receive well-intentioned, as well as *not* well-intended, tips regarding the crime. Accordingly, while chasing these leads, it becomes easy to follow the operative theory in front of them rather than consider the actual facts of the case. When this happens, unless there is a major break that shifts the focus back to the crime scene evidence, the odds improve that the investigation will become an unresolved cold case.

In violent crimes, murder does not happen in a vacuum. It has victims and perpetrators. To achieve the end result, the perpetrator must actualize a motive with a method when given the opportunity to do so. Here, in part, is the rub for the perpetrator. For, despite the self-perceived cleverness of the perpetrator, an examination of the crime scene evidence for what is *and what is not* at the scene, the perpetrator will ultimately leave a telltale record regarding the motive and relationship between victim and perpetrator. That is, when the investigator measures the pieces of direct, circumstantial, and physical evidence against known crime subtypes, the facts should indicate whether in whole, or in combination, the crime was *power-assertive, power-reassurance, anger-retaliatory*, or *anger-excitation (sadism)*. Furthermore, the subtypes will provide additional information regarding whether the crime was likely purposeful, fantasy driven, revenge, or pleasure killing. Further descriptions of the four identified subtypes are discussed below.[1]

Perpetrator Subtypes

Power-Assertive Type

In the nonsexual power-assertive type, power is a conceptual term that denotes a process of creating notions, ideas, and symbols that reflect thought. Here, the perpetrator chooses to take a criminal action for achieving control and dominance of an individual or a situation. Commonly, nonsexual power-assertive murders are committed for greed, investment, contract, domestic dispute, politics, or as a simple drive-by shooting. In these instances, the detached relationship with the victim may be minimal and require little or no direct contact with the victim. For instance, the murder could be completed by simply shooting the victim in a place and manner that meets the perpetrator's needs. In contrast, the sexual power-assertive rape/murder, by its nature, has an inherent emotional involvement that increases the probability of percussive injury to the victim. That is, given the increased emotionality, the perpetrator's needs are satisfied only through direct injury to the victim, such as, hitting, bludgeoning, stabbing, strangulation, and so forth.

Power-Reassurance Type

In the nonsexual power-reassurance type, the acquisition of control, dominance, and mastery becomes enhanced through daydreaming and fantasy development. Here, the scripts and usurpation of power are limited only by the inadequacy of imagination. The criminal activity, which may result in the death of the victim, may include impersonation of heroic or professional occupations, stalking the rich and famous, infant kidnapping for a pretend family, or hostilities that make the perpetrator feel important and potent. In contrast, the sexual power-reassurance type uses fantasy to create desired or ideal relationships with targeted or opportunistic victims. Primarily, the victims are either younger, older, or somehow considered "damaged goods" by the perpetrator. Herein, the victim choice, by their age or condition, lessens the inherent challenge to his power that could be produced by a healthy and appropriate-aged person. Often, due to his need for validation, the perpetrator will ask the victim for approval and rating of the exhibited performance. Accordingly, this type of perpetrator is sometimes referred to as "the gentleman rapist." However, when the preplanned assault goes awry, the loss of power prompts a violent reaction upon the victim. As a result, the crime may show a disorganized scene and possible post-mortem sexual activity.

Anger-Retaliatory Type

In the nonsexual anger-retaliatory type, the emotional outburst against the target is to punish a perceived wrongdoing, real or imagined, committed against the aggrieved perpetrator. Most often, the violence is percussive (hitting, stabbing, strangulation, etc.) upon the victim until the perpetrator has sated the precipitating anger. An exception to the percussive violence is the crime of arson. Here, for instance, the perpetrator may burn down a rental apartment or home because of an eviction. Notwithstanding, the goal of the perpetrator is to punish, get even, and retaliate against the victim. Generally, the target victim is one who has the ability to condemn, censure, ridicule, or prompt a feeling of injury to the aggressor. In this category, the types of victims may be a person, business, group, landlord, child molester, and so forth. In contrast, the sexual anger-retaliatory type is often nettled by and simultaneously attracted to women. Accordingly, while using women to further his dependency/hatred, the perpetrator uses them as foils and scapegoats for explaining his own failures. Often, the targeted victims are the same age or older than the perpetrator, for it is generally this group that has the power to humiliate or scold. An exception to the age range would be a younger woman who may be a clerk in a store that refuses his credit card, the stepdaughter who threatens to expose sexual abuse, or a female supervisor. Most often, the primary target victims within this group are mothers, aunts, wives, and girlfriends. However, due to the pathological connections between the perpetrator and victim, the killing of the primary target becomes unacceptable. Hence, the perpetrator may seek a substitute target for which to act out the crime intended for the primary target. In the crime, the percussive violence may continue into post-mortem activity. Following the emotional catharsis, the perpetrator will position the body with eyes away from the point of egress. Likewise, the perpetrator feels no guilt and exits the crime scene with a feeling of well-being and cleansing.

Anger-Excitation Type

In the nonsexual anger-excitation (sadism) type, the prolonged and ritualized process of human destruction is the goal unto itself. Here, despite a myriad of methods and schemes, the core elements of sadism are dependency, dread, and degradation of the victim. Although extensive fantasy may be used, it is not required with the nonsexual anger-excitation type. The victims may be known or stranger, male or female, and adult or child. Within this subset, the crimes may be parental torture of children (burning, starving, bindings, etc.), male torture of a rival suitor for a love object (humiliation, bondage, beheading, etc.), and war-related killing of soldiers (beating, burning, incomplete strangulations, staged beheadings, sexual mutilations, tossing live prisoners into a fire pit). In contrast, the sexual anger-excitation type increases the fantasy component into elaborate scenarios designed to break the body and mind. Here, operative schemes are devised to confuse the victim by "con games" that offer false hope and then destroy that hope. Again, the satisfaction of these killings is gained in the process of the killing, not the death itself. Often, victim selection is from symbolic categories or characteristics, such as hair color, size, age, or fetish interests. Victims are often prostitutes, drug users, nurses, children, students, and matriarchs. Methodically, the perpetrator will exact sexual pleasures through secondary sexual mechanisms such as bondage, insertions, and so forth. In addition, the anger-excitation perpetrator may engage in acts of necrophilia or cannibalism.

Summary

The following information provides additional information about the four subtypes of offenders that may be encountered during the course of an investigation. Remember that in some cases characteristics may overlap to a degree or you may see two subtypes emerging.

Power-Assertive
   Assault is preplanned.
   Forceful aggression and intimidation.
   Grasps and maintains control over victim.
   Uses exaggerated machismo overreaction.
   Search for virility, mastery, and dominance.
   Language is directive and commanding.
   Injury to victim is purposeful, not recreational.
   Sexually related violence is percussive (beating, cutting, strangling).
   Brings weaponry to crime scene and takes away after the killing. Often,
      weapons are part of normal image (a gun, knives, ropes, etc.).
   Although violence may be severe, there is no mutilation of the body.
   Murder does not "count" unless someone knows; feels the need to brag.

Power-Reassurance
   Preplanned rape with unplanned overkill of the victim.
   Prompted by fantasy and overidealized seduction and conquest.

Seeks verbal reassurance from victim (e.g., the gentleman rapist).

When victim does not yield to planned seduction, the fantasy collapses and an emotional explosion results in killing.

Often, post-mortem mutilation.

Tends toward disorganized crime scene.

Victim selection may be younger or older than the perpetrator. Also, the age range may be similar, if victim is perceived as "damaged goods."

Weapons may be clothing, fist, and knives.

If sexual behavior occurs, it is likely to be post-mortem.

Body may have insertions.

Anger-Retaliatory

Assault is situational planned.

Stylized violent burst of attack.

Violent assault and overkill of victim.

Victim's eyes away from egress.

Nettled by poor relationships with adult women.

Assault precipitated by scolding from woman.

Victim is often a scapegoat/substitute for the intended victim.

Victim is chosen because she lives or works in area near offender.

Victim may be preselected pending the perpetrator's impulsive reaction to an anger/challenge.

Although perpetrator may drive to the crime location, he approaches the last 200 feet by foot.

Anger-Excitation (Sadism)

Homicides are preplanned and designed to inflict terror and pain upon the victim.

Satisfaction is found in the killing continuum, not in the death.

The insatiable appetite is predicated on dependency, dread, and degradation.

In the search for domination and mastery, overt sexual dynamics may become delayed and muted. Instead, there is a rise of secondary sexual mechanisms, which allow emotionally laden power concepts to become activated and satisfy the crushing of the prey.

The victim selection may be male/female that fits perpetrator's needed symbolic category, such as prostitutes, nurses, children, students, and matriarchs.

Complementary fetish interest may be long blond hair, specialized shoes, large breasts, or tawdry clothing.

Once a victim has been encountered by con and/or ruse, perpetrator will attempt to isolate for control.

As fantasy system is implemented, perpetrator may show vacillating
    mood shifts, with a methodical approach at terrorizing the victim.
Prior to killing, there may be evidence of burning, cutting, washing,
    bruising, and ligature marks.

Unlike natural, accidental, or suicide deaths, homicide is the only manner of death that has post-crime behavior. That is, although the victim's body is dead, the perpetrator still derives satisfaction from the killing. Unwittingly, the perpetrator's post-crime behavior continues to leave evidence for the investigator to capture and use for identification and eventual prosecution.

Inasmuch as the crime scene evidence is the beginning and nexus for the investigation, the evidence, by presence or absence, compared with the appropriate crime subtype, becomes the gold standard for evaluating the relevance of other data, information, and understanding for the case.

The fact that a homicide/murder was committed with a motive, in a particular method, and at a specific time and location indicate that the perpetrator had sufficient cause to target and kill the victim. Whether the perpetrator may have had a great deal or limited exposure to the victim, he or she found cause, method, and time to aggress against the target. These actions prior to the killing are pre-crime behaviors. Given the nature of the victim, it is possible that any number of people may have wanted the victim dead. Accordingly, while looking into each of these possible suspects, the investigator can determine the victim–suspect relationship, conflict between the parties, and the intended benefit to the suspect for killing the victim. Again, using the standard created by the crime scene, one can measure the crime scene crime subtype to that of the pre-crime behavioral suspect list. In fact, the crime subtype of the crime and the suspect should be the same. In particular, if the crime is determined to be power-assertive, so should be the motivational and relationship structure of the suspect.

Again, contrary to conventional thought, the murder is not over when the body dies but when the perpetrator stops deriving satisfaction from the killing. In some instances, this may be days or years! Accordingly, since these behaviors follow the killing, these actions are called post-crime behaviors. Here, the investigator can take the same subjects listed in the pre-crime behavior suspect list and fill in for each suspect whether they benefited with greed, power, silencing a secret, sexual gratification, or hatred. Again, as in the pre-crime behavior analysis, the investigator uses the crime evidence and subtype of the crime to measure against the post-crime suspects. When completed, the primary suspect's pre-crime and post-crime behaviors should match the crime description and analysis. For example, if the crime was power-assertive, the primary suspect should show power-assertive characteristics for both pre-crime and post-crime behaviors. In addition, if the primary suspect is within the pool examined, the pre-crime and post-crime entries should contain a number of weighted linkages to the crime. If not, this could indicate a direction for further investigation or the primary suspect has not been included in the list.

In a given list of five possible suspects, if one particular person has numerous entries that are significant to a motive and relationship with the victim, this person should be examined on the post-crime behaviors to determine the quantity and quality of a perceived or real gain made by that person. Often, dependent on the type of killing, these items could range from 25 to 40 entries. Alternatively, if none of the other four suspects on the list have any pre-crime or post-crime issues beyond possibly disliking the victim, because of, for example, a bad car deal, they can be algebraically crossed off to clear the field of extraneous clutter.

Note: It is possible that one or more persons may have been involved in the killing. If so, each of the persons should have listed key items and a relationship with one another.

In reference to the primary suspect, once the data have been collected and properly entered into the schematic diagram, directional vectors can be drawn from the pre-crime behavior through the crime standard and transverse into the post-crime behaviors. Thus the vector represents the connection *before, during,* and *after* the crime. Accordingly, this can be done a number of times at different points of congruency. In effect, this means that the primary subject, through actions and words, helps identify himself to the exclusion of all others.

Methods

As previously mentioned, the first stage of the process is to identify the crime characteristics and behaviors. Generic examples can be seen in Table 10.1.

Crime Behavior

The crime behavior exhibited and performed at the crime scene is pivotal to all behavior preceding and following it. Accordingly, as the standard, it is first established between the pre-crime behavior and post-crime behavior. The data for crime behavior should include time of notification, location and position of body, injuries sustained (blunt force trauma, gunshot wounds, stabbings, strangulation, etc.), post-mortem manipulation of the body, and presence or absence of collateral evidence (clothing, money, body parts, etc.). Finally, this section should include the autopsy findings for the primary and secondary causes of death.

Table 10.1   Peri-Crime Behavior Examples

Pre-Crime Behavior	Peri-Crime Behavior	Post-Crime Behavior
	Notification:	
	• Date	
	• Time	
	• Location, etc.	
	Scene:	
	• Organized	
	• Disorganized	
	• Items missing, etc.	
	Body position:	
	• Normal	
	• Staged or posed	
	• Unusual findings or potential signature issues	
	• Autopsy findings	
	Cause of death:	
	• Gunshot wound	
	• Stabbing	
	• Strangulation	
	• Other	
	Wound pattern(s)	
	Etc.	

Pre-Crime Behavior

This category extends to all persons reported or developed by investigators who may have had conflict with or in fact caused the death of the victim. Dependent on the type of risk factor for the victim, this number may vary from one to ten or more. For the purposes of data entry, this section should be located on the left of the crime behavior column. Each suspect should be listed individually across the top of the section with room to enter significant points of interests below the name.

Often, the information listed here is circumstantial and in need of documentation. Accordingly, the source of the information should be noted.

Most often, the supplied information refers to relationships between the victim and mentioned suspect. Sometimes it can be relationships gone awry, jealousy, fear, hatred, love, control, greed, sexual behavior, business conflict, or a myriad of other potential reasons. Again, it is extremely important to note whether the tip or witness knows firsthand of the alleged facts or whether it came via an undocumented route or through the rumor mill.

Note: Commonly, the witness's observation, heard conversation, or tidbit of information would not stand alone as a piece of evidence. However, when linked with other pieces of collateral evidence into a network, it can become relevant and upgraded into a credible statement.

Predicated upon the aforementioned comments, it still remains that one, two, or three unkind remarks regarding the victim do not a killer make! In fact, the primary suspect should demonstrate either overt or underlying angst, motive, or reason to benefit from the victim's death.

Post-Crime Behavior

Following the crime, the killer may act with stealth or unwitting brashness to benefit from the miscreant deed. Frequently, despite being alert and having made attempts at being cautious, the perpetrator will yield intelligence and knowledge to the underlying psychopathology underwriting the crime. Hence, dependent on the subtype style, the perpetrator, by behavior, may have with cavalier bravado revealed his true nature.

Again, dependent on the subtype of murder, the post-crime behaviors may vary: bragging about the killing, inappropriate behavior at the funeral, diminution of the victim and exaggeration of their own importance, attempt to establish an alibi, attempt at interjection into the investigation, creating false scenarios, new relationship or marriage, money or insurance gains, silencing secrets known by victim, improved power base as a result of the victim's death, disconnect between affect and word content (smiling while stating that he is devastated at the loss of his wife), change in lifestyle, or satisfaction that the victim is dead.

Case Study 1[2]

To illustrate this method of suspect identification (suspectology), we are going to use a case from Hudson, Wisconsin. In 2002, a small Midwestern town experienced a double homicide of a 39-year-old, highly respected funeral director and a college-aged intern. Both victims were shot and found in the office of the funeral home. Aside from the bullet wounds and shell casings, there was no physical evidence of value found at the scene, such as fingerprints, DNA, or theft or plundering of the scene. In fact, it appeared that the assailant entered the premises with purposeful intent, acted out, and left the building. The bodies were discovered approximately 15 minutes later by the local coroner who came to do regular business. *Later, during a roadblock search, a witness stated that he had seen a thickly built man, wearing a white T-shirt, black pants, and a brown corduroy hat, leave the building and entering a large car at about the time of the killings.* Flummoxed by the unusual murders, the investigators began searching for leads in the case. Eventually, they had a number of potential leads related to a wide variety of possible motives, including the local priest *who had refused to give last rites to the victims at the murder scene.* Despite these suspect leads, the examination of facts came to naught in moving forward, except for one, Father Ryan Erickson (Fr. R.E.), who could not be eliminated. That is, while the others could be algebraically eliminated as suspects, the attempt to eliminate Fr. R.E. from the list was thwarted by his persistent presentation of red flags. Utilizing this case study as an illustration of the suspect identification process, Table 10.2 shows an abbreviated array of crime behavior concerning

Table 10.2   Peri-Crime Behavior Outcomes for Case Study 1

1. February 5, 2002, at 13:40 h, a 911 call was placed from the funeral home, indicating a need for help with an apparent murder of two bodies.
2. When police arrived, they secured the building and discovered two dead bodies in the office of the building.
3. The funeral home director, age 39, was found sitting in the office desk chair with a bullet wound to the forehead. He was dead.
4. The second victim, a college intern, age 22, was found slumped over the back of a second chair. He had been shot in the head, with a grazing wound to the right little finger. He was dead.
5. A third bullet was found behind a broken mirror. (It is believed that the first shot to the intern injured the finger and lodged in the wall behind the broken mirror.)
6. There was no evidence of defense wounds and/or resistance from the two victims.
7. The rest of the office and building was undisturbed. (The victims' coats were left on the back of the chairs, and the mobile telephone remained upright in place.)
8. Although the second victim's wallet was in plain sight, it was left in place. There was no evidence of robbery or theft.
9. The only physical evidence left at the scene was spent firearm shells. There was no evidence of fingerprints, DNA, or footprints.
10. Later, a witness reported that while stopped at a street corner at the time of the offense, he observed a thickly built male wearing a brown corduroy hat, white T-shirt, and black pants walk from the funeral home to a large black car.
11. A very tight police perimeter was placed around the crime scene, and very few persons (need-to-know basis) learned what happened to the victims and how.
12. The autopsy results confirmed that both victims died from gunshot wounds to the head.

Table 10.3   Pre-Crime Behavior Outcomes for Case Study 1

1. For some months prior to February 5, 2002, the church secretary advised that a parish priest, Fr. R.E, had been observed in the upstairs of the church aiming an imaginary gun and firing at parishioners whom he did not like.

2. For a few years, the funeral home director and family attended the church where the subject was a parish priest. Although accepted by the director's family, the priest was viewed with some reserve because of what appeared to be theatrical and odd behaviors. Nevertheless, on occasion, the priest was invited into the family home for gatherings.

3. As a highly respected and personable leader in the community, involved in business and church activities, the funeral home director was well known to have been the go-to guy for remedying problems. As such, he would honorably confront any problem and seek remediation. This was also true with church issues. Accordingly, the funeral home director and priest would "lock horns" on various issues.

4. Although the funeral home director knew that the priest was a gun aficionado, stocked the rectory refrigerator with squirrel meat, and became overzealous on some issues, he did not comment on these matters. However, it is now known that when a young high school parishioner came to him and reported the priest for giving alcohol to young men for sexual favors, the funeral director became highly alarmed and confronted the priest about the behavior.

5. Prior to the victims' death, the priest later confided to a friend that he and the funeral director had a major verbal battle.

6. Although not proven as fact, the circumstantial inference is that the funeral director gave the priest 12 hours to reassess his position, advise the bishop, and resign. Otherwise, the funeral director would advise the bishop himself and take action.

7. On February 4, 2002, it is known that the funeral director reorganized his schedule to accommodate a special meeting at 13:00 hours with a "special" person who was not specifically identified by name. *Given the perceived need to keep confidential the nature of the discussion with the parish priest the previous evening, it is believed that the funeral director scheduled the meeting with him to force the final solution.*

8. Per the bishop, the parish priest did not mention the funeral director, and/or admit, discuss, or infer any personal wrongdoing.

9. Fr. R.E. kept his job.

this case study, followed by Tables 10.3 and 10.4, which reflect the pre- and post-crime indicators, respectively.

Table 10.5 lists the categories of information together in one table, so correlations can be made. It shows the vectors in place that bound Fr. R.E. to be the one and only person who could have committed the murders. To expound further, let us examine the correlations that can be found in Table 10.5. The correlations between the pre-, peri-, and post-crime behavior displayed by the subject as well as the shifts in the subject's behavior will be addressed. It is important to note here that the hope for an investigator is to observe significant differences in pre- and post-crime behavior, such as if the subject did not drink prior to the crime and then began drinking afterward. This simple fact could be an indicator, paired with other circumstantial evidence, that

Table 10.4   Post-Crime Behavior Outcomes for Case Study 1

1. February 5, 2002, 14:30 hours, Fr. R.E. advised a group of local nuns that there had been a tragedy at the funeral home and the victims had been shot dead. At this time, the SWAT team had not completed the search of the building. Furthermore, save for only a few detectives, the cause of death was highly privileged information that was kept secret.

2. February 5, 2002, 16:45, Fr. R.E. was called to give last rites to the victims at the funeral home. He refused.

3. February 5, 2002, 18:00, Fr. R.E. told the church secretary that he did not know what to say to the funeral director's family. Nevertheless, he did go with a friend and paid an uncomfortable visit.

4. Several days later, Fr. R.E. conducted the funeral services for the victims.

5. In the search for possible leads, the detectives interviewed Fr. R.E. and asked whether anyone had confessed or hinted about the motives for the murders. In response, Fr. R.E. suggested that the funeral director and his secretary may have been having an illicit affair. This lead later proved to be untrue.

6. Later, when police learned of the inside information related to the murders that was shared with the nuns, Fr. R.E. claimed several different sources for the information. Again, this proved untrue.

7. When asked about his further thoughts regarding possible motives for the killings, he indicated that he had heard that the funeral director was possibly linked to the Mafia. Not true.

8. When asked about his whereabouts at the time of the killings, Fr. R.E. became flustered, offered numerous contradictory statements, and could not positively account for several hours of time.

9. When asked about his providing alcohol to minor boys for sexual behaviors, he denied any impropriety. Later, he advised that he was simply offering them sex education.

10. Fr. R.E. denied committing the murders.

11. Fr. R.E. provided numerous firearms and swords to police.

12. Fr. R.E. complained/bragged about being a primary suspect in the murders.

13. Fr. R.E. was moved to a different parish.

14. When asked to participate in a second interview, Fr. R.E. claimed to be too busy. However, a call to the bishop changed his mind.

15. Armed with a search warrant to search the rectory, detectives found a brown corduroy hat, weapons, a computer with hundreds of deleted sexually explicit e-mails to young boys, and photographs containing child pornography.

16. Fr. R.E. admitted to a friend/parishioner that he and the funeral director had had a strong argument the night before the killings.

17. When asked what should happen to the killer who committed the crime, he opined that that person should commit suicide.

18. Several weeks later, Fr. R.E. committed suicide by hanging.

Table 10.5 Consolidated Pre-, Peri-, and Post-Crime Behavior Outcomes for Case Study 1

Pre-Crime Behavior	Peri-Crime Behavior	Post-Crime Behavior
1. For some months prior to February 5, 2002, the church secretary advised that a parish priest, Fr. R.E., had been observed in the upstairs of the church aiming an imaginary gun and firing at parishioners whom he did not like.	1. February 5, 2002, at 13:40 hours, a 911 call was placed from the funeral home, indicating a need for help with an apparent murder with two bodies.	1. February 5, 2002, 14:30 hours, Fr. R.E. advised a group of local nuns that there had been a tragedy at the funeral home and the victims had been shot dead. *At this time, the SWAT team had not completed the search of the building. Furthermore, save for only a few detectives, the cause of death was highly privileged information that was kept secret.*
2. For a few years, the funeral home director and family attended the church where the subject was a parish priest. Although accepted by the director's family, the priest was viewed with some reserve because of what appeared to be theatrical and odd behaviors. Nevertheless, on occasion, the priest was invited into the family home for gatherings.	2. When police arrived, they secured the building and discovered two dead bodies in the office of the building.	2. February 5, 2002, 16:45, Fr. R.E. was called to give last rites to the victims at the funeral home. He refused.
3. As a highly respected and personable leader in the community, involved in business and church activities, the funeral home director was well known to have been the *go-to guy* for remedying problems. As such, he would honorably confront the problem and seek remediation. This was also true with church issues. Accordingly, the funeral home director and priest would "lock horns" on various issues.	3. The funeral home director, age 39, was found sitting in the office desk chair with a bullet wound to the forehead. He was dead.	3. February 5, 2002, 18:00, Fr. R.E. told the church secretary that he did not know what to say to the funeral director's family. *Nevertheless, he did go with a friend and paid an uncomfortable visit.*
	4. The second victim, a college intern, age 22, was found slumped over the back of a second chair. He had been shot in the head, with a grazing wound to the right little finger. He was dead.	4. Several days later, Fr. R.E. conducted the funeral services for the victims.
	5. A third bullet was found behind a broken mirror. (It is believed that the first shot to the intern injured the finger and lodged in the wall behind the broken mirror.)	5. In the search for possible leads, the detectives interviewed Fr. R.E. and asked whether anyone had confessed or hinted about the motives for the murders. In response, Fr. R.E. suggested that the funeral director and his secretary may have been having an illicit affair. *This lead later proved to be untrue.*
	6. There was no evidence of defense wounds and/or resistance from the two victims.	

Continued

Table 10.5 (Continued)   Consolidated Pre-, Peri-, and Post-Crime Behavior Outcomes for Case Study 1

Pre-Crime Behavior	Peri-Crime Behavior	Post-Crime Behavior
4. Although the funeral home director knew that the priest was a gun aficionado, stocked the rectory refrigerator with squirrel meat, and became overzealous on some issues, he did not comment on these matters. However, it is now known that when a young high school parishioner came to him and reported the priest for giving alcohol to young men for sexual favors, the funeral director became highly alarmed and confronted the priest about the behavior.	7. The rest of the office and building was undisturbed. (The victims' coats were left on the back of the chairs and the mobile telephone remained upright in place.) 8. Although the second victim's wallet was in plain sight, it was left in place. There was no evidence of robbery or theft. 9. The only physical evidence left at the scene was spent firearm shells. There was no evidence of fingerprints, DNA, or footprints.	6. Later, when police learned of the *inside information related to the murders* that was shared with the nuns, Fr. R.E. claimed several different sources for the information. Again, this proved untrue. 7. When asked about his further thoughts regarding possible *motives* for the killings, he indicated that he had heard that the funeral director was possibly linked to the Mafia. Not true.
5. Prior to the victims' death, the priest later confided to a friend that he and the funeral director had a major verbal battle.	10. Later, a witness reported that while stopped at a street corner at the time of the offense, he observed a thickly built male wearing a brown corduroy hat, white T-shirt, and black pants walk from the funeral home to a large black car.	8. When asked about his whereabouts at the time of the killings, Fr. R.E. became flustered, offered numerous contradictory statements, and could not positively account for several hours of time.
6. Although not proven as fact, the circumstantial inference is that the funeral director gave the priest 12 hours to reassess his position, advise the bishop, and resign. Otherwise, the funeral director would advise the bishop himself and take action.	11. A very tight police perimeter was placed around the crime scene and very few persons (need to know basis) learned how and what happened to the victims. 12. The autopsy results confirmed that both victims died from gunshot wounds to the head.	9. When asked about his providing alcohol to minor boys for sexual behaviors, he denied any impropriety. Later, he advised that he was simply offering them sex education. 10. Fr. R.E. denied committing the murders. 11. Fr. R.E. provided numerous firearms and swords to police. 12. Fr. R.E. complained/bragged about being a primary suspect in the murders.

Table 10.5 (Continued)   Consolidated Pre-, Peri-, and Post-Crime Behavior Outcomes for Case Study 1

Pre-Crime Behavior	Peri-Crime Behavior	Post-Crime Behavior
7. On February 4, 2002, it is known that the funeral director reorganized his schedule to accommodate a special meeting at 13:00 hours, with a "special" person who was not specifically identified by name. *Given the perceived need to keep confidential the nature of discussion with the parish priest the previous evening, it is believed that the funeral director scheduled the meeting with him to force the final solution.*		13. Fr. R.E. was moved to a different parish.
8. Per the bishop, the parish priest did not mention the funeral director, and/or admit, discuss, or infer any personal wrongdoing.		14. When asked to participate in a second interview, Fr. R.E. claimed to be too busy. However, a call to the bishop changed his mind.
9. Fr. R.E. kept his job.		15. Armed with a search warrant to search the rectory, detectives found a brown corduroy hat, weapons, a computer with hundreds of deleted sexually explicit e-mails to young boys, and photographs containing child pornography.
		16. Fr. R.E. admitted to a friend/parishioner that he and the funeral director had had a strong argument the night before the killings.
		17. When asked what should happen to the killer who committed the crime, he opined that that person should commit suicide.
		18. Several weeks later, Fr. R.E. committed suicide by hanging.

indicates involvement in the commission of the crime. We will now move on to the assessment of Fr. R.E.'s behavior.

The appropriate manner in which to approach a correlation analysis between pre-, peri-, and post-offense behavior is to first examine the known facts of the case; that is, those facts that are inherent to the crime and the crime scene itself. To begin the analysis of the scene, one must consider the several factors listed in Table 10.1. These factors, including but not limited to notification issues, scene issues, body position, unusual findings, autopsy findings, cause of death, and wound patterns, will dictate to the evaluator and subsequent investigator(s) possible motives for the crime, as well as the typology of the offender they are seeking.

For the purposes of this analysis, we will mention only the case facts pertaining to the aforementioned factors. All the following facts can be located in the peri-crime behavior listed in Table 10.2. The notification date, time, and location were as follows: On February 5, 2002, at 13:40 hours, a 911 call was made from the funeral home (the crime scene), indicating that there had been a murder. At the scene, investigators discovered two dead bodies: that of the funeral home director, age 39, and that of his college intern, age 22. The scene itself was highly organized: there was no evidence that the bodies were staged, no robbery, no pre-mortem torture, no post-mortem disfigurement of the bodies, and so on. The offender simply walked in, shot, and walked out. The autopsy subsequently concluded that both victims had expired due to gunshot wounds to the head.

This crime meets the criteria of a power-assertive type. Likewise, the pre-crime and post-crime behaviors of the primary suspect, Father Ryan Erickson, are also the power-assertive type.

Note: Although sexual issues were integral to the pre-crime, the crime was nonsexual. (See the section "Typology Research" and endnote citations for a full description of the subtype and indicators.)

As the facts of the crime itself have now been established, let us turn to the process of correlating the pre-, peri-, and post-offense behaviors. When pursuing a power-assertive offender, investigators must keep in mind one critical aspect of such an individual's personality: The crime does not "count" unless someone knows. That is, the offender feels an intense need to brag about his actions. Therefore, one of the most telling indicators of Fr. R.E.'s involvement is the fact that he informed a group of local nuns of a murder at the funeral home and told them that the victims were shot to death. This was at 14:30 hours, a time prior to police releasing any information pertaining to the crime to the public.

Now, let us correlate the pre- and post-crime behavior to the facts of the crime. The first issue to be addressed is the weapon used to commit the crime, which was a gun. With regard to pre-crime behavior, it was noted that the church secretary often saw Fr. R.E. in his office pointing an imaginary firearm and firing at parishioners he did not care for. With regard to post-crime behavior, Fr. R.E. provided numerous firearms to the police. (See Table 10.3 and Table 10.4.)

The remainder of the pre- and post-crime behaviors displayed by Fr. R.E. is primarily emotional in nature. The motive behind the murders was ultimately discovered to be that the funeral home director was going to report Fr. R.E. for sexually abusing a young boy. The precipitating factor (and pre-crime behavior) that triggered the murders was a meeting that took place between Fr. R.E. and the funeral home director on February 4, 2002, during which the funeral home director confronted Fr. R.E. about the abuse.

The post-crime behavior displayed by Fr. R.E. becomes increasingly erratic in nature. Following telling the nuns about the murder, Fr. R.E. was called to the funeral home to administer last rites but refused. However, Fr. R.E. did indeed perform funeral services for both victims later in the week. When police interviewed Fr. R.E. later in the week, he again demonstrated his power-assertive tendencies in that he broke the confessional seal by intimating that the funeral director and his secretary may have been having an illicit affair. Not only was this meant to throw investigators off track, but being questioned by the police stroked the suspect's ego, made him feel important, and feel the need to brag. Following this incident, Fr. R.E. continued to offer police conflicting reports regarding his whereabouts at the time of the crime, how he had first heard about the murders and was able to pass along that information to the nuns, and he attempted to throw off the police again by claiming that the motive for the shootings may have been related to the Mafia. In the end, when asked what he believed should happen to the person that committed the murders, Fr. R.E. asserted that this person should commit suicide. It was ultimately discovered that Fr. R.E. was indeed sexually abusing young boys; and a few weeks after his last interview, Fr. R.E. committed suicide by hanging.

Contrary to the overt intention of the primary suspect, the examination of the pre-, peri-, and post-crime behaviors became the critical evidence that identified him as the perpetrator. Ironically, the perpetrator, not the investigators, provided the crucial evidence supplied against the primary suspect! That is, despite efforts to thwart the investigation and potential arrest, it was the proffered lies, deceptions, and diversions offered by the perpetrator that led to the conclusion. Again, like the firefly and the fire, the perpetrator becomes identified and consumed by his malicious greed and his own actions.

As indicated in Table 10.5 and Figure 10.1, the greater the number of vector connections between the primary suspect and the crime, the greater the probability that this perpetrator, among all other suspects, had a motive, method, and opportunity to commit the crime against this *particular* victim. Eventually, often by their own actions, deeds, and words, the evidence reaches critical mass where a reasonable person would conclude that the perpetrator is guilty of the crime, to the exclusion of all others.

Figure 10.1 is a representation of a correlation chart. The chart is meant to be read from left to right across the columns labeled Pre-Crime Behavior, Peri-Crime Behavior, and Post-Crime Behavior. The arrows in the first two rows should additionally clarify this method. The numbers represented in each box are the numbers represented in Table 10.5 within each respective column. While the traditional correlation methodology is to draw lines between related items, for the purposes of visual clarity, we elected to instead

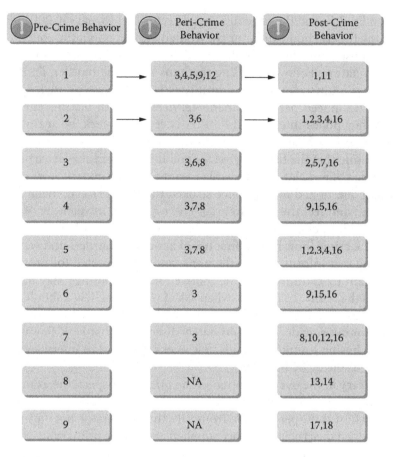

Figure 10.1 Crime behavior correlations for Case Study 1.

create this diagram. This diagram may also be useful for juries during trial, as it more clearly depicts correlations drawn between the pre-, peri-, and post-crime behaviors. It is also important to note that despite the fact that correlations begin in the diagram with pre-crime behavior, the correlations are fluid; for example, if one were to begin with post-crime behavior and move in the opposite direction toward pre-crime behavior, the numbered correlations would remain the same.

Let us now explore how Figure 10.1 may be used to describe correlations between pre-, peri-, and post-offense behavior to investigators or a jury/prosecutor. For the purposes of this explanation, the relationship between pre-offense behavior number 1; peri-offense crime scene factors 3, 4, 5, 9, and 12; and post-offense behavior factors 1 and 11 will be discussed from Figure 10.1. As can be seen in Table 10.5, pre-offense behavior number 1 is described as follows:

For some months prior to February 5, 2002, the church secretary advised that a parish priest, Fr. R.E., has been observed in the upstairs of the church aiming an imaginary gun and firing at parishioners whom he did not like.

This pre-offense behavior is related to the following peri-offense crime scene factors:

3. The funeral home director, age 39, was found sitting in the office desk chair with a bullet wound to the forehead. He was dead.
4. The second victim, a college intern, age 22, was found slumped over the back of a second chair. He had been shot in the head, with a grazing wound to the right little finger. He was dead.
5. A third bullet was found behind a broken mirror. (It is believed that the first shot to the intern injured the finger and lodged in the wall behind the broken mirror.)
9. The only physical evidence left at the scene was spent firearm shells. There was no evidence of fingerprints, DNA, or footprints.
12. The autopsy confirmed that both victims died from gunshot wounds to the head.

Finally, the pre-offense behavior can be correlated with post-offense behavior factors 1 and 11, which are described as follows:

1. February 5, 2002, 14:30 hours, Fr. R.E. advised a group of local nuns that there had been a tragedy at the funeral home and the victims had been shot dead. At this time, the SWAT team had not completed the search of the building. Furthermore, save for only a few detectives, the cause of death was highly privileged information that was kept secret.
11. Fr. R.E. provided numerous firearms and swords to the police.

The pre-offense behavior of Fr. R.E., that is, pointing an imaginary gun at parishioners whom he did not like, demonstrates both his capacity to, at the very least, imagine committing murder, and the weapon he would most likely use to commit the murder: a gun. The peri-offense crime scene factors, primarily the weapon used to kill the victims, a gun, are consistent with Fr. R.E.'s pre-offense behavior. Finally, as a power-assertive individual committed these murders, Fr. R.E. felt the need to brag about the killings as is typical with a power-assertive personality. As such, the post-offense behavior of telling the group of nuns about the murders that had occurred, as well as revealing the manner in which the victims were killed, can be correlated to the pre-offense behavior number 1. The relationship between bragging to the nuns and the imaginary shootings of disliked parishioners is behaviorally logical as both acts are indicative of a power-assertive personality type who feels the need to exert power, control, and dominance over his victims.

The purpose of the aforementioned explanation is to convey the importance of correlating pre-, peri-, and post-offense behaviors. Individually, these behaviors may be insignificant to investigators. However, when the behaviors of each person of interest are mapped chronologically and as a whole, the collective behaviors will ultimately identify the perpetrator. That being said, it is critical for investigators to thoroughly develop accurate pre-, peri-, and post-offense behaviors and timelines for all potential persons of interest. Generally speaking, the greater the dichotomy between pre- and post-offense behaviors, the greater the chance that the individual in question is the perpetrator of the crime that is being investigated.

As stated earlier in the chapter, the purpose of the peri-crime behavior column is to provide evaluators and investigators with an accurate psychological portrait of the perpetrator by analyzing the various elements of a crime scene. By examining notification issues, scene issues (organized versus disorganized), body positions (staged versus natural), unusual findings or signatures, autopsy findings, and wound patterns, a perpetrator subtype can usually be identified. To review, the four subtypes are *power-assertive, power-reassurance, anger-retaliatory,* and *anger-excitation.*

Once a subtype has been classified, it then behooves the investigator to examine the correlations between pre-crime and post-crime behaviors of persons of interest who are consistent with the subtype classification. The person of interest who displays the most correlations between pre-crime, peri-crime, and post-crime behaviors is, in most cases, the perpetrator. Conversely, if there is a distinct lack of correlations between pre- and post-crime behaviors, the model may be useful in the elimination of persons of interest. As can be seen from the diagram, Fr. R.E. displayed a significant number of correlations between pre-crime, peri-crime, and post-crime behaviors. His behavior also became increasingly erratic, culminating in his suicide. Therefore, given the number of correlations and the broad spectrum of behavior, it can be safely deduced that Fr. R.E. did indeed commit the murders at the funeral home.

In some instances, where multiple suspects cloud the field of vision in the investigation, a schematic matrix can clarify the issue and return the investigative search to a manageable level. Likewise, where cases may be partly or completely circumstantial, the methodology can provide evidence for case resolution.

The Scott Peterson case is a well-known investigation and trial that was primarily circumstantial in nature; that is, given the absence or sparseness of direct physical evidence, the investigation of the subject's double lifestyle, misleading statements, improbable scenario (fishing on Christmas Eve), making of cement blocks, altered physical appearance, accumulated cash, and Viagra "from brother" for a trip to Mexico. Accordingly, when the issues were interwoven with a myriad of further circumstances, a crime pattern emerged that was unique to the crime and him as the perpetrator. Again, with multiple bits of circumstantial evidence related to or inferred from the crime that could not be explained or eliminated, the jury refuted his defense claims and held him accountable for the crime beyond a reasonable doubt. Likewise, in the case illustration and many more cases that result in convictions, the relevance and weight of evidence related to *who, what, when, where, how,* and *why* become critical for identifying the perpetrator's *motive, method,* and *opportunity.*

The aforementioned approach can be used to bolster and clarify a weak physical evidence case.

Case Study 2

See Appendix C.

Conclusion

The protocol described in this chapter and illustrated both here and in Appendix C was created to maximize the available evidence in a case. To avoid the pitfalls incorrectly focusing on who appears to be the *right suspect,* this approach capitalizes on the perpetrator's behavior and psychopathology to identify him as the person responsible for the crime. For more information and research material regarding this process, and the utilizing of these subtypes to identify suspects, one should review the following section and the material listed in Appendix E.*

Typology Research

1. Bennell, Craig, Bloomfield, Sarah, Emeno, Karla, and Musolino, Evelyn. (2013). Classifying serial sexual murder/murderers: An attempt to validate Keppel and Walter's (199) model. *Criminal Justice and Behavior, 40*(1), 26–39.
2. Copson, G. (1995). Coals to Newcastle? Part I: A study of offender profiling (Police Research Group Special Interest Series, Paper 7). London: Home Office Police Department.
3. Copson, G., Badcock, R., Boon, J., and Britton, P. (1997). Articulating a systematic approach to clinical crime profiling. *Criminal Behavior and Mental Health, 7*, 13–17.

---

* Although the research by Bennell, Bloomfield, Emeno, and Musolino (2013) opposes the effectiveness of the subtype process by Keppel and Walter, a new study recently completed has validated the concept with a 95 percent probability of being statistically significant. One of the keys to the second study is that it evaluated over 900 cases versus the 53 cases assessed by Bennell et al., therefore increasing the probability of being more valid. This new research should be published by the end of 2014 or early 2015.

4. Douglas, J. E., Burgess, A. W., Burgess, A. C., and Ressler, R. K. (1992, 2006). *Crime Classification Manual*. Lexington, MA: Lexington Books.
5. Folino, J. O. (2000). Sexual homicides and their classification according to motivation: A report from Argentina. *International Journal of Offender Therapy and Comparative Criminology, 44*(6), 740–750.
6. Geberth, V. J. (1996). *Practical Homicide Investigation: Tactics, Procedures, and Forensic Techniques* (3rd ed.). Boca Raton, FL: CRC Publishing.
7. Geberth, V. J., and Turco, R. N. (1997). Antisocial personality disorder, sexual sadism, malignant narcissism, and serial murder. *Journal of Forensic Sciences, 42*(1), 49–60.
8. Groth, A. N., Burgess, A. W., and Holmstrom, L. L. (1977). Rape: Power, anger, and sexuality. *American Journal of Psychiatry, 134*, 1239–1243.
9. Godwin, M. (2002). Reliability, validity, and utility of criminal profiling typologies. *Journal of Police and Criminal Psychology, 17*(1), 1–18.
10. Goodwill, A. M., Alison, L. J., and Beech, A. R. (2009). What works in offender profiling? A comparison of typological, thematic, and multivariate models. *Behavioral Sciences & the Law, 27*(4), 507–529.
11. Hazelwood, R. R., and Burgess, A. N. (1987). *Practical Aspects of Rape Investigation: A Multidisciplinary Approach*. New York: Elsevier North-Holland.
12. HITS murder form. (1995). Seattle, WA: Washington State Attorney General's Office.
13. Holmes, R. M., and Holmes, S. T. (1996). *Profiling Violent Crimes: An Investigative Tool*. Thousand Oaks, CA: Sage.
14. Holmes, S. T., and Holmes, R. M. (2002). *Sex Crimes* (2nd ed.). Thousand Oaks, CA: Sage.
15. Hunter, J. A., Hazelwood, R. R., and Slesinger, D. (2000). Juvenile-perpetrated sex crimes: Patterns of offending and predictors of violence. *Journal of Family Violence, 15*(1), 81–93.
16. Johnson, G. (1994). VICLAS: Violent crime linkage analysis system. *RCMP Gazette, 56*(10), 5–22.
17. Keppel, R. D. (1995). Signature murders: A report of several related cases. *Journal of Forensic Sciences, 40*, 658–662.
18. Keppel, R. D. (1997). *Signature Killers*. New York: Pocket Books.
19. Keppel, R. D., and Birnes, W. J. (2009). *Serial Violence: Analysis of Modus Operandi and Signature Characteristics of Killers*. Boca Raton, FL: CRC Press.
20. Keppel, R. D., and Birnes, W. J. (2003). *The Psychology of Serial Killer Investigations: The Grisly Business Unit*. San Diego, CA: Elsevier.
21. Keppel, R. D., and Birnes, W. J. (1995). *The Riverman: Ted Bundy and I hunt the Green River Killer*. New York: Pocket Books.
22. Keppel, R. D. and Walter, R. (1999). Profiling killers: A revised classification model for understanding sexual murder. *International Journal of Offender Therapy and Comparative Criminology, 43*(4), 417–437.
23. Keppel, R. D., and Weis, J. P. (1994). Time and distance as solvability factors in murder cases. *Journal of Forensic Sciences, 39*, 386–401.
24. Maniglio, R. (2010). The role of deviant sexual fantasy in the etiopathogenesis of sexual homicide: A systematic review. *Aggression and Violent Behavior, 15*(4), 294–302.

25. McCabe, M. P., and Wauchope, M. (2005). Behavioral characteristics of men accused of rape: Evidence for different types of rapists. *Archives of Sexual Behavior, 34*(2), 241–253.

26. Morneau, R., and Rockwell, R. (1980). *Sex, Motivation, and the Criminal Offender.* Springfield, IL: Charles C. Thomas.

27. Pardue, A., and Arrigo, B. A. (2008). Power, anger, and sadistic rapists: Toward a differentiated model of offender personality. *International Journal of Offender Therapy and Comparative Criminology, 52*(4), 378–400.

28. Robertiello, G., and Terry, K. J. (2007). Can we profile sex offenders? A review of sex offender typologies. *Aggression and Violent Behavior, 12*(5), 508–518.

29. Santtila, P., Pakkanen, T., Zappala, A., Bosco, D., Valkama, M., and Mokros, A. (2008). Behavioral crime linking in serial homicide. *Psychology, Crime & Law, 14*(3), 245–265.

30. VICAP form. (1991). Washington, DC: Federal Bureau of Investigation.

31. Warren, J. I., Hazelwood, R. R., and Dietz, P.E. (1996). The sexually sadistic killer. *Journal of Forensic Sciences, 41*, 970–974.

32. Warren, J., Reboussin, R., Hazelwood, R. R., Cummings, A., Gibbs, N., and Trumbetta, S. (1998). Crime scene and distance correlates of serial rape. *Journal of Quantitative Criminology, 14*(1), 35–59.

33. Woods, L., and Porter, L. (2008). Examining the relationship between sexual offenders and their victims: Interpersonal differences between stranger and non-stranger sexual offences. *Journal of Sexual Aggression, 14*(1), 61–75.

34. Woodworth, M., and Porter, S. (2000). Historical foundations and current applications of criminal profiling in violent crime investigations. *Expert Evidence, 7*(4), 241–264.

Endnotes

1. Keppel, R. D., and R. D. Walter. 1999. Profiling killers: A revised classification model for understanding sexual murder. *International Journal of Offender Therapy and Comparative Criminology*, 43(4): 417–437.

2. Hudson Police Department, Hudson, Wisconsin. 2005. See also documentary, "Fifth Commandment," *Forensic Factor V*, Discovery Channel of Canada, 2009.

Investigative Interviewing

Issues and Concerns Relating to Cold Cases

11

JAMES M. ADCOCK AND SARAH L. STEIN

In the recent past, the topic of interviewing, especially "interrogations," has come under much scrutiny by social scientists from all over the world, and we do not intend to include any of the issues that have surfaced regarding terrorists or waterboarding, as that has nothing to do with cold case investigations. In Great Britain, Holland, and other countries, the term *interrogation* is no longer allowed or used, as they have renamed the entire process for witnesses and suspects "investigative interviewing."[1] This reaction to law enforcement's manner of gaining information from witnesses and suspects appears to have surfaced due in part to the reported "false confessions" found in criminal cases from the United Kingdom and other countries, as well as the United States. The Innocence Project has reported that in its exonerated cases (312),[2] a false confession was also found in 25 percent (approximately 60) of them. So, is this a real problem? Yes, to a certain extent it is, especially when vulnerable persons of interest or at-risk types of people (primarily mentally deficient or juveniles) are interviewed by an authoritative figure.

But let's go beyond confessions to the entire interviewing and interrogation process as we know it today. Criminal investigation textbooks have throughout the years consistently written about the same thing with regard to both interviews and interrogations. Concerning interviews, these textbooks instruct the reader to answer the major questions of who, what, when, where, how, and why; to understand the different types of witnesses from the talkative to the timid, to the reluctant to the deceitful, and the one who refuses to talk; and about how to conduct the canvassing interview. Furthermore, they would describe the four-step process found in the cognitive interview, frequently correlating it with the interview process conducted during a hypnosis session. All of this is very helpful for the investigator, albeit elementary.

As for interrogations, the authors of these criminal investigation books have also remained somewhat on the same track. For example, ample information about how to conduct a proper Miranda rights warning, how to set up an interrogation room, reasons why some people confess and some do not, methods of approach that may include accusatory tactics to getting the suspect to feel guilty, to overwhelming physical evidence that puts the suspect at the scene—all geared toward obtaining an admission or confession of guilt. And while these two words, *interviews* and *interrogations*, have long been a part of our vocabulary, the word *interrogation* is becoming less popular because of the connotations it reflects.

In their attack on the interrogation process, researchers have unequivocally placed the Reid technique[3] at the top of their list as the biggest contributor to the problem of false confessions. Although we do not intend to use this medium to debate this issue, we do want to say that after attending the Reid regular and advanced courses in interviews and interrogations, there is no doubt that the interrogation process taught can be psychologically demanding. However, Adcock firmly believes that if fault is to be placed, it is not so much the technique as it is the person conducting the interrogation, because in all likelihood, the interrogator used a variation of the Reid technique and did not follow the steps exactly as they were taught. As with polygraphs and polygraph examiners, the end results are only as good as the examiner. Besides, no one should be convicted on a confession alone; there should always be corroborating evidence, which the detectives are obligated to obtain to support the confession. The bad guys lie to us all the time, so why should a suspected admission or confession be any different? In our experience with confessions, there is always a little bit of truth where the confessor has confabulated (filled in fictional pieces of the puzzle) so as to not appear all bad. Therefore, a confession or an admission that is only partially correct needs to be validated through additional investigation or supporting physical evidence.

On the Reid website,[4] a short article describing why people confess was posted in the "Investigator Tips" section. The article discusses the motives as being for tangible gains, protecting a loved one, low intelligence/youthful offenders, coercion, duress, mental illness, and faulty memory. It emphasizes that even though these are not all-inclusive, every case must be evaluated on its own merits along with the "totality of the circumstances," not just the confession. Reid then suggests that investigators carefully consider the following:

1. The suspect's condition at the time of the interrogation
   a. Physical condition (including drug and/or alcohol intoxication)
   b. Mental capacity
   c. Psychological condition
2. The suspect's age
3. The suspect's prior experience with law enforcement
4. The suspect's understanding of the language
5. The length of the interrogation
6. The degree of detail provided by the suspect in his confession
7. The extent of corroboration between the confession and the crime

8. The presence of witnesses to the interrogation and confession
9. The suspect's behavior during the interrogation
10. The effort to address the suspect's physical needs
11. The presence of any improper interrogation techniques

The meat of any investigation falls into three sources of information: the physical evidence, behavioral actions of the actors involved, and the informational pieces of the puzzle brought together primarily through interviews and interrogations. Without a doubt, the proper conduct of interviews is paramount to any investigation, especially a major case. Courses being taught to law enforcement are traditionally referred to as "interviews and interrogations," yet the majority of what is taught focuses on interrogation with very little dealing with the actual interview process of victims and witnesses.[5] One needs to be proficient in conducting proper interviews before one can become an effective interrogator. We also believe this is another contributing factor to cases remaining or becoming cold and unresolved.

The problem is not just the lack of utilizing proper interviewing techniques but also the lack of proper case management, where significant witnesses are totally overlooked and never interviewed. One case in particular comes to mind that baffles us to this day: Throughout the entire case file numerous witnesses were telling the police and others that actors A, B, and C were involved in the killing of a person and, in fact, even one of the three had been overheard telling someone he was there and saw it. Yet none of them were ever interviewed then or later. Granted, these witnesses were not exactly the most reliable types in our society because they were prostitutes and drug addicts, but usually when there is that much information pointing in the same direction, one should suspect there is some truth there. And, at a minimum, the information should have been checked out and invalidated, if nothing else. It was missed most likely because no one was carefully reviewing the information in the file to ensure all that needed to be done was in fact being accomplished; this all goes toward the belief that we need first-line supervisors in detective units reviewing ongoing cases on a regular basis. They are not there to second-guess and micromanage the detectives but to ensure they remain on track, do not form tunnel vision, and economize their time through prioritization of leads and a solid investigative plan.

All of this pertains to the interview process and how we go about obtaining information from the numerous types of witnesses. In many neighborhoods, the people who live there are reluctant, or adamant, about not talking to the police. They have to live there; you don't. They either have a high disregard for the police, or they are fearful of retaliation from the bad guys if they do speak to police. However, with cold case investigations, time is on our side because this fear of harm may be gone and is no longer a viable threat when you return months to years later.

Interview Process

Let us return to the interviewing process as a tool for detectives. The object of the interview is to obtain information about what happened, how, why, who did it, and so forth. In order to effectively utilize this tool, the interviewer needs to have a full grasp of the types of questions (e.g., open, closed/direct, and suggestive or leading) and when to ask them.

The first of these is the *open-ended* line of questioning. Open-ended questions are those that do not allow a yes or no response but rather are open so that the respondent tells a story of what they saw, heard, and so forth. An example of this would be: "Tell me everything that happened here." These types of questions are eliciting a full response from the witness. These are then followed by clarifying type questions to fill in any gaps that may exist in the witnesses' story (e.g., time gaps, people not further identified, qualifying phrases).

Closed/direct questions are designed to elicit a specific position or answer from the person. An example of this would be: "Did you have any contact with the victim prior to 1900 hours?" As you can see these questions nearly always elicit a *yes* or *no* answer with no clarification until the interviewer asks. Unless you are seeking this type of direct response, these questions should only be used after the open questions have been fully explored and answered. Generally, these are not used until you are near the end of the interview and need to be more direct in order to obtain the truth of what happened.

The last of these is the leading or suggestive type question. These are really dangerous because in the process of asking the question the interviewer is telling the witness what they want to hear as a response. For example, "Was the getaway car a red Buick?" versus "What color and type of vehicle was used for the getaway?" These are particularly problematic when interviewing children because of the possibility of putting words in the mouths of the young witnesses or victims, suggesting to them the answers we are looking for.

The most important point here is to utilize the open-ended questions as much as possible. We need to hear what they saw and what they heard, not what we think they saw or heard. When interviewing victims or significant witnesses who probably saw what happened but are either traumatized or reluctant, consider utilizing the cognitive interview. It is especially helpful in assisting the eyewitness (or victim) to recall what they saw during an event. The cognitive interview is a four-step process:

Step 1—Reconstruct the circumstances of the event. The interviewer begins by asking the witness to reconstruct how the incident began and to cite those circumstances they see surrounding it. This might include the environment, weather, lighting, cleanliness, and so forth.

Step 2—Instruct the witness to report everything. In this question, they are asked to relate everything and to not omit any details, suggesting to the witness that even the smallest piece could have evidentiary value.

Step 3—Conduct a recall of the events but in different order. It is here that the interviewer instructs the witness to recall from different points within the timeframe in question, and they may be asked to reverse the order of events.

Step 4—Change perspectives. In this question, the witness is asked to change his or her perspective or role to someone else in the incident to consider what that person might have seen from another angle/perspective.[6]

Although over the years we have read about this process, nowhere have we heard of anyone actually using it, particularly not in the United States. Granted we have not talked to every police officer in the country, but I see little utilization of the cognitive interview except in Great Britain where the technique is used a lot. It is interesting to note that Vriji[7] has suggested that the cognitive interview technique can also be very helpful with suspect interviews. With this concept, he writes that utilizing the "reverse order" step will cause the deceptive person to trip up and make mistakes in his or her statement. When this happens the interviewer should concentrate more on those areas in search of a confession. This does have some potential of being a good technique.

Regardless of the technique, as stated by Reid, the detective should always evaluate the confession in light of the "totality of the circumstances" and validate all admissions or confessions through follow-up investigation.

Behavioral Analysis Interview

One of the better techniques used to assist the detective in determining whether a person is being deceptive is the behavioral analysis interview (BAI).[8] While Vriji would totally disagree, it has merit as a valid process of obtaining "indicators" of deception. Note that we said "indicators," those things that are a sign of possible deception, not absolute, just a sign that needs further clarification and investigation to either validate or invalidate what is being said. According to Horvath, Blair, and Buckley,

[the BAI is] the only questioning method that has been developed specifically to help investigators sort those who are likely to be "guilty" from those who are not. In its typical application the BAI is a pre-interrogation interview that is used to focus interrogational effort; however, it also can be used independently in order to circumscribe investigative efforts in those cases in which there is a fixed and relatively large number of "suspects."[9]

The BAI incorporates a series of questions geared to elicit responses that may cause the interviewee to provide either verbal or physical behaviors that a properly trained interviewer can evaluate as either being deceptive or truthful. Again, these are indicators—nothing more than an indication of possible deception. The interviewer is taught to ask a set of questions while noting the verbal and physical behaviors exhibited by the interviewee. In the beginning, the interviewer asks the usual demographic questions of the person, looking at neutral ground issues where one would expect truthfulness to prevail. Then he goes on to the series of questions where the verbal and physical behavioral responses are noted.[10]

Reason for the Interview
    What is the person's understanding of the purpose for this interview?
History/You
    The interviewer tells the person what she or he is investigating and
        tells the person that if they committed the crime they should tell
        the interviewer now.
Knowledge
    The interviewer then asks the person if they know who did commit
        the crime.
Suspicion About Others
    "Who do you suspect committed this act?"
Vouch for others
    Then the person is asked to name those who they believe should be
        above any suspicion—those who could not have committed the act.
Attitude
    The person is asked how they feel about being interviewed concern-
        ing this crime.
Credibility
    What do they think really happened, for example, was the money really
        stolen? Was the victim forced to have sex? The person is asked,
        "When the accuser says you did steal the money, are they lying?"
Opportunity
    The interviewer then asks the person of all the people they know who
        had the best opportunity to commit the crime.
Motive
    Ask the question, "Why do you think someone did this?"
Think
    Ask, "Did you ever think of doing something like this even though
        you didn't go through with it?"
Objection
    Have the person tell the interviewer why they would not have done
        anything like this.

Punishment

Ask the person what they think should happen to the one who committed this crime.

Investigation Results

Ask the person how they think this investigation will end with regard to him.

Second Chance

The interviewer then asks the interviewee if the person who did this deserves a second chance.

Alibi

At this point the interviewer elicits an alibi from the interviewee.

Tell Loved Ones

"Did you tell your family that you were being interviewed regarding this crime?"

This list is not all-inclusive; it provides optional questions that may assist in determining truthfulness versus deception. These include questions about whether the interviewee believes anyone else might name them as the suspect, what do they think would eliminate them as a suspect, have they ever been questioned in the past about this type of crime, has anyone approached or talked to them about this incident, would they be willing to undergo hypnosis to recreate for the interviewer about where they were and what they were doing at the time of the incident, and what would be the easiest way to commit an act like this. Again, all these questions are geared toward observing verbal and nonverbal behaviors.

Prescriptive Interview

When it comes to interviews and interrogations, you can never receive too much information. It is for that reason, before we get into murder typologies and interrogation strategies, that we want to include information from Chapter 3 of the *Crime Classification Manual* by Douglas et al., titled "Prescriptive Interviewing: Interfacing the Interview and Interrogation with Crime Classification."[11] This manual should be on the bookshelves of all detectives, read, and used as a guide when dealing with these types of crimes, whether hot or cold. And, as we stated, the interfacing of this manual with the prescriptive interview is paramount.

Preparing for this type of interview involves an extensive amount of investigative effort, especially considering that you may only get one chance to interview/interrogate the suspect because once she or he asks for an attorney, you can no longer interrogate them. Therefore, the better prepared you are, the higher the likelihood of obtaining an admission or confession. And with cold cases there is absolutely no reason for you to even initiate an interview with any suspect until you have successfully prepared yourself for the interview by going through these four steps:

Data Collection
> Comprehensive and meticulous data collection system must be implemented to reconstruct each element of the crime. This is a principal factor in determining that all the elements have been met as described by law.

Assessment
> Assessing the relevancy of the data to the crime is required. Objectively judge the value of the information and determine if it can apply to the elements of the crime.

Analysis
> Detectives must do more than just determine that each element is intact. This requires organizing and dissecting the information, thereby observing the complex web of interrelated components of the crime. For example, I may "see" a set of stairs before me; however, I observe that there are exactly 16 steps covered with a distinctive color and quality of carpet. In addition, the carpet is soiled and cluttered with specific toys and items of clothing, suggesting the presence of children of corresponding ages. The condition of the carpet and disarray of clothing and toys may suggest the housecleaning habits of the owners and even imply an economic stratum. It is during this phase of preparation that meaning and substance are assigned to the (criminal) act and the actor. Armed with this enhanced understanding, the fourth step is applied.

Theorizing
> Theorizing assumes the challenges of identifying the motivation underlying the criminal thought process and reconstructing the crime. It attempts to mentally crystallize the interwoven thread of thought that the criminal mind uses to justify his crime and general behavior.

The preparatory phase of the interview is preeminent in conducting a successful interview. There is no substitute for this principle, and it should never be sacrificed for convenience or expediency. Success is tantamount to preparation.

At the onset, it was stated that the interfacing of the prescriptive interview process with the crime classification is paramount. Classifying the crime (utilizing the manual) integrates all preparatory steps of the interview. It is the precursor to humanizing the offender and revealing his thought process. It includes the accumulation and assimilation of data compiled during the investigative phase for the purpose of conducting a criminal investigative analysis (also referred to as a psychological profile). It is here where the criminal investigative analyst will review and analyze area photos, maps, sketches, crime scene photos, victimology, and all incident-related reports to formulate a profile of the criminal personality. A close examination of this information will begin to reveal behavioral characteristics of the offender, thereby exposing major personality traits.

The process applied by the criminal investigative analyst may suggest the cause or motive for the crime and offer implications of the offender personality, as suggested by the method selected to commit the crime. An assessment of the offender's behavioral patterns can unmask an undercurrent of emotional deficiencies and needs. An improved understanding of these emotional deficiencies and needs can provide a solid foundation for the interviewer. This foundation will support the strategic construction of approaches and appeals to be tailored for this offender. The upcoming section on murder typologies and interrogation strategies will show how some of this comes to the surface.

Consider, for example, the advantage an interviewer would have when he has in his possession the following personality characteristics of the suspect that were extracted from the analysis of a disorganized lust murder:

- Of average intelligence and a high school or college dropout
- Probably unemployed or blue-collar, unskilled occupation
- Financially dependent on a domineering female
- A previous criminal record of assault-related offense
- Probable voyeuristic activities
- Probable pornography interest and collection
- Alcohol or drugs exhibited in his behavior
- Keen sense of fantasy
- Inability to carry out preplanned activities
- Difficulty in maintaining personal relationships with a female for an extended period of time
- A need to dominate and control relationships
- Sexually inexperienced
- Never married, or a brief, combative marital relationship
- Sadistic tendencies
- Controlled aggression but rage or hatred
- Confused thought process
- Feels justified in his behavior while feeling no remorse or guilt
- Defiant of authority
- Low self-esteem
- Frustration from lack of direction of control of life
- Combustive temper

- Impulsive
- Deep anxiety

Douglas et al. go on to write that while considering these characteristics in concert with investigative activities confirming some of the biological and descriptive information provided, an interviewer can begin to observe the offender. The interviewer may recognize and exploit certain personality characteristics and associated emotional deficiencies. In pondering the offender's behavior, thought processes, and aligned emotions, the interviewer is now better prepared to design various approaches to conform to the offender's personality.

This process assists the interviewer in stepping out of his world and into the foreign territory of his adversary. If the offender decides to cooperate, it will be because he can justify his decision from his perspective. There is only one frame of reference that is important in the offender's decision-making process: his own. And if the interviewer successfully influences the offender to conform, it is because an alliance was forged in the offender's territory.

Although prescriptive interviewing is not a panacea for the challenges in obtaining confessions, it is still one more precision instrument to be used in swaying the balance of justice in society's favor. A prescriptive interview will enhance law enforcement's efforts to persuade serious offenders to escort us into the caverns of their torrential minds, surrender their secrets, and expose their culpability. Douglas et al. conclude by writing that it is hoped that the successful use of this method will both promote the cause of justice and deter effects of recidivism.

Murder Typologies and Interrogation Strategies[12]

As a prelude to murder typologies and interrogation strategies, there is a difference between hot and cold case investigations as it pertains to interview and interrogations. To start, every sound interview should have as much background information on the person being interviewed as is possible, and when it comes to suspects, this is even more important. In a hot case, little background information is known prior to victim and witness interviews, placing the interviewers at a disadvantage. As to suspects, a little more is usually known before the interrogation, but in many situations not nearly enough to conduct a proper interrogation. But time is frequently limited, and the pressure is on to interrogate and get that confession. As a result, many of these are conducted without adequate knowledge of the suspect, his background, his beliefs, his behavioral traits, or his strong and vulnerable areas that could be challenged.

On the other hand, cold cases present different problems with some advantages over the hot ones. Due to the time that has passed, witness interviews can be a challenge to the investigators as they attempt to get these people to recall events of years gone by. To their advantage, however, is that more often than not, with the passage of time these witnesses seem to be more likely to discuss the event today than they were several years ago. Relationships have changed, people have moved, and it is now less threatening and easier to talk. In interrogation of a suspect, the passage of time is a great advantage to the detective. It is here that this interrogation is conducted only when the detective is ready; therefore the detective will have obtained all the background information that possibly exists; she or he will know the strengths and vulnerabilities of his suspect; she or he will also know how to approach the suspect, all without the pressures that come to bear if this was a hot case that needed an immediate resolution. Furthermore, due to the passage of time, the suspect may feel more confident and comfortable that you had not questioned him as a suspect, and this comfort is now gone when you do interrogate him. So, with cold case investigations, time is on your side.

In Chapter 10, where suspectology and the pre-, peri-, and post-offense behavior issues are addressed regarding suspect identification, we provided a revised classification model that was designed by Keppel and Walter relating to sexual murders (the same models can and have been successfully utilized in nonsexual type murders; in fact the two case studies provided in this book were nonsexual type cases): power-assertive, power-reassurance, anger-retaliatory, and anger-excitation. Certain techniques are suggested to maximize results in conducting an interrogation of these types of murderers. Since these are cold cases, the detectives have ample time to develop a good suspectology and design the pre-, peri-, and post-offense behavior model concerning the persons of interest, which should in turn lead to a productive interrogation. Utilizing their design and keeping in mind the prescriptive interview methodology described earlier, the following procedures are suggested.

Power-Assertive (PA)

Characteristics: Rape is planned, whereas murder is not. Offender uses aggression and demands to justify his manhood, and uses intimidation to maintain a machismo appearance. He targets his own age group and leaves an organized crime scene. He will bring the weapon to the scene and leaves with it. He will also set boundaries to his actions (e.g., he will not entirely remove the head). No mutilation of the body, but signs of beating, cutting, strangling may be evident.

Who is he? He's domineering. He takes pride in his image as a man and is likely to be well built. He may drive a pickup truck or sports vehicle. He's antisocial and a school dropout. If he has a military record, it is likely poor. He'll brag about his crime in a bar for glory points. He has a phobia of being labeled a "pervert." He'll use weapons such as guns, knives, and ropes.

Interrogation strategies/approaches: Silent, fishing, direct, accomplice, degrading, blame, pride. The interrogator should establish and maintain control. Challenge the suspect's manhood. Suggest that real men own up to their mistakes; enter prison as a man. Allow the suspect to brag. Perhaps provide the suspect with a chair that is lower in height than yours.

The Achilles' heel for the PA is the acquisition and demonstration of the power image. That is, he wants to be viewed as a John Wayne–type of character. Depending on the amount of threat presented in the interview session, he may attempt to bluff his way through with exaggerated machismo behaviors. Conversely, if he is situationally intimidated by the setting, he will hide the bluff and defer to the power of the police. When opening the interview, you should ask him why he is being interviewed or polygraphed. Ask him to explain what the accusations are against him. Ask him about his background, including age, work history, friendship patterns, group loyalties, values, beliefs, and sexual orientation and behaviors. Although one needs to control for grandiosity and exaggeration, let him brag about his manliness.

With the promise that you will revisit the issues more in detail later, let him give a brief overview of the offense. Upon completion of the review, you should start through the story again with complete detail being given. While doing so, you should jump questions in and out of order. (It is far more difficult to lie under these conditions.) Start showing him inconsistencies in his story. Point out that you would like to believe him man to man, but his role is being challenged. Therefore, if he can explain this or that, there is the potential of being redeemed. (In brief, you are playing the ego games by challenging his masculinity. That is, by locking him into the masculine standards that were implicitly agreed upon earlier, you are corralling him into a small fenced paddock. The next thing is to only open one door for him to walk out unscathed. That is, he needs to tell the truth, like a real man!)

If and when the suspect becomes attenuated and caught up in saving his power image, it might be the time to use one of several approaches to force him into the final gate.

Silent approach—Simple eye contact without verbalization.
Fishing approach—"I'd like to hear how you planned it."
Direct approach—"You didn't mean to shoot the grocer, or did you?" "You were having sex and didn't mean to choke her to death, or did you?"
Accomplice approach—Fear of offender's partner making a deal; shifting the blame on them.
Blame approach—Stupid errors by accomplice.

Pride approach—"Smart crime; it took brains to do it."

Degrading approach—"Somebody had to do the thinking for you."

We all make mistakes approach—"However, at the end of the day, are you going to be a man or a mouse? Sometimes, a man makes mistakes and stands up and takes the medicine. At least, under these conditions, he has still saved his manhood."

Note: Often, the good cop–bad cop routine works with this type of offender. However, it can certainly be successful with a single interviewer.

Power-Reassurance (PR)

Characteristics: The offender lives in a scripted fantasy world and feels threatened if reality breaks into the fantasy. He acts out fantasies for verbal reassurance from the victim. Rape is planned, whereas murder is not. Murder is typically a result of a failed rape, which leads to overkill and post-mortem mutilation. Sexual activity usually occurs post-mortem. There are often wounds to the breasts and groin/thigh areas. The body may have insertions. He avoids women in his own age group and targets those older or younger, and chooses familiar locations. He commits attacks during night hours and leaves a disorganized crime scene.

Who is he? He's a loner and a "weirdo." He is likely to conduct stalker activities prior to the attack. He is concerned about his sexual competence and seeks reassurance and the need to justify his power. If he has a military record, the offender was likely a passive soldier who took orders well. Weapon of choice may be clothing, fists, and knives.

Interrogation strategies/approaches: Statement, identification, social, religious. Suspect is concerned about power and is impulsive. He'll justify the crime by blaming the victim. You may try approaching suspect by arranging chairs close together. Like the PA, the PR is concerned about power. However, he wants unconditional affirmation through fantasy-driven behaviors. Generally, this type of offender tends to be somewhat disorganized and impulse driven. (Although he may have the plan for the offense in his mind, the particular moment and victim may be opportunistic.) Often, since the offender has already justified the crime in his own mind, when it goes awry, it becomes the fault of the victim. (Nevertheless, do not assume that the crime was unsuccessful for him.)

For the PR, the chairs should be arranged so that the interviewer can close in and touch the suspect. That is, after moderating the suspect's emotional temperature, a review of the facts in place, the interviewer may need to show care and understanding for the offender. In doing so, the offender can show understanding of how the victim helped to mislead him into the situation. The following methods may be helpful in facilitating the PR to admission:

Statement approach—"You just borrowed the items, not really stealing them. It sounds like (the victim) was coming on and tantalizing you."

Identification approach—"I would have done the same thing! Man, when a girl comes on to you!"

Social approach—"Lots of people do what you did. Research has shown that 97% of men feel that women who lead them on ... need to and should be hit!"

Religious approach—"There are no limits to forgiveness."

Anger-Retaliatory (AR)

Characteristics: Rape and murder are planned. Typically, the offender commits the attack in a familiar location. The crime is driven by a need to seek revenge against a woman of power (or a substitute for one) through anger, sparking a burst of violence. He targets women in the same age group or slightly older. It is a frenzied attack. He leaves a disorganized scene.

Who is he? He's impulsive, self-centered, and pathologically attached to women. He usually has superficial relationships and becomes estranged from marriage or has a history of domestic abuse. If he has a military record, it may show a discharge for behavioral issues. He usually attacks in areas with which he is familiar.

Interrogation strategies/approaches: Have knowledge of his history and past relationships. Allow suspect to talk about himself and interrupt him with questions. Bring up women from his past that may have controlled him, who he'll have resentment against. Suspect feels as though females wrongly victimized him; seeks revenge and feels no guilt. He may have substituted a woman rather than attack the actual female figure who "wronged" him.

The critical factor for this type is a catharsis of emotion acted out onto the intended (or substitute) victim. The perpetrator imagines that he has been unduly "victimized," which justifies a retaliatory response. When acting out the crime, the amount of anger can be somewhat measured by the pre- and post-mortem activity. When his appetite has been sated, he emotionally cools and leaves the victim in a position that denotes ultimate contempt and subjugation. After taking a memento, he will exit the crime scene with feelings of triumph, calm, and wellness. He can be very socially engaging shortly thereafter; he may develop a sense of maudlin attachment to the victim and display inappropriate sentimentality. This can be accomplished because he does not feel any guilt.

When preparing to interview this type of perpetrator, you should seek out the female person(s) who have nettled him in the past. Upon opening the interview, let the perpetrator describe himself. Most often, he will embellish his feats of masculinity and relationships with women. Again, ask about all of the different areas of identity. (Those previously listed under PA.) In an overview, let him explain his relationship/knowledge of the crime. Again, when going through for the second time in detail, the interviewer should jump the questions in a nonsequential style, which will break the prepared story. This will also frustrate the perp. Also, the interviewer can start to challenge his credibility and threaten his portrayed self-image by introducing contradictory and challenging comments made by the controlling women in his life. For example: "Your mother said that you never amounted to much because you drank and caroused around. She claimed that you were a bully who just never grew up." These points of reality will start to agitate him and make him relive his anger against her. This anger should be built upon. Eventually, he will again feel belittled and trapped. This makes it easier for him to explode from within, to save his own face, and claim the crime. In the anger-retaliatory type, the interviewer must *never* believe that the perpetrator feels guilt. He is feeling aggressive, not shameful, despite the display of emotion and rationalization.

Anger-Excitation (AE)

Characteristics: Rape and murder are planned. The crime is sadistic in nature. The extended torture and killing can be ritualistic. Satisfaction stems from inflicting terror and pain rather than the death itself. It is a crime of luxury. The body may be disposed of in an unfamiliar location. A con or ruse may be used to lure the victim. There may be signs of cutting, bruising, and ligature marks.

Who is he? He may appear as an average person, conducting a normal life. He is likely well educated and financially stable. He can separate a normal lifestyle from his criminal activities. He seeks domination and mastery. There may be sexual or nonsexual emotions. The fantasy fuels the ritualistic attack. He's methodical in his actions.

Interrogation strategies/approaches: Most difficult to get a confession. Suspect will try to victimize you. He has a high IQ and will play games. He'll try to size up the interrogator. Therefore, you must prove yourself. Probe suspect for facts in a way so that he feels clever.

The suspect is sadistic and pleased with what he has done. He feels as though he is better than you and thus you should be in awe of him. He'll reveal partial truth.

The AE type is by far the most diabolical to interview. In brief, he is "satisfied" by the process of administering dependency, dread, and degradation. Independent of the perpetrator's level of sophistication, his goal is to achieve a sense of mastery, control, and domination. (This can also be extended into the interview room with you. It is often acted out in game-playing with the interviewer. Since he feels inherently superior to you, you are the mouse and he is the cat. Accordingly, only when you start to appreciate his greatness will he reward you with partial truths and snapshot bits and pieces.)

When preparing to interview the AE, this is the time to do your homework and practice interviewing. You may want to consult an expert. (Even so, the likelihood of a full confession is almost nil.) Consider yourself fortunate if you are able to identify the emotional dead spots. For, despite their upbringing, these offenders learn to emotionally blunt affective feelings, which may cause some hesitancy to fully acting out. Inasmuch as the psychopath can only pretend to have common social bonds with others, it is essential for him to "read" the person with whom he is dealing and give the appropriate learned response. He does not feel spontaneous and comfortable in a vacuum. He needs feedback to manipulate the intended target. Therefore, at the interview, you are the intended victim. He will read your body language, words, and flow of logic with the intended goal of measuring and surmounting you. Again, his innate weakness is the pathological need to be superior and master of all. Therefore, use his high IQ (average for AE is 119) against him.

Summary

There is no guarantee that the aforementioned strategies will gain an admission or confession, but without them a confession is highly unlikely. These strategies should be used as a guide to the events in the interrogation room. Through the victimology report, one begins to understand the victim and looks for why this particular victim was selected; to know your victim is to be familiar with your suspect. The same theory applies to the suspectology, and the pre-, peri-, and post-offense behavior models. It all goes toward a level of pre-interrogation preparation that hot cases normally do not allow for. The cold case is an exception to murder cases and should be used to the advantage of the detective.

Endnotes

1. Shepherd, Eric. 2007. *Investigative Interviewing, the Conversation Management Approach*. Oxford University Press: New York.
2. Innocence Project. www.innocenceproject.org. Accessed January 8, 2014.
3. Reid, John E. & Associates, Inc. www.reid.com. Accessed August 25, 2009.
4. Reid, John E., et al. 2009. "Motives for False Confessions," *Investigator Tips*, July–August.
5. In July 2006, Adcock attended the 3-day Reid Technique of Interviewing and Interrogation and the 1-day Advanced Course on the Reid Technique of Interviewing and Interrogation courses. Except for differentiating up front the differences between interviews and interrogations (nonaccusatory versus accusatory), both courses focused almost entirely on interrogations of suspects,

including how to detect behavioral (verbal and physical) indicators of deception. Although these types of indicators are important to the interviewer of victims and witnesses, nowhere were they taught how to conduct a proper nonaccusatory interview, one designed to obtain the facts and circumstances of what happened, where, when, who, how, and why. I can only guess that it was assumed the attendees knew how to conduct a proper interview.

6. Zulawski, David, and Douglas E. Wicklander. 1993. *Practical Aspects of Interview and Interrogation*. CRC Press: Boca Raton, FL; pp. 160–161.
7. Vriji, Aldert. 2008. *Detecting Lies and Deceit, Pitfalls and Opportunities*, 2nd ed. John Wiley & Sons: West Sussex, UK.
8. Reid, John E., et al. 2006. The Reid Technique of Interviewing and Interrogation. Handouts provided at the Reid Interviews and Interrogations course, July.
9. Horvath, Frank, J. P. Blair, and Joseph P. Buckley. 2008. The behavioral analysis interview clarifying the practice, theory and understanding of its use and effectiveness. *International Journal of Police, Science and Management, 10*(1), 101.
10. Reid, John E., et al. 2006. From the Reid Technique of Interviewing and Interrogation Workbook provided at their seminar in July; p. 33.
11. Douglas, John E., Ann W. Burgess, Allen G. Burgess, and Robert K. Ressler. 2004. *Crime Classification Manual*, 2nd ed. Jossey-Bass: Hoboken, NJ. All of the information in this book relating to the prescriptive interview is referenced and reprinted with permission by John Wiley & Sons, Inc.
12. Keppel, Robert, and Richard Walter. 1999. Profiling killers: A revised classification model for understanding sexual murders. *International Journal of Offender Therapy and Comparative Criminology, 43*(4), 417–437. Obtained from Richard Walter with permission in 2007.

Cold Cases and Staged Crime Scenes
Crime Scene Clues to Suspect Misdirection of the Investigation[*]

12

ARTHUR S. CHANCELLOR AND
GRANT D. GRAHAM, SR.

Introduction

After the preliminary screening of a cold case has been completed and a decision is made to reopen the investigation, one of the first steps is to *read the file*, paying particular attention to the autopsy and forensic analysis reports; crime scene photographs and examination; and the statements of police, suspects, witnesses and victims; particularly, whoever discovered the body or made the initial report to police.

We have several main goals when reviewing these particular reports. First is the standard review to gain an understanding of the event itself and of the crime scene; and how it was found based on the photographs, sketches, various technical reports, and lists of all physical and forensic evidence that was identified and collected. The second goal is to examine the scene through the actions and behaviors displayed by the offender and determine what they did before, during, and after the event. These pre-incident, incident, and post-incident behaviors can provide important investigative information regarding consistency with statements, physical evidence, conditions, timelines, coincidental behaviors, or claims of coincidental occurrences. Any inconsistencies should be verified and may provide important evidence that the offender attempted to alter or stage the scene. This includes the addition, removal, or changing of any physical evidence and may include post-mortem mutilation, posing the body, or other similar interaction with the victim at the scene. Changing or altering the scene or post-mortem interaction with

[*] This article was originally published January 2014 in *Investigative Sciences Journal*, volume 6, no. 1, accessible at www.InvestigativeSciencesJournal.org. It is our intent to give it a chapter in this book because many cold cases may have staged crimes scenes that are misdirecting the efforts of investigators causing the cold to become even colder.

the victim are all examples of staging; and if scene alterations are not recognized during the preliminary investigation, it may completely change the interpretation of the crime and cause detectives to develop false theories and go off into misleading directions.

Most detectives have probably come into contact with offenders who have altered a scene; however, most police literature, case studies, and training in this area is really limited to examples of homicide cases in what Geberth defines as "the perpetrator changes elements of the scene to make a death appear to be a suicide or accidental in order to cover up a murder."[1] Although this statement is true regarding an offender's attempts to mislead a homicide investigation, staging can include other activities and different crimes, which may include arson used to cover up evidence at a crime scene or positioning a body in a sexually stylized manner to degrade or humiliate the victim or to shock society. Staging actually takes on many forms and is attempted for many different reasons; the scene altercation is really only dependent on the offender and the dynamics of each individual event or scene. To better understand the concept of staged crime scenes and "staging," this chapter takes a second look at the general definitions of a staged crime scene and characterizes these events into distinct categories based on motives and general intent of the offender.

General Definition

One of the problems with the concept of staged crime scenes is the definition as to what exactly constitutes staging or a staged crime scene. In current professional literature there are several variations. For instance, Geberth provides a somewhat general definition by stating, "Staging is a conscious criminal action on the part of an offender to thwart an investigation."[2] The *Crime Classification Manual*[3] provides a more detailed and specific definition: "Someone purposely alters the crime scene prior to the arrival of police. There are two reasons that someone employs staging: to redirect the investigation away from the most logical suspect or to protect the victim or victim's family."

Whereas both of the previous definitions are generally correct, the authors believe they are also overly broad and do not adequately define or explain the staging act itself, as well as all of the potential offender scene alterations that have nothing to do with misdirecting a police investigation. To enable investigators to better recognize and understand the acts of crime scene staging, this article offers a new terminology to both define and categorize different types of staging based on the offender's motivations and behaviors. The combined offender behaviors and motivations place the offender into one of two categories known as *primary staging* and *secondary staging*.

An additional and separate category of scene alteration, which is carried out by someone other than the offender and is not intended to misdirect a police investigation, is defined as a *tertiary scene alteration.*

A primary staged scene is defined as

> an intentional and purposeful altering or changing of physical evidence or other aspects of the crime scene, and/or providing false information to the police relative to the incident, with specific criminal intent to misdirect or divert a police investigation away from the true facts and circumstances of the crime.

The important difference between this new definition and other previous broader definitions are the phrases "intentional and purposeful" and "with the specific criminal intent to misdirect or divert a police investigation." This new definition focuses on the offender and his or her motive behind the scene altercation and should be seen and understood as *perpetrator driven activity.* The second important change in the previous definition involves a very important aspect of misdirection of a police investigation, which is the offender providing false information to the police. This is an important element in almost all staged crime scenes because so many times it is the offender that actually reports the crime to the police and must therefore provide an explanation as to what happened, giving them an opportunity to enhance or supplement any scene alteration that may be present with false information they believe will further justify or explain the staged version of events they want investigators to see and believe. In essence, the offender sets the stage for a false reality based on their fantasy of what the scene should look like to represent their version of events. Examples include effort to point out any physical evidence that may be present or missing, or offer other explanations as to how the crime was actually committed. Hazelwood and Napier[4] have defined these false statements and efforts to lie to the police to initiate or continue with the misdirection of the investigation as *verbal staging.*

Based on the individual circumstances of each crime scene, primary staged scenes can be further placed into one of two subcategories known as *ad hoc* and *premeditated.*

Ad Hoc Primary Staged Scenes

An ad hoc staged crime scene is basically what the name implies; it is an intentional effort to misdirect the police, undertaken or completed by the offender, but without forethought and preplanning. In other words, the staging takes place *after the fact* of some crime or event. There are a couple of basic differences between this type of staged crime scene and the others covered later in this article. The main difference with ad hoc scenes is the clear lack of *premeditation* or prior planning and the impulsivity involved in the staging, or actual alteration of the scene. An ad hoc staged crime scene would typically result from efforts of the offender to cover up criminal acts, omissions, or negligent activity by staging the scene to provide an alternate explanation as to what really happened. Therefore, the altered or changed physical evidence and subsequent statements or explanations offered by the offender is almost always related to some type of self-preservation effort to divert police attention away from themselves and onto someone or something else.

Often these types of staged scenes do not necessarily reflect added evidence, as much as it reflects missing evidence or an otherwise altered scene. Examples of common ad hoc staging efforts would include child abuse deaths wherein the offender suddenly and thoroughly cleans the residence; temporary removal of other children prior to police arrival; or the victim is bathed, redressed, or repositioned in bed to alter the way the scene and the child would be seen by the authorities. In cases such as drug abuse deaths, the scene might be cleaned up and all illegal substances removed. The victim may then be repositioned to resemble an accidental or natural type death, such as an accidental drowning in a bathtub. On more than one occasion a female victim was removed from the scene, undressed and left out in public and posed in a sexualized manner to resemble a sexual homicide.

One of the better examples of an ad hoc type staged crime scene is illustrated in the following case example.

Case Study 1

A frantic young couple reported that on the previous evening person(s) unknown entered their apartment and kidnapped their 4-month-old baby from her bedroom. The parents claimed that the father was away working a double shift and the mother had put the child to bed around 9 p.m. the night the child was kidnapped. When the mother woke up in the morning, she discovered the child missing with the front door closed but unlocked. She immediately called her husband who came right home and called the police. The parents claimed to have no idea what happened to their child and could not think of any potential suspects. The kidnapping report initiated an immediate response from all of the local police agencies.

A detailed crime scene search was initiated, but no signs of forced entry or other physical evidence consistent with the parents' claim were discovered. During the background investigation of the family, relatives and friends reported that the wife was not known to keep a very clean house and there was actual concern about the general welfare of all of their children. Yet, the house at the time of the scene processing was orderly, neat, and clearly had been recently cleaned. The mother's statements to police claimed of spending the previous days engaged in normal family activity and portrayed herself as a normal and caring parent. However, this was not the general feeling of friends and neighbors, who portrayed the mother as neglectful and inattentive to all of her children. Eventually, the parents were confronted with the conflicting information and the mother confessed that the child actually died from neglect. The mother had been on the computer almost nonstop for almost an entire week and had never checked on the child. Most likely it had literally starved to death, while the mother played on the Internet. She discovered the child dead in her crib the previous evening and called her husband who managed to sneak away from his job and returned home. He took the child, wrapped it in a blanket, and then took the child to an open rural area and threw the child's body into a nearby pond where it was later recovered. The husband and wife later pled guilty to various offenses regarding the death and disposal of their daughter.

In this case example, as with many other ad hoc type staged scenes, the mother had no real intention to murder her child. But, once she made the discovery she had no idea how to explain the child's death. Rather than admitting to any wrongdoing, the mother and father impulsively formulated an ad hoc plan to explain the child's disappearance and demise. While the husband took control of the child's body, the wife went through and completely cleaned their house from top to bottom. Their decision was an attempt to deflect attention onto an unknown intruder and thus escape or deflect any suspicion, blame, and responsibility for their actions.

Rather than being forced to provide any details, information, or explanation as to what happened, they claimed no knowledge as to the exact circumstances surrounding the event. By maintaining that the mother was asleep and the father wasn't home, they believed they created an easily manageable explanation of events. The complainant's lack of knowledge or inability to remember what exactly happened is a frequent finding in these types of events because it is easier for the guilty party to maintain their story if they do not have to recount any details.

However, because the explanation of events are basically created on the run and not planned out in any great detail, inconsistencies are usually much easier for investigators to recognize and uncover. One of the key features of this type of staged scene is the nature of the description of events and the "evidence" left behind or presented to the investigators at the scene. Interestingly, there seems to be an overwhelming need for the offender who stages an ad hoc scene to paint themselves in the most positive manner by pointing out how responsible they were, what precautions they may have taken to prevent such accidents, or express frustration at the event taking place when they were not around to do something to prevent the occurrence.

For those offenders who do place themselves at the scene at the time of the incident, it is not unusual for them to claim a vigorous but unsuccessful physical resistance against an unknown attacker, but was somehow overpowered or injured and could not resist any further.

Case Study 2

A 16-year-old girl reported that her boyfriend dropped her off in front of her house minutes before her scheduled curfew. As she was walking toward the house, she was approached from behind by a young man who covered her mouth to prevent her from calling out and then forced her back into the street where a pickup truck, driven by another unknown male, pulled up. She was forced into the extended cab backseat area of the pickup truck, her head covered by some type of clothing articles, and then driven to an apartment complex where she was forced from the truck, then into one of the apartments and was raped.

The victim claimed to have physically resisted the assault but was overpowered by the combined efforts of both offenders. Afterward she was forced back into the truck and driven to a remote area of town where she was taken out of the truck and raped again. This time, however, the victim claimed to have attempted escape by running away but was quickly recaptured in an open field, and the two men then teased and tormented her by dragging her through some grass and mud, and then "punished" her attempts to escape by burning her stomach twice with cigarettes. She was eventually released near a convenience store where she called her parents and reported the crime.

As part of the initial investigation the boyfriend was contacted and only after a few minutes confessed that the event did not happen the way the victim claimed. The boyfriend stated that they had actually engaged in consensual sexual intercourse together earlier in the evening. Afterward, the boyfriend discovered the condom he was wearing had broken open and the girlfriend immediately concluded that she was pregnant. The girl could not face telling her parents that she was pregnant and after thinking for several minutes formulated a plan to stage a rape. In order to stage the rape, she believed she needed evidence of more than one man's semen. Convincing the boyfriend to follow along, the two set out to locate another man to have sex with the girl in order to obtain additional semen. They made contact with two men waiting outside a bar in a pickup truck. The boyfriend offered the girl to them for sexual relations. The men readily agreed and escorted the pair onto their apartment and the "victim" went willingly inside, disrobed and began to have sexual relations with one of the men. However, the process was taking too long for the girl and she demanded the man stop, which he did. The girl then got dressed, returned to the parking lot where the boyfriend was waiting in his vehicle and they drove off. However, because the man had not climaxed, the girl still did not have the necessary evidence that she believed was necessary to support her claim of events.

As a result, the two went back to town looking for other possible "candidates." Another man was eventually located outside of a convenience store. The girl approached him with offers of sex and then the two went into the nearby bushes and engaged in sexual intercourse and the man climaxed inside her. Now that the "victim" had the necessary physical evidence, the boyfriend dragged her through some mud and grass, and she burned herself on the stomach with cigarettes to validate "torture" by the suspects. The boyfriend had let her out at a convenience store where she called her parents and made the claim of rape. She reported the kidnapping and rape to the police and was able to describe the vehicle the men were driving in good detail, but was only able to provide a basic description of the suspects and did not think she would be able to identify them in the future. Based on the description of the vehicle and statement of the boyfriend, the two men who were approached outside the club were actually located and during an interview confirmed the unusual story.

The previous case demonstrates the impulsive and unplanned nature of the ad hoc type staged crime scene. The victim's plan, although somewhat more intricate than many, was still made on the run with the intent to deflect blame from the victim and divert attention from the real events. However, because the victim was not the real victim of a crime, she had to concoct a story in a limited period of time that she thought would be believable based on her limited life experiences. In this case, we can see many of the other markers of an ad hoc type staged scene. These include the victim portraying herself in the best possible light and whatever happened was beyond her ability to control or avoid. According to the victim, she was returning from a date before her curfew; she was attacked literally at her own house, by two much stronger males; although she had physically resisted and even tried to escape she was overpowered and could not possibly resist what eventually happened to her. This case was unusual in that the victim was not able to use the evidence that was available to her and instead had to manufacture evidence through consensual sex with other men. The physical injuries were self-inflicted and amounted to what the victim thought would corroborate her claim. She relied mostly on the false information provided to the police to substantiate her allegations.

From an investigative perspective, the reported verbal, sexual, and physical behaviors of the "offenders" during the incident did not make sense and cast doubt on her claim almost immediately. What this case study clearly demonstrates is what a victim attempting to make a false complaint or stage a scene is willing to go through in order to deflect attention away from themselves and onto some other person or thing.

Premeditated Primary Staged Scenes

The second subcategory of the primary type staged scene is the premeditated. In direct contrast to the ad hoc scenes, the premeditated staged scene may be meticulously planned ahead of time by the offender and run the gamut from fraudulent burglary or theft reports, to false rape complaints, and even homicides. The important characteristic difference regarding the premeditated staged scene is the amount and type of physical evidence that is often provided to establish what is being portrayed. The evidence provided or the scene alteration is really only limited by the intelligence, imagination, and overall life experiences of the offender. Whereas ad hoc staging tends to point away from the actual act and onto other unknown factors or persons, premeditated primary staging tends to have clear evidence that focuses the police onto the act or event being portrayed. In these cases, the offender wants the police to have a clear understanding as to what happened, leaving little to no chance the evidence will not be found or misinterpreted. It is not unusual in these situations for the offender to be the one that actually points out the evidence to the police to ensure it is found.

In the following case study, an offender planned to stage a burglary with the intent of filing a fraudulent insurance claim.

Case Study 3

A student returned to his dormitory following a 10-day school break and reported that while he was gone, someone had entered his dormitory room and had stolen a very expensive piece of jewelry and a stereo. The "thief" had also packaged other items, as if ready to steal, but they were apparently left behind. An examination of the scene noted no signs of forced entry to the doors, but the victim believed someone entered through his second-floor window. Furthermore, the scene examination noted there was no disturbance of the ground directly underneath the "victim's" window, nor at any other location around the entire building.

Inside the room were an empty stereo cabinet and several large plastic bags full of personal and school items belonging to the victim that appeared as if the perpetrator was going to take them away as well. The victim then brought out a small jewelry box that still had numerous pieces of quality gold jewelry but claimed an expensive diamond engagement ring for his girlfriend was missing. The plastic bags of personal items were also examined and found to contain a few common clothing items as well as several of his textbooks. The theft of the stereo and jewelry could be expected, but the theft of the school texts did not make any sense at all as these were neither high-valued items or of any particular interest to a lot of other students.

A canvass of the other occupants of the dorm eventually located the "missing" stereo in another student's room. The other student reported that he had actually purchased the stereo from the "victim" several days prior to the school break. It was his intent to take it to a girlfriend's house off the campus but he had not had a chance to do so. During his interrogation, the "victim" confessed to staging the scene prior to leaving for break. His intent was to file a claim for his loss with the jewelry store where he had also purchased insurance for the ring. The student was charged with filing a false police report.

In Case Study 3, the "victim" expected a police report would be generated based on his complaint but never expected anyone to actually do a follow-up investigation. He therefore provided what he thought was evidence of a break-in; his window was unlocked, his personal property was in disarray, and some property was even "prepackaged" to steal, and he reported the loss of a few valuables. In his mind, this was what he would have expected to find if someone had actually broken into his room. The evidence provided was very basic, and tended to focus on the break-in and actions of the offender inside the room.

There is seemingly no limit to the lengths and methods an offender will pursue in support of their premeditated staged offense. The end result of their planning is based on their life experiences, and personal interpretation of how the scene and associated evidence should appear to achieve their desired outcome, which is commonly to get away with and sometimes also benefit from the crime as demonstrated in Case Study 4.

Case Study 4

A brother and sister team planned to defraud a major tourist amusement park out of a large sum of money by claiming the sister had been attacked and raped while inside the amusement park. As part of their plan, the sister first had consensual sex with an unsuspecting male partner. The brother and sister then went straight to the amusement park where they walked to a location out of public view. The brother then physically assaulted his sister by striking her repeatedly in the face with his fists and ripping her clothing. Subsequently, the brother left the scene and his sister caught the attention of a park security guard and reported that while walking near a restroom she had been kidnapped, dragged into a hidden area, and sexually assaulted by an unknown offender. The police were summoned and the victim taken to the hospital where she was examined. Semen was recovered during the examination, which tended to confirm the victim's claim of assault. The scheme was undone when the previous consensual partner found out about the incident and he reported to the police to avoid being implicated. The pair were both tried and convicted of filing a false report. Their motive for fabricating the entire incident was a planned lawsuit against the amusement park.

The premeditation or planning of the above event can be seen by the intended victim engaging in consensual sex hours before the event so they would be prepared with physical and forensic evidence when they went to the amusement park. The last step was only the physical trauma that was inflicted immediately before the report. The two offenders believed the semen found in her body during the medical examination and the physical trauma would substantiate their claims. As we have seen from the two previous examples, some premeditated events are much better planned than others, and the amount and type of evidence provided to stage a premeditated scene is only dependent upon the offender and their intelligence, criminal experience, maturity, life experiences, and motive behind the event.

Since many offenders are not real victims and are likely to have never actually participated in a previous criminal act, the offender often makes a mistake by presenting too much evidence at the scene in what can be described as exaggeration. Leaving too much evidence tends to lead to conflicting evidence as to what happened. One common and very simple example of exaggeration is an offender who plans to murder a victim and then make it appear to be a suicide. The victim is then shot in the head and invariably they place the gun into the victim's hands to make it very obvious to the police that the victim shot themselves. In reality, the gun is not always found in the victim's hand, so it's really only important to the police that the weapon used was located in the immediate area of the victim. Of additional importance is the physical condition of the firearm: safety on/off, slide forward or locked to the rear, hammer cocked or forward, and other functional attributes related to the operation of the particular weapon as well as any related trace evidence. The condition of the firearm is sometimes overlooked and can be an important indicator that a scene has been staged.

In addition to providing an overabundance of physical evidence, the offender may design a scenario or explanation that attempts to play upon perceived police and societal prejudices and offender stereotyping. An example of this effort to play upon a perceived police prejudice is seen in the well-publicized case of Susan Smith from South Carolina who falsely reported that an unknown black offender carjacked her vehicle with her children inside. In addition to the sympathy generated by the kidnapping of a young mother's children, Smith played on the perceived police and societal prejudices by identifying the offender as a black male. In reality she drove her vehicle to a lake and with the children inside, allowed the vehicle to submerge into the lake, and the children were drowned.

As previously stated, staging appears across the full spectrum of crime, but there are three crimes or events that are used as themes to misdirect the police investigation more often than others. These are the interrupted burglary or home invasion, suicide, and sexual homicides. So whenever the investigator is confronted with these crimes a careful look for any signs of a false report or staged event should be considered.

All of the aforementioned case studies for primary staged scenes, whether they are ad hoc or premeditated, provide a very important key to an offender's understanding of the police investigative process. As such, the suspect's staged scene and the false story are not generally designed to last through a long-term investigation; rather, the main goal is to get through the initial police observation of the scene and the preliminary criminal investigation without arousing any suspicions. If they are successful, there is actually a very good chance there will be no follow-up investigation and their version of events will be accepted; therefore they will get away with their crime.

When looking at a cold case, there is also a third goal behind reviewing the initial crime scene and preliminary investigative reports, that is, to identify the motive or the reason behind the crime. From an investigative perspective, once we understand the motive we can then start to identify or narrow down a possible suspect. Whenever the motive of the crime cannot be clearly established we look very carefully at the scene for any evidence that the scene may have been staged and the investigation misdirected from the outset of the preliminary investigation.

One of the more common scenes is a homicide that is staged to resemble a home invasion or interrupted burglary. In these cases, the scene has been altered to resemble someone rifling through the scene looking for some valuables. The problem many times in cold cases is there appears to be multiple or even conflicting motives noted during the investigation.

As an example of multiple motives one only has to look at the JonBenét Ramsey case wherein the 6-year-old daughter of a wealthy businessman was murdered inside her home. But the parents first reported that the child was abducted based on a three-page ransom note. Yet, hours later in a search of the residence the victim was found deceased in a room in the basement. Her discovery inside the house is curious, as she was found with a ligature around one of her wrists as if she had been at one time been bound. It is unclear why the offender would have to tie up a 6-year-old in order to maintain control over her. She also had suffered a skull fracture and died of ligature strangulation. Since many other indicators of staging existed, the immediate question was if this was a kidnapping, then why leave the body behind to be found. If the motive was murder or even sexual assault of the child, then why leave the handwritten note behind, which gave the police their only real forensic evidence. Moreover, the presented offender was so clever they entered the house at some point (which was never really established), went up to the second floor of the house, removed the child without causing her to wake or call out, then took the child down two flights of stairs where the body was found. At some time after she was removed from her bedroom, the child experienced some severe blunt force trauma and was strangled and left in the basement. The offender then left the scene and was so resourceful that they left no signs they were inside the house. But, the same offender was so unprepared that everything used in the commission of the crime originated from the scene. The handwritten note was written from a pen that was recovered by police inside the kitchen and came from a writing tablet that was also in the kitchen area. The ligature and piece of wood used as a garrote also came from the house.

The last question we always ask in this case is exactly what was the motive behind the entire incident. Sexual assault? Kidnapping? Murder? Even today, the exact motive behind the entire incident is still unclear, therefore this case and other similar cases should be looked at as a staged scene.

Hazelwood and Napier[5] identify the issue of recognizing the motive very clearly: "In staged scenes the investigator is confronted with the necessity to determine the motive for two different behaviors. (1) The original act that necessitated the staging and (2) The staging itself." Hazelwood and Napier continue to say: "In staged crimes, learning the motive will more often than not lead to the person responsible." Thus, establishing the motive not only helps to determine the scene has been staged, but also leads to discovering the impetus leading up to the staging, ultimately leading to identifying the offender.

So, from an investigative standpoint the first task is to recognize that the scene was staged or the crime did not happen in the manner reported. We then have to look at the original crime and who is most likely to be considered a suspect. For instance, if we determine the victim did not commit suicide as the scene initially indicated, we now have to look at the event as a murder and shift our attention to determine the motive behind the murder and who is likely to benefit or would have a reason to commit the crime. So many times in cold cases we see signs that the detectives first did not recognize the scene may have been staged or if they recognized the scene was staged did not follow up and focus on the original crime itself.

One of the last goals in reviewing the file is to look at all of the verbal, physical, or sexual behaviors displayed by the offender before, during, and after the crime. In looking at their behavior, we are hopefully picking up many clues of the offender's intelligence, life experiences, criminal sophistication, or criminal experience. Considering these behaviors in combination with the motive will tell us a lot about the offender, or will present inconsistencies that point to a false report or a staged scene to misdirect the investigation. Again, one of the better examples is in the JonBenét Ramsey case where we have a dichotomy of offender behaviors that typically points to a staged scene or false report.

In the JonBenét case, we are presented with a suspect that displays organized offender behavior by being so intelligent and organized to be able to enter a residence, remove a child from her bedroom, commit a murder, hide her body, and then leave the residence without leaving any sign or evidence of their presence. Yet, this same offender is so disorganized and unprepared to commit the crime that everything used to commit the crime and leave the note originated from within the crime scene. Also, with all of this work and effort the real motive for the crime cannot even be determined.

Showing *proprietary interest* during the crime is another inconsistent offender behavior during normal criminal acts. An example of proprietary interest shown by the offender is a murder scene where the wife is killed and her possessions are thrown around, ransacked, or damaged. Yet, in the same house the husband's personal property is left untouched. It appears as if the offender wantonly destroyed or had little concern over the wife's property but exercised care not to damage or even disturb the husband's property. Many times, at the end of the scene examination or case review, a detective may find that despite the appearance of forced entry or ransacking of the scene, the only real crime that was committed was the murder of the victim.

Secondary Staging

There are many other offender behaviors encountered at crime scenes that can be grouped into the general concept of staging but are not intended to misdirect a police investigation or divert attention away from the offender. The difference with these types of scenes is the absence of motive to mislead or deceive; rather the impetus for the scene alteration is more closely related to the psychological and crime scene signature aspects of the offender. Such change in provocation for this type of staging behavior requires a different perspective when examining the scene, and thus a different definition in which to classify these events, known as secondary staging, and is defined as

the intentional alteration or manipulation of the crime scene or the victim by an offender that is unrelated to misdirecting or diverting the police investigation.

Such alteration takes in a very wide range of possible offender behaviors from simple acts such as placing something over the victim's head, to posing the victim into sexually provocative or embarrassing positions, insertions of foreign objects into the body, or other post-mortem mutilation of the victim. These actions may be a part of fulfilling the offender's fantasy or intended to shock and offend society, humiliate or degrade the victim, or even for some other ritualistic or symbolic meaning only understood by the offender. In secondary staging, the scene alteration is performed strictly for the benefit of the offender. Three common examples of secondary staging are known as *depersonalization, body posing,* and *symbolic/ritualistic.*

Depersonalization

Perhaps the most common and easily recognizable example of secondary staging is depersonalization, defined by Geberth[6] as "the actions taken by a murderer to obscure the personal identity of the victim. The face may be beaten beyond recognition, or the face of the victim may be covered." Since the head and face are the most recognizable aspects of our normal appearance, when covered, the victim is transformed from a person the offender may know, love, or had a personal relationship with to just an anonymous body. This behavior of covering the face of the victim by some item at the scene has been interchangeably used in professional literature staging, depersonalization, or psychological undoing.

Other more extreme examples of depersonalization include post-mortem mutilation of the victim's body and typically involve the face or in some cases the actual removal of a woman's breasts or genitals, also referred to as defeminization, defined by Geberth[7] as "divesting of female quality or characteristics." These more extreme actions are seen as a way to essentially change the victim into a nonperson or to *depersonalize* them.

Body Posing

Body posing is perhaps the best known, most recognizable, and probably the most documented example of crime scene staging; likewise, the vast majority of professional articles on criminal investigative analysis, offender profiling, and crime scene signature analysis involve this aspect of this type of offender behavior. Although they are extremely well documented and studied, they really only make up a small percentage of all homicides. Different efforts to determine the frequency of these incidents by Keppel and Weiss,[8] Hazelwood and Napier,[9] and Geberth[10] have all agreed that they are actually very rare occurrences. Generally speaking, these events tend to take place within the context of a sexual homicide, which Geberth[11] has defined as a scene where there "is evidence of sexual activity observed in the crime scene or upon the body of the victim." Geberth further stresses that a "sexual homicide is not a case with just sexual overtones, but is the overriding motive for the death. The term 'posing' in the context of a sexual homicide is deliberate offender efforts to manipulate or pose the victim into a sexually provocative position within the crime scene." Because the nature of the crime involves positioning the victim into sexually provocative positions and may include elements of bondage, insertion of foreign objects, or post-mortem mutilation, they tend to be well publicized and studied.

Prominent public placement or display and body posing of the victims is another example of a secondary staged scene. One of the best known examples would be the Hillside Strangler serial murder investigation during the 1970s in Los Angeles, California. In those cases, female victims were kidnapped, raped, sadistically tortured, and then murdered. Their bodies were then transported to residential neighborhoods, and left naked in public areas where the neighborhood residents found them. The bodies were clearly left to humiliate and degrade the victim as well as to demonstrate the offender's power and the incompetence of the police. Each succeeding placement of the victims added to the offender's sense of power and accomplishment, while continuing to emphasize the inability of the police to catch them.

The common thread prevalent in these behaviors with regard to crime scene staging is the staging activities are not intended to misdirect the police investigation; more notably, as previously stated, they are intended through some internal or psychological motivation to shock and offend society, humiliate or degrade the victim, or for some other symbolic reason only understood by the offender.

Symbolic or Ritualistic

The third general example of secondary staging are those scenes that are staged or altered for some symbolic or ritualistic reasons by the offender for reasons other than to fulfill a fantasy or misdirect a police investigation. One example is the famous case of John List.

John List Case Study

On November 9, 1971, John List methodically killed his entire family—his wife, mother, and his three children. He initially shot and killed his wife and mother and then as his children came home from school he murdered each one. List went to the bank and closed his own and his mother's bank accounts, and then placed the bodies of his wife and children on sleeping bags next to one another, with rags/towels covering their faces, in one room of the house and attempted to clean up the scene. He also wrote a five-page letter to his pastor explaining why he had murdered his family leaving instructions for their cremation and religious services. List was experiencing financial difficulties making only $5,000 dollars for the year and foreclosure proceedings had begun on his home. In his other notes he confessed that he killed his family to spare them from experiencing poverty as well as sparing them from ever losing their souls from the evil influences in the world. To delay discovery of the bodies and his crime, he had stopped milk, newspaper, and mail deliveries saying the family was going to North Carolina for a few weeks. The bodies were eventually discovered almost a month later, all lying next to each other with religious music playing over the home's intercom system.

In the List case, the scene was altered after the victims were killed and all moved to one room where they were all together and then symbolically laid out next to each other with religious music playing in the background, and the offender wrote notes confessing to the murders. But, the staging was not related to misdirecting the subsequent investigation; rather it was an example of symbolic staging that List felt the need to arrange for his own personal reasons.

When discussing ritualistic crime scenes, many times we tend to associate them with the occult, satanic ceremonies, or some other religious reasons. However, *ritualistic* also refers to instances where the offender's crime scene behavior is repeated and noted from one scene to another. This example of ritualistic behavior is also known as the crime scene signature, wherein the offender implants his individuality into the scene through his own repeated behavior. This repeated behavior may be realized by how or where the victim is posed and through the various types of post-mortem offender behaviors at the scene and the offender's interaction with the victim. Thus, recognizing the presence of Secondary Staging can lead to identifying some of the best individualistic offender behavioral evidence. If similar behavior is repeated in any additional crimes, this may be the basis of recognizing or identifying the offender's particular crime scene signature and potentially linking cases together.

It is important to consider that not all sexually staged scenes fall into the category of secondary staging and that the theme of "sexual connotations" may be used as a ruse by the offender to cover the true nature of the crime; thus, bring us back to the motive of specific criminal intent to mislead the criminal investigation in primary staging. As such, staging a murder scene to resemble some type of sexual homicide by removing some of the victim's clothing, posing them into a sexually stylized position, or insertion of a foreign object into the body is a very well established theme. So much so that any instance where the death appears to be sexually motivated should be carefully examined for signs of staging. In many instances, when reviewing a cold case in what the initial detectives believed was a sexually motivated crime, there may be clear signs of staging, basically because of the lack of corresponding offender behavior that is consistent with a true sexually motivated crime.

In the case of those scenes that are staged to resemble a sexual homicide, the correct categorization would be of an ad hoc or premeditated scene rather than a sexual or symbolic staged scene, since the purpose was to misdirect the police, rather than to humiliate or degrade the victim.

Tertiary Scene Alteration

There is one last general aspect of scene alteration that needs to be considered when it is carried out by family members or other persons that may initially find a body in an embarrassing or degrading situation: seeking to spare the family or the victim any embarrassment. Geberth is very clear on this point stating, "Staging should not be used to describe the actions of a family member who may innocently cover or redress a loved one found nude or who has died in an otherwise embarrassing situation."[12]

Although unintentional and noncriminally motivated actions could potentially change the nature of the scene, they do not fall into the primary or secondary staging definition unless there was specific criminal intent or purpose behind the scene alterations. Such potential criminal intent could be established, for example, when a suicide scene is intentionally changed to resemble a homicide or an accident to ensure that the "victim's" life insurance policy with a suicide clause will still pay.

The other noncriminal alteration, that is, accidental, incidental, or innocent, to the original crime scene by family members or other witnesses are better referred to as *artifacts*. Here, the artifact may be something altered or added to the scene after the fact, but has no real evidentiary or behavioral value and has no criminal intent to mislead or secondary staging motives. The term for these types of actions is *tertiary staging*, which is defined as an alteration or change to the scene made by someone other than the offender that is incidental to the crime and done without specific criminal purpose or intent to misdirect the police investigation.

Because tertiary scene alterations are generally not completed by the offender, such activity should be identified and clarified, but generally has no other real evidentiary or behavioral importance. The importance in identifying this type is staging is to discover the true nature of the actual crime and ensure the investigation is not sidetracked.

Conclusion

There is very little statistical data available to determine the actual number of staged scenes that are attempted each year, and due to the nature of these types of incidents it is difficult to gather data. Most of the information collected on this subject therefore is based primarily on the personal or antidotal experiences of detectives or authors of professional literature. However, Schlesinger et al. (2012) completed a review of 946 homicides supplied by the Federal Bureau of Investigation (FBI) Behavioral Science Unit from across the United States and found 79 cases or 8.35 percent were staged to misdirect the criminal investigation, or primary staging. Alternatively, 91.64 percent of the cases reviewed (867) were not staged to mislead police.

Of the primary staged scenes in this study 25.31 percent (20 cases) used arson as the staging method. Verbal staging, defined in the study as filing a false missing person police report to cover the murder, occurred in 21.51 percent (17) of the cases. The study went on to further classify 17.72 percent (14) as burglary/robbery/breaking and entering themes, 13.92 percent (11) as accidents, 7.59 percent (6) as suicides, 5.06 percent (4) as homicide–suicide, and one case (1.26 percent) primary staged "as a sexual homicide by exposing the victim's genitals."

Although this study gives great insight into the prevalence of staging, it is limited to homicide investigations. What's abundantly clear is that staged scenes are and will continue to be an investigative issue that affects the fact-finding outcome of a criminal investigation.

The ability to recognize attempts of misdirecting the police at the earliest stages of a crime or preliminary investigation provides a greater understanding of what may have actually happened. This type of information is invaluable for investigators as they develop their case. When looking at cold cases we always look at the possibility that the original theory of the crime and how the case was investigated was based on a staged or an altered scene and false information to support that alteration.

Endnotes

1. Geberth, Vernon J. 1996. The staged crime scene. *Law and Order Magazine*, 44(2).
2. Geberth, Vernon J. 2006. *Practical Homicide Investigation* (4th ed.) CRC Press/ Taylor & Francis: Boca Raton, FL.
3. Douglas, John E., Burgess, Ann W., Burgess, Alen G., and Ressler, Robert K. 2006. *Crime Classification Manual: A Standard System for Investigating and Classifying Violent Crimes* (2nd ed.). Jossey-Bass: San Francisco, CA.

4. Palerma, George B., and Kocsis, Richard N. 2005. *Offender Profiling: An Introduction to the Sociopsychological Analysis of Violent Crime.* Charles C. Thomas: Springfield, IL.
5. Palerma and Kocsis, *Offender Profiling.*
6. Geberth, *Practical Homicide Investigation.*
7. Geberth, *Practical Homicide Investigation*
8. Keppel, Robert D., and Weis, Joseph G. 2004. The rarity of "unusual" dispositions of victim bodies: Staging and posing. *Journal of Forensic Science,* 49(6), 1308–1312.
9. As quoted by Palerma and Kocsis, *Offender Profiling.*
10. Geberth, Vernon. 2010. Crime scene staging: An exploratory study of the frequency and characteristics of sexual posing in homicides. *Investigative Science Journal,* 2(2).
11. Geberth, *Practical Homicide Investigation.*
12. Geberth, The staged crime scene.

Evaluation Reports and Legal Considerations

13

JAMES M. ADCOCK AND SARAH L. STEIN

Introduction

In this chapter, we first discuss the official reporting of information found during the case file evaluation, then on to the legal considerations that have to be made. There are basically two types of reports that an evaluation team may prepare, depending on the target audience of either investigators or prosecutors. A report for the detectives is usually more investigatively oriented, as it addresses areas of concern to the detectives that will help them establish all the elements of proof. It will also contain a detailed investigative plan for an accurate resolution. The other type of report is usually for a prosecutor, wherein you are asking for a prosecutorial determination. Utilizing the latter depends on whether a prosecutor has been assigned to the team and is fully aware of the intricacies of the investigation and therefore fully prepared to prosecute accordingly.

Report Formats

The format of reports to police detectives will vary from case to case based on the amount and type of information available. While keeping in mind that your responsibility is to review the file for solvability factors, identify witnesses and suspects, locate and identify any and all evidence, develop crime theories, and prepare a strategic investigative plan, you must thoroughly document your findings and substantiate them with footnotes that relate directly to the sources of your information for verification. Each of the categories mentioned should be addressed in the report, preferably as tabbed sections following a basic overview of your findings.

This overview report, which serves as a cover letter to the supporting documents, may have the following headings (these will be explained in the following paragraphs):

Basis for Evaluation
Background Information
Synopsis of Results
Methodology
Attachments

The "Basis for Evaluation" section will reflect how you came to review the particular case, when, where, and so forth. The next section would address the background information of the case that might include the abduction, subsequent murder, and finding of the body. A short summary of who, what, where, when, how, and why, if known, should follow. In the "Synopsis of Results" part of this report, one might start by stating something to the effect that "barring the receipt of additional information and/or evidence to the contrary, the evaluation team proffers the following theory or theories of the crime." Basically, state what you think happened, answering all the pertinent questions. The facts stated should be supported by footnotes with direct citings from the case file.

Next, describe the methodology that your team utilized to evaluate this case; basically how you followed, for example, the cold case evaluation model. The report should end with a listing of all the attachments, consisting of the victimology summary; timelines; evidence issues; witness list; persons of interest with pros and cons; pre-, peri-, and post-crime behaviors; interrogation strategies; and a comprehensive investigative plan. The key element for the detectives will be the comprehensive investigative plan where leads are identified, prioritized, and supported by footnotes from the case file. Although it is totally out of your control, the fact remains that some may not like the concept of having outsiders (nonpolice) reviewing their case files, and others may decide not to pursue the investigation for other reasons. It is just one of those things we have to live with. To my knowledge, out of the 12 cases we worked on in New Haven, Connecticut, only 4 are presently being pursued further by the respective departments.

The goal of the cold case process is to obtain a conviction, not just make an arrest. So if you are not fortunate enough to have a prosecutor on your team to advise your investigative actions accordingly, then consideration and focus of the report will change somewhat. This puts you in the position of having to brief the district attorney on the merits of the case to convince him or her that it is prosecutable. Therefore, the format of the report to the district attorney needs to be somewhat different from the evaluation report to the detectives.

The Prosecutor

The first thing a prosecutor is going to look for is whether the elements of proof of the crime have been fully met. Being able to demonstrate this is paramount.

Since the goal of the cold case process, as mentioned earlier, is to obtain a conviction, not just an arrest, two suggestions are made: (1) ensure completeness and accuracy of the investigation by utilizing the scientific method where all possible theories of the crime have been explored; and (2) present the case to the prosecutor in an organized manner that demonstrates the elements of proof for the crime(s) and fully documents the case file information. The easier it is for the attorney to understand, the more likely he or she will proceed with a prosecution.

This first element, utilizing the scientific method, has already been described, but we will reiterate the importance of using this method. By disproving all other theories of the crime, you take away from the defense any and all possible motives it might conjure up to confuse the jury. Your case becomes very thorough and solid for prosecution.

The second element requires organization of the data in a format the lawyers can work with. Attorneys approach their cases by having the right amount of information that proves the elements of the offenses charged. This could be done in the form of a case book or report designed specifically by law enforcement for presentation to the prosecuting attorney, making sure that all the elements of proof are provided. For the purposes of this chapter, let's take murder as the offense, and specifically the statute from the State of New Jersey (*N.J.S.A.* 2C:11-3a(l) and 3a(2), Revised 06-14-2004).

> The defendant is charged by indictment with the murder of (insert name of victim). Count of the indictment reads as follows: (Read indictment)
>   A person is guilty of murder if (he/she):
>
>   (1) caused the victim's death or serious bodily injury that then resulted in the victim's death; and
>   (2) the defendant did so purposely or knowingly.
>
> In order for you to find the defendant guilty of murder, the State is required to prove each of the following elements beyond a reasonable doubt:
>
>   (1) that the defendant caused (insert victim's name) death or serious bodily injury that then resulted in (insert victim's name) death, and
>   (2) that the defendant did so purposely or knowingly.
>
> One element that the State must prove beyond a reasonable doubt is that the defendant acted purposely or knowingly.
>   A person acts purposely when it is the person's conscious object to cause death or serious bodily injury resulting in death.
>   A person acts knowingly when the person is aware that it is practically certain that (his/her) conduct will cause death or serious bodily injury resulting in death.[1]

Now, let's take this statute and view the three primary elements of proof, with "motive" being added. It is here that you will be able to fully illustrate the documentation you have to support your conclusions.

Death occurred. Supported by a death certificate, coroner's or medical examiners report, photographs of the deceased, and so on.

At the hands of the accused. Supported by an admission or confession, which are subsequently supported by named witness statements, physical evidence, and all other data that point toward the accused as the one who did the killing.

Purposely or knowingly. Many statutes require that the accused committed this act purposely and knowingly. Therefore, all statements and accounts that relate this part of the story should be collected and collated under this heading.

Motive. While motive is always a very important piece of information, it is not always clear during the course of an investigation. The more information you have documented, the stronger the case.

The strength of the information provided under these headings will make a difference of whether the prosecutor will even go to trial. The amount of information you have in these categories testifies to the fact that you utilized the scientific method and disproved all other theories of the crime, thereby promising the likely success of your efforts in the form of a solid conviction.

Once the elements of proof are well documented, your report to the prosecutor should follow a logical sequence as it might be presented in a legal proceeding. One way to do this would be to follow the format designed by a colleague of ours, Steve Chancellor.[2] At our cold case seminars in New Haven, Connecticut, Chancellor would present different cases he had evaluated, and provided with this presentation a format for a report that fully and logically documented the events in question. His report format is well suited for briefing prosecutors. In preparing these reports, Chancellor utilized the following template.

Review and Analysis

This report was prepared based on a review of all of the associated case documents, including individual police reports, statements, investigative notes, and other evidence accumulated during the course of this investigation, as provided by the requesting agency. The resulting analysis and opinions reached in this case were based solely on that material in conjunction with sound investigative principles. The receipt of additional materials, evidence, and/or information not previously provided may result in altered findings and opinions.

OPINION

Based on the available information, this homicide is best categorized as a personal cause type, wherein the murder was directly related to some type of interpersonal interaction, conflicts, or other "personal" motives between the victim and offender. This type of homicide is often seen in interfamilial homicides such as domestic, matricide, or fratricidal type incidents. This opinion is based primarily on the lack of any other evidence or information indicative of any other potential motive such as burglary, home invasion robbery, or sexual assault.

CRIME ANALYSIS

Victimology Assessment

One of the first steps in the review and analysis process is to conduct a victimology assessment relating to the victim. The purpose of a victimology assessment is to determine what, if anything, elevated an individual's potential for becoming the victim of a violent crime and then to place the victim on a risk continuum from low to moderate to high. This assessment is based on both factual and subjective criteria about the victim, but generally speaking, it is the overall lifestyle of the victim and the situational dynamics present at the time of the crime that are the primary focus in making the assessment.

The victimology assessment is based on such factors as victim's age, overall health and physical characteristics, marital status, maturity level, education, work and employment history, socioeconomic level, childhood and family background, current family living conditions, ties to the local community or neighborhood, residence type and location, general overall life experiences, their ability to handle stressful situations, and other personality characteristics.

CRIME SCENE EXAMINATION (DESCRIBE THE CRIME SCENE EXAMINATION RESULTS)

Part of any homicide investigation and analysis is the identification of likely suspects. For this analysis three factors were used to identify possible suspects. These factors are known as the *motive, opportunity,* and *means.* In simplistic terms, we are looking for who has a reason or motive to murder, who has the chance to commit the crime, and who has the ability or tools necessary to commit the crime. Each of these areas is discussed in detail below.

Motive

The motive is basically the actual underlying cause or reasons behind the death of the victim. There is always a reason (motive) behind the perpetrator's actions. Some of the more common motives for homicide include monetary gain, revenge, jealously, love, sex and marriage, and/or some other interpersonal conflict between victim and offender. Often, especially in personal conflict type homicides, there are multiple motives in play. (*Note:* There are some crimes in which the actual or underlying motive is only understood by the perpetrators themselves and may never be clarified until they are captured. Infamous examples include the well-publicized Son of Sam, the Tate-LaBianca murders committed by the Manson family, and the Zodiac murders.)

Opportunity

Opportunity simply refers to the chance or ability to actually commit the crime. For instance, if the homicide occurs at a specific time at a specific place, yet the suspect is known to be at another location and thus does not have the opportunity to commit the crime, they must be eliminated as a suspect, no matter the motivation. The only other possibility was if the suspect was involved with a coconspirator who agreed to kill the victim while the main suspect established an alibi.

Means

The "means" or ability to commit the murder, such as a murder weapon or the key or combination to an outside lock to allow access to the victim.

SUGGESTED COURSE OF ACTION

The following recommendations are presented to your agency as a suggested course of action in order to aid in the successful resolution of this investigation. It is intended as guidance only and does not reflect any legal obligation or requirement for your agency to accomplish. It is possible that these recommendations and suggestions may change, prove unnecessary, or will be deemed inappropriate, if/when additional information or evidence was not provided by your agency for the actual review and analysis.

> The investigative plan should be considered a living document, meaning it is subject to change or alteration as circumstances develop during the investigative process.
> The following investigative leads have been identified and are suggested for successful resolution of this investigation. The leads are not placed into any specific order or priority list unless otherwise noted.
> - Forensic evidence (list all physical evidence, lab results, etc.)
> - Other investigative leads (all leads that need to be accomplished)

A sample report utilizing this method can be found in Appendix D.

Legal Considerations

In Chapter 3, about concepts for initializing a cold case squad, it was suggested that a prosecutor be included as a cold case team member and legal advisor. With cold cases there comes a magnitude of legal issues that will need resolving to ensure a conviction is obtained. These will vary from case to case and from jurisdiction to jurisdiction, and there may be changes in the statutes over time. In the previous section, it was explained how a cold case unit, without an assigned attorney, can increase its odds of presenting a solid case to the prosecutor through the utilization of different reporting formats. In this section, we will assume that the prosecutor is satisfied that your presentation shows that the case may be prosecutable, and he or she needs to explore how to go about prosecuting the case. As a backdrop, the Martha Moxley case from Greenwich, Connecticut, will be used to illustrate the legal hurdles encountered in the prosecution of Michael Skakel some 25 years later for the murder of Martha Moxley.

General Considerations

In order to prosecute, the tasks to be accomplished are going to be jurisdictionally specific; therefore the reader is cautioned to fully discuss all the potential issues with their respective prosecutor before moving forward with the follow-up investigation. In any case, there are specific considerations that need to be made, the first of which is whether the elements of the crime(s) have been met by the information provided in the case file. For the purposes of this book, let's assume they have been fully met. Next is whether there is any physical evidence: Where is it, what potential does it present, and has the chain of custody been maintained over the passage of time? Your prosecutor does not need any surprises in court regarding mishandled or mislabeled evidence that could contribute to the value of the evidence.

It will be necessary for the attorney, as it was for the detectives, to physically eyeball the evidence maintained for the investigation. Utilizing the evaluation model will be extremely helpful in this phase because every item of physical evidence has been logged and all data regarding each piece are correlated. For example, the log will identify when the item was collected, the chain of custody, whether it was examined and by whom, whether it was sent to a crime lab, results of all testing, and finally what testing might be accomplished today with the advancements in forensic science technology. Keep in mind that new technology could create additional legal hurdles for the prosecution, and those new techniques need to be adequately researched before venturing in that direction.

As noted by Schubert,[3] do not assume that just because the evidence supervisor cannot locate a particular piece of evidence that the evidence is in fact lost, as it could have just been misplaced but still be within the confines of the secured evidence depository. A thorough search by the detective might uncover the location of any misplaced evidence. Furthermore, where possible (and if not already accomplished), consider having the evidence reevaluated with today's forensic technology, as this could produce new results and help to refute any defense theories of the crime.

Prosecutors are ethically and legally bound to bring cases to a grand jury only if they believe that there is probable cause that this particular defendant committed a particular crime, and that there is sufficient evidence that if charges are pressed they can prove each element of the crime beyond a reasonable doubt. This is the same standard that is applied in every case, but much more difficult in cold cases where the necessary evidence and witnesses may no longer exist or are difficult to locate.

Cold cases are typically very complex cases because (1) they were not solved initially; (2) they have been repeatedly investigated by many investigators, each with different theories of the cases; and (3) often with the identification of different persons of interest who, for one reason or another, were not charged. These factors are potentially exculpatory to the person finally charged and may create reasonable doubt in the mind of a jury.

Nonhomicide cold cases may run into problems with statute of limitations. In most states, there is no statute of limitations for murder, but other crimes committed along with the homicide may be barred from prosecution. In addition to the time bar, statutes also change with time, and the defendant must be charged in accordance with the homicide statute at the time the crime was committed. This was a major issue in the Martha Moxley murder case, which occurred in 1975 at a time when Connecticut's statute of limitations for homicide was 5 years. Additionally, in capital cases, the law pertaining to aggravating factors that enhance the penalty for murder to the death penalty may change and only those aggravating factors at the time of the crime can be considered. Last, in some rare cases, the defendant may have been a juvenile at the time of the crime and is now an adult. Although this does not necessarily prohibit prosecution of the defendant as an adult, the determination of whether the person is to be tried as a juvenile or an adult is a complex legal issue.

The prosecutor needs to research, evaluate, and consider any lesser crimes associated with the case. This is all part of preparing the prosecution for every possible scenario that may come to light through the defense. As with the investigation, the scientific method approach, where all theories are identified and addressed, will go a long way toward securing a conviction.

Cold cases typically have evidentiary issues that may have a significant impact on prosecuting the case.

Chain of Custody

The rules of evidence require that physical evidence presented at trial be the same evidence that was collected at the crime scene. Proof of this is made by demonstrating by written record each time the evidence changed hands. Any missing link in the chain of custody permits the defense to challenge the integrity of the evidence, causing in some cases the complete exclusion of the item.

Memory of Witnesses

If a witness testifies that he or she can no longer remember a fact about a case, it is possible to refresh the memory by reading previously recorded statements. In cold cases, however, the witness, so many years older, may no longer recall anything about the incident, and thus police records cannot be used to create a memory that does not exist. Prior statements to the police can in certain circumstances be used as the past recollection recorded; however, recent Supreme Court decisions have greatly curtailed testimonial hearsay statements (*Crawford v. Washington*, 541 U.S. 36 [2004]).

Loss of Evidence

Evidence is occasionally lost or destroyed in the course of time. The loss of evidence has obvious impact on the ability to prove each element of the crime beyond a reasonable doubt. However, evidence that is deliberately destroyed creates the defense argument that the evidence would have been exculpatory for the defendant and therefore the defendant's due process rights have been violated. In some cases, the willful destruction of evidence may result in dismissal of the charges.

Other

What about your witnesses? How reliable are they today versus at the time they were originally interviewed? Were their initial statements written, and did they sign their statements, or were they possibly recorded electronically? As previously mentioned, the passage of time frequently helps the cold case investigation process and this should be used to your advantage. Consideration might be given to utilizing hypnosis to help significant witnesses recall what they saw or to try to engage the witness with the cognitive interview process as a means of assisting their recall.

What about the age of the defendant at the time of the murder versus now? As reflected in the Martha Moxley case, which will be described next, Michael Skakel was barely 15 years old at the time of the murder, but was 39 when he was arrested. Do you try him as a juvenile or as an adult? Skakel's defense attorney filed motions claiming that there was a statute of limitations of 5 years in effect in 1975, but the trial court denied the motion. These and many other legal decisions will have to be made, and the more thorough the prosecutor is in searching out these possibilities, the more likely she or he will obtain the conviction.

The Murder of Martha Moxley (A Case Study)

To illustrate some of the legal considerations of a cold case, we use as a backdrop the murder of Martha Moxley that occurred on October 30, 1975, in Greenwich, Connecticut. Some 27 years later, Michael Skakel was convicted of her murder. The case and the trial drew national attention, but what was not evident were the legal hurdles and legal preparations that went into presenting this very difficult case to a jury. One of the attorneys for the state was Christopher L. Morano, formerly of the Connecticut State's Attorneys' Office, Rocky Hill, Connecticut.

Over the years, even before this case came to trial, Morano had lectured at the Henry C. Lee Institute of Forensic Sciences on how a prosecutor should go about preparing and prosecuting a cold case. His lecture focused on the role of the prosecutor as being two-pronged: (1) what laws existed at the time the murder was committed versus (2) what laws exist today that may present problems in the prosecution. Read "Martha's Story" about the legal hurdles encountered and the trial procedures utilized by the prosecutors in this case.

Martha's Story[4]

On October 30, 1975, in the town of Greenwich, Connecticut, the night before Halloween was commonly known as "mischief night" or sometimes "doorbell night." On this particular evening, 15-year-old Martha Moxley and her friends set out for a night of harmless pranks—spraying shaving cream and throwing eggs and toilet paper around the neighborhood before stopping at the home of Tommy and Michael Skakel.

The Skakel brothers were well known in the neighborhood for their behavior and lack of discipline—and also because they were the nephews of Ethel Skakel-Kennedy, widow of the late Senator Robert F. Kennedy. The Moxleys and Skakels lived in Belle Haven, a gated community in Greenwich, an affluent area of town where Hollywood actors lived and former President George Bush grew up.

Sometime between 9:30 and 11:00 that night, Martha left the Skakel house. Home was only 150 yards away, but Martha never made it. Martha's body was found the next day under a tree in her back yard. Her jeans and underwear had been pulled down, but there was no apparent evidence of sexual assault. She had been beaten so hard with a 6-iron that the shaft had shattered. A jagged piece of it was used to stab her through the neck. Police later learned that the club was part of an expensive Toney Penna set, which had belonged to Tommy and Michael Skakel's mother, Anne. Mrs. Skakel had died of cancer two years earlier, leaving her husband Rushton to raise their large and reportedly unruly family. Their son, Tommy, then 17, was said to be the last person seen with Martha. According to Martha's diary, she had fended off several past attempts by Skakel to "get to first and second base," said Martha's mother, Dorothy Moxley. The day Martha's battered body was found, Greenwich police did a cursory search of the house with Rushton Skakel's permission, but they never obtained a warrant to do a thorough search. This lack of a warrant in the investigation led to accusations of "special treatment" for the well-connected, influential family.

The Skakels stopped cooperating with police in early 1976 and have since refused to be interviewed. Emanuel Margolis, the family's attorney, said Tommy Skakel, now in his early 40s and living in Massachusetts, has always insisted he had nothing to do with the murder. But police had other suspects besides the Skakels. They questioned a young neighbor of the Moxleys and a 24-year-old tutor living with the Skakels. They also considered transients off Interstate 95. "We have a circumstantial evidence case, with no witnesses," said Donald Browne, the Special State Prosecutor. "Unfortunately, we have circumstances that point in several different directions." Perhaps new DNA tests done on evidence from Martha's clothing will point investigators in a certain direction, he said.

For years, nothing was mentioned about the case publicly. Residents of Greenwich did not speak of the terrible crime which had gone unsolved. Meanwhile, in 1983, the *Greenwich Time/Stamford Advocate* hired a freelance writer named Len Levitt to write an article on the case. The article appeared to be "so controversial" at the time that the publishers shelved it until 1991 when a rumor started floating around Greenwich that William Kennedy Smith (then facing a rape charge on which he was acquitted in Palm Beach, Florida) knew something about the murder. This rumor proved to be untrue, but sparked curiosity into Martha's unsolved murder. The article stirred new public interest.

The case regained national attention in 1993 when *A Season in Purgatory*, Dominick Dunne's best-selling novel based on the murder, was published. Dunne, who later wrote extensively about the O.J. Simpson trial, encouraged Mark Fuhrman to investigate the case. Throughout the years, Greenwich police and the state prosecutor never stopped searching for clues. But leads were few and far between, and the investigation appeared to be going nowhere.

In September 1994, Detective Frank Garr retired from the Greenwich Police Department. Garr left to take a job with the State Prosecutor's Office as an investigator, taking the Moxley file with him to work on the case full time. Several years later, former Los Angeles police detective Mark Fuhrman started to write a book about the case. Fuhrman had gained notoriety when his controversial testimony allegedly tainted the prosecutions' case against O.J. Simpson. Throughout his investigation of Martha's murder, Fuhrman promised that his book, *Murder in Greenwich*, would name the killer. But Greenwich authorities did not welcome this "outsider." "I have no reason to talk to Mark Fuhrman," snapped one investigator who refused Fuhrman's request for an interview. Authorities told Fuhrman they would not cooperate because they did not want to jeopardize their ongoing investigation. "What they are actually doing," Fuhrman said, "is hiding old mistakes." He continued, "If you know there was a mistake and you leave it that way because you won't allow yourself to say or admit that you made a mistake, then that's a catastrophic mistake."

Retired police detective Stephen Carroll, one of the few cooperating with Fuhrman, agreed that investigators made mistakes but insisted that the Skakels did not get special treatment. "Mistakes happened," Carroll said, "because of inexperience." The department had not handled a murder in 30 years. "I think it was bungled from the first moment," author Dominick Dunne said. "It was a small community then. And this was an amazingly rich family."

Fuhrman's interest in the case gave Moxley's family new hope that the murderer would finally be brought to justice. "He really has stirred things up, and if he can focus attention on the case, we're grateful to him," said the victim's mother, Dorothy Moxley. "That's my life, these days," she said, "The hope that someday we'll know who did this." Fuhrman's book *Murder in Greenwich* was released in 1998 and publicly named Tommy's younger brother, Michael Skakel, as the prime suspect.

At the same time another book, *Greentown*, was published. Written by a Greenwich native, Timothy Dumas also pointed to the possible involvement of one of the Skakel brothers in the crime. In May 1998, a three-judge panel approved prosecutors' request for a grand jury investigation. The state's chief court administrator then appointed Bridgeport Superior Court Judge George N. Thim to investigate evidence gathered by the Greenwich police and the state attorney's office. Such grand juries, it should be noted, are rare in Connecticut and are only used when other investigative procedures have failed. In such a grand jury case, Judge Thim was able to subpoena witnesses to testify about the killing. Prosecutors in Connecticut do not have subpoena power and have complained they have been paralyzed in the Moxley case because they have been unable to force witnesses and suspects to speak with them.

The grand jury interviewed more than 50 witnesses in connection to the case. Some reportedly former residents and staff of the Elan School in Poland Springs, Maine, where Michael Skakel allegedly confessed to the murder while undergoing rehab. The grand jury held hearings behind closed doors for 18 months, and officially ended on December 10, 1999. Judge Thim then had 60 days to decide whether he believed there was enough evidence to make an arrest.

On January 19, 2000, at a 9:00 a.m. conference held in Bridgeport, Connecticut, prosecutors announced that an arrest warrant had been issued for "an unnamed juvenile." Attorney Mickey Sherman told reporters that his client, Michael Skakel, was the person in question and that Skakel was on his way to Connecticut to surrender to authorities. Later that same day, Michael Skakel surrendered to Frank Garr of the State Prosecutor's Office at the Greenwich Police Department. Skakel was booked on charges of murder (as a juvenile) and posted $500,000 bail before being released.

On May 4, 2002, the trial began in Norwalk, Connecticut, and took four weeks. On June 7, 2002, after 4 days of deliberations, the jury found Michael Skakel guilty as charged. Bail was revoked, and Michael was confined to Garner Correctional Institution in Newtown, Connecticut, awaiting sentencing on August 9, 2002. Mickey Sherman immediately announced that he would appeal.

Then, on August 29, 2002, after 2 days in court, Michael Skakel was sentenced to 20 years to life in prison. On January 14, 2006, the Connecticut State Supreme Court unanimously upheld the murder conviction of Michael Skakel.

The major obstacle was Skakel's age (15) at the time of the murder. Should he be tried as an adult or as a juvenile? The prosecution won its argument that he should be tried as an adult. Thoroughly evaluating the laws at the time of the crime and how they may have changed over time coupled with evaluating the pros and cons of various decisions that could be made are all paramount to mounting a good prosecution.

It seems that many of us in society are visual people in that we can relate better to what we see than what we hear. Therefore, the ability to provide demonstrative-type evidence to the jury will go a long way toward convincing the jury of the merit of the case. In earlier chapters, we mention the value of the diagram to illustrate the pre-, peri-, and post-crime behaviors analysis; in this chapter, we discuss the format of reports as being comprehensive and persuasive. In the Skakel case, the Connecticut prosecutors went down a new road and presented an interactive multimedia presentation the likes of which had never been seen before. "As witnesses were testifying, prosecutors displayed on a large screen photographic evidence, maps, diagrams of the murder scene, and other demonstrative evidence that they were able to summon from a CD-ROM."[5] This process of presenting the evidence in the case from the beginning to the end of the investigation not only made it more compelling to watch, but also made it believable, as the jury was captivated by the presentation and were able to see for themselves what was being presented.

The defense has argued unsuccessfully that the multimedia presentation, especially during the prosecution's closing, convicted Skakel. On the other hand, the prosecution will argue the circumstantial evidence coupled with Skakel's own words were what defeated him in the eyes of the jury. There is, however, no doubt that the interactive multimedia presentation was crucial in that it provided the evidence of the case in demonstrative manner that all could see and understand.[*]

Conclusion

The bottom line is that cold cases are not as easy to prosecute as hot cases where the evidence and witnesses' memories are fresh. Cold cases present a challenge to us all and especially to those who are charged to investigate and prosecute within the confines of the law, then and now. The best approach is to have a prosecutor on the cold case team, and when that is not possible, a prosecutor should be brought on board as soon as possible to ensure a prosecutable case and not just an arrest that may never get into a courtroom.

Endnotes

1. www.judiciary.state.nj.us/criminal/charges/homicide2.doc. Accessed September 1, 2009.
2. Steve Chancellor is a retired U.S. Army Criminal Investigation Command (CID) agent, a former detective with the Mississippi State Police, and director of the Mississippi Bureau of Investigations Cold Case Unit, Batesville. At the time of this writing, he is employed by the U.S. Army CID in Atlanta as a civilian advisor to the organization.

[*] On November 21, 2013, the *New York Times* reported that a judge in Connecticut had ordered Michael Skakel be released from prison and put on bail to await a possible retrial. This was predicted upon the judge's belief that Skakel did not receive a fair trial in May 2002 as his lawyer failed to adequately represent him. Regardless of the results of these most recent motions and hearings, the fact remains that cold cases present a challenge to our legal system.

3. Schubert, Anne Marie. 2004. In *Cold Case Homicides*, Chapter 5, Richard H. Walton, Ed. CRC Press: Boca Raton, FL.
4. http://www.marthamoxley.com. Accessed August 31, 2009. Courtesy of marthamoxley.com and Tom Alessi.
5. Carney, Brian, and Neal Feigenson. 2004. Visual persuasion in the Michael Skakel trial: Enhancing advocacy through interactive media presentations. *Criminal Justice Magazine, 19*(1).

Conclusion

14

JAMES M. ADCOCK AND SARAH L. STEIN

In this book we have provided the reader with some concepts as to how and why we find ourselves in the middle of having over 185,000 unresolved murders since 1980. And we have given, as a possible remedy, the utilization of three cold case evaluation models to be used as a guide to help solve some of those unresolved cases. There is no question that organization with supervision is absolutely critical for the process of investigating these crimes if we are to reduce the number of unsolved murders. In cold cases, organization and utilization of the methodology as prescribed in the scientific method are paramount to conducting a good evaluation and follow-up investigation that will lead to the conviction of the offender.

In the book titled *Death Investigation*, Adcock wrote about utilizing the scientific method but realized that this method was geared almost entirely to science-based projects. Therefore, he developed The Scientific Method for Investigators.[1] Although this process targets ongoing or hot cases, if followed, it can be applied very effectively to cold cases as well.

The Scientific Method for Investigators

1. Obtain from witnesses the accounts of what happened.
2. Based on these accounts anticipate the questions you will be asked by others so you can properly collect and record the physical evidence.
3. Collect and record the physical evidence.
4. Formulate hypotheses about the events that occurred and anticipate the questions you will be asked.
5. Determine whether or not the witness statements are consistent with the physical evidence; gather more information or evidence as needed.
6. Through the process of verifying witness statements and admissions/confessions consider the evidence at hand and disprove as many hypotheses as you can.
7. Formulate an assessment (final hypothesis) to a reasonable degree of certainty, recognizing the existing limitations.

Where do we go from here? As we look forward to lecturing and meeting other detectives from various jurisdictions to teach them and learn from them about how they cope with the cold case problem. We feel it is imperative that we have a constant exchange of information and ideas so we can improve on the processes we presently use. We must continue to strive to resolve these cases and from them, hopefully, learn why they did not get resolved in the beginning, setting the stage for future training that will assist in reducing the number of cold cases. Although some cases will never be resolved due to a lack of evidence or witnesses, many are full of valuable pieces of information that will lead to a resolution and a conviction. But these leads have to be explored beyond just the physical evidence capabilities. The key is organization of the information and adequate guidance from experienced supervisors.

As a sidelight, it is interesting to note that in the many adventures of Sherlock Holmes there are several comments and quotes that are very pertinent today to the art and science of criminal investigation. So, in parting ways, we would like to leave with you food for thought by providing Sherlock Holmes's Seven Vital Lessons,[2] coupled with our comments regarding each:

> "One should always look for a possible alternative and provide against it. It is the first rule of criminal investigation." (Dr. Watson in "The Adventure of Black Peter," an investigation set in 1895.)
>   - Looking for that "alternative" goes not only to validating your theory of the crime and making a better case for the prosecution but also helps to eliminate theories the defense may raise at trial.
> "I never guess. It is a capital mistake to theorize before one has data. Insensibly one begins to twist facts to suit theories, instead of theories to suit facts." (Derived from statements made during "The Sign of Four" and "A Scandal in Bohemia," both set in 1888.)
>   - Oh how true! Do not guess, let the evidence tell you what has happened, and always look for the "alternative." The pieces of the puzzle must fit.
> "Use your time sparingly. Determine what you have. Then determine what you need. Then look for what you need in the place where it must be." (Watson's chronicles do not provide this axiom, and it is possible that he never heard it until after his last recorded adventure with Holmes. However, it has been stated often during the Sherlock Holmes Mystery Weekends at The Victorian Villa Inn, Union City, Michigan.)
>   - Our time is precious and sometimes costly, so if you are properly and adequately organized you will save time.

"There is nothing so important as trifles. Never trust to general impressions, but concentrate yourself upon details." (Derived from statements made during "The Man with the Twisted Lip," set in 1889, and "A Case of Identity," set in 1888.)

- Sometimes the little nuances of an investigation are the "trifles" and they should be fully explored. Collectively these details make the case.

"Singularity is almost invariably a clue." (From "The Boscombe Valley Mystery," set in 1888.)

- I interpret this to mean that when one specific thing stands out by itself, it is most likely a significant "clue" to be evaluated and further explained. If you do not use it, the defense counsel will.

"It is a mistake to confound strangeness with mystery. The most commonplace crime is often the most mysterious, because it presents no new or special features from which deductions may be drawn." (From in "A Study in Scarlet," Watson's first recorded case with Holmes, set in 1881.)

- A lot of this is self-imposed by the investigators through their prejudices, improper techniques, or lack of attention to details. Do not make it out to be something it is not. Look beyond the forest for the individual trees.

"When you have eliminated the impossible, whatever remains, however improbable, must be the truth." (From "The Sign of Four," Watson's second recorded case with Holmes, set in 1888.)

- Ah, the scientific method at work. Again and again I have stated that you must apply the scientific method to your investigation and/or evaluation. As you eliminate other possible theories of the crime, your theory becomes prominent and foremost as the truth to what really happened.

Remember, with all of these cases, no stone should be left unturned and no family should be left wondering what happened to their loved one.

Endnotes

1. Adcock, James, and Arthur S. Chancellor. 2013. *Death Investigation*. Jones & Bartlett Learning: Boston, MA.
2. Adapted from John C. Sherwood's essay "Sherlock Holmes's Seven Vital Lessons" (2009). As found in Dean Jones' dissertation submitted as partial requirement for the award of MSc in Police Science and Management at the Institute of Criminal Justice Studies, titled "Reviewing the Reviewers, The Review of Homicides in the United Kingdom."

Appendix A: Establishing a Police Gray Squad to Resolve Unsolved Homicide Cases[*]

Take a quick mental inventory of your area and think about the homicide cases that made the news for a while. Did all of them have suspects who were arrested, prosecuted, and adjudicated? Were there any that slipped through the cracks because no suspects developed early in the case? How many unsolved homicides are there in your county? If your inventory struck one or more cases you might be interested in the experimental program in Tulsa, Oklahoma, that challenges a select group of citizens to come up with answers.

Before looking at the program you might want to continue with your assessment of the situation. Are there more unsolved cases than your personnel can reasonably work on? Have all of the unsolved cases been reviewed annually to determine if witnesses and evidence are still available? If you are on top of things, you will find that all of the cases are open and still being pursued. On the other hand, you may find that some unsolved homicides are still assigned to detectives who have retired or been reassigned years ago. You may not be able to locate hard copies of the case file in your working case section.

What can you do if the inventory places you in the second situation of dealing with missing files and stale assignments? First, you need to establish whether you really want to open up this job of resolving the unsolved cases. If you are the decision maker you may decide it is just too much work. You may be working under orders from above to get the old cases moving or reacting to outside influences requesting action. Whatever the reason that brought you here to the decision, you have to gauge the level of commitment to the project. It will be time consuming and, in some cases, traumatic to revive the old investigations.

Hopefully, you will choose to revisit the unsolved homicide cases in your area to bring about a resolution. Leaving them be brings up some unpleasant descriptions of inaction. So, just what can you do with the old cases using your current personnel? You can crack the whip, wheel in the overtime

---

[*] Provided by Detective Eddie Majors, Tulsa Police Department Gray Squad (Cold Cases), Tulsa, Oklahoma, on January 11, 2010.

money barrel, or look to other resources. The Tulsa Police Department chose a combination of the three, with emphasis on the third option.

The department's goal was to form a specialized squad of volunteers who work under loose supervision on the unsolved cases. Squad members would be selected for their personal skills and adaptability. They would be given full authority to review any unsolved homicide as long as the lead investigator approved. And, in some circumstances, they would be given authority to contact other agencies and witnesses regarding the cases.

Selecting squad members was relatively easy. When word was spread in the city about the volunteer project, applications flooded in. This was not a file clerk, paper-copying group, although at times it seems everyone does that. It was more of a think-tank concept. The department soon had a retired businessman-volunteer who was content to organize case files into an orderly system. He scratched his head more than once as detectives brought in unsolved homicide files, in boxes, file drawers, and assortments of binders.

By quietly going through boxes of reports and diagrams he established an existence in the squad. The role he played in the squad was much more important than an organizer. He quietly opened the door from the outside, into the semisecret circle of the homicide detectives. It was months before he was really accepted in the squad. The first sign of acceptance was a lunch invitation to eat with the squad. From that day on, the barriers fell and others would follow in his footsteps.

Once the door was open to the squad others were selected from the growing list of volunteers. Team coordinators could be open to unusual applications. A practicing general surgeon indicated he would like to work with the squad. He brought a new term to homicide detectives: anal retentive.

A retired engineer/land surveyor completed the application and was quickly selected. His computer drawing skills soon endeared him to crime scene detectives. A medieval history professor emeritus from the University of Oklahoma drew the squad's attention with his multipage curriculum vitae. He was quite accomplished in writing for publication. The professor's first summary of a complicated case drew considerable attention from supervisors in the detective division. He used footnotes to call attention to crime scene photos and reports.

The selection process for new squad members should remain open. You never know when you will find jewels on the surface. Three new gray squad members in Tulsa were also selected for their unique skills. A retired postman with insomnia created and built a database of all Tulsa homicide cases beginning in 1963. A graphics and mapping supervisor for a government agency began an exchange of digital graphics and photos between the department and outside organizations. And, finally, an energy marketer for a large oil company rounded out the squad by beginning a chronological review of all unsolved cases from 1970.

As the selection process for new squad members was continuing there was considerable attention given to their blending in with regular homicide squad members and supervisors. Job assignments and pairing of tasks was critical because a small slip could set the project back years. There is no room for groupies in the squad who are there just to feed on the excitement. Each person, paid or volunteer, must have a job and stick to it.

Gray Squad members were selected for their self-starting and creativeness in problem solving, much the same as the regular homicide detectives. More tension was observed during the project when volunteers required too much supervision or partnership than any other time. They were accepted most when they came in quietly, did their work, and left. The work grew from limited access in cases to a true partnership between them and the regular detectives. As their involvement increased, the need for their initial background checks and waivers grew more apparent to supervisors. They became part of the investigative squad, recognized on the street by uniformed officers as the Gray Squad.

One question asked by many of the department representatives looking at the Gray Squad concept is "How do you handle the hours?" The Tulsa Police Department's guidelines for volunteers recommend a minimum number of hours per month. The Gray Squad supervisors found it easier to be more flexible with working hours, probably due to the flexible lives of the homicide squad members. Call outs in the middle of the night, weekends, and holidays are the rule, instead of the exception.

Volunteers in the squad are more comfortable when they can work at home or in their own offices. They often have their own computer systems and specialty programs that aid them in doing their assignments. Some volunteers have preferred the seclusion of their own place to sink into thought while analyzing complex details of events from years ago. For whatever reason they choose, flexibility seems to be the key to their happiness. The retired squad members do not want to punch the clock, but they do want some discipline of days they work. Maybe that serves to get them moving out of the house a day or two a week.

Squad meetings for Gray Squad members have been very inspirational as members present their cases or projects to the whole squad. Some of the members only see each other during the meetings, although they read about the accomplishments in newsletters and monthly reports. Gray Squad members should also be invited to participate in command staff briefings when they have been working on particular cases under discussion or review.

The squad meetings and command staff briefings are also a forum to present new ideas or concepts developed while working the unsolved cases. The Tulsa Police Department Homicide Squad found many new techniques developed by Gray Squad members were applicable to new cases. Breaking homicide cases are now started with a system of organization, labeling, and presentation that was developed by the Gray Squad for unsolved cases. Using the system enables supervisors or others in the squad to pick up a case from any detective's desk and find reports quickly and efficiently.

Some Gray Squad members are advancing toward another level of case management and presentation while working on the unsolved cases. They have begun using digital reproductions of old crime scene photos, aerial photos, maps, and sketches in combination with written materials to organize volumes of information. Their goal is to prepare the way for whole homicide investigations to be stored on individual compact computer disks. This task, if presented from the outside, would probably be laughed off by homicide squad members as unworkable. But the ideas, presented by people they work with and trust, begin to take on merit.

The open-minded approach to new concepts and methods has not come quickly or easily. It has come because the managers of the Gray Squad were willing to bring in freethinking people from the outside and tell them there was a job to be done. They did not describe how to do the job because that would have only cloned another homicide detective with the same training previous ones received. Managers of the Gray Squad program should be just as willing to open the door and let the squad interact.

The managers and supervisors of the Gray Squad program will want to see a return for their investment. Is this group of outside people worth the time and effort we have to devote to them? The simplest way of looking at the Gray Squad is the number of cases they have solved, or caused to be solved. Of course, this is the path most administrators will choose to take, since it is easily quantifiable.

There will be other cases that are reviewed and found to be unsolvable with the information and manpower available. The case may require travel or testing that is out of reach of the department's budget. Then, there are cases listed as unsolved when the known suspect is deceased. If there is no possibility of prosecution, the administrator may elect to close the case. The administrator may find satisfaction in reviewing the numbers of solved or resolved cases. There will be an enormous amount of pride and respect attached to a project that shows a sincere desire to remember homicide victims, their families, and friends.

Beyond the moment there are other reasons for establishing a police gray squad. Each person, each community, longs to make their mark on the future. By bringing new minds and ideas into the law enforcement agencies of our country, we can expand the use of technology and processes to include new breakthrough developments.

References

Heim, Roy. 1991. Concepts for the Gray Squad. Tulsa Police Department Homicide Squad Report.

Huff, Mike. 1998. 1998 Homicide Squad Annual Report. Tulsa Police Department.

Appendix B: Dutch Victim Assessment Form—Victimology

Victim Assessment Form

1. General

First and last names:	
Sex:	man/woman

Nickname:

Date of birth: Place of birth: Country of origin: Nationality:

Address and domicile: How long has victim lived here: With whom has victim lived here: Relation to other inhabitants: Who has keys to the living:

Description form filled out and attached:	yes/no
Prior arrests/antecedents:	yes(attached)/no
Any reports in BPS:	yes(attached)/no
Informant CIE:	yes/no

2. Childhood and Upbringing

Relationship diagram made and attached:	yes/no
Who took care of the victim during childhood:	
Social economic status of the family:	
Striking with regard to the way of upbringing:	
Relationships within the family: Noteworthy changes among these relationships:	
Remarkable events during childhood (divorce, incest, death of family member, etc.):	
Relation to child protective services:	
Sort of neighborhood victim grew up in:	
(Religious) Beliefs or cultural backgrounds: Does victim have certain ideals? Does victim actively enforce these ideals?	

3. Marital status and (Family) Relations

Family diagram made and attached:	yes/no
Timeline of events concerning family and partner made and attached:	yes/no
Timeline victims (intimate) relations made and attached:	yes/no
Married/living together/single? Been married? Reason of divorce (if applicable): Children? Raised by whom and how?	
How did partners interact? Domestic violence?	

Did victim have extramarital relations? With whom and when? Was this known to others?
Did the family have certain habits? How were they reflected? (Visiting dates, birth-, family-, holidays, outings, reunions, etc.)
Did victim have much contact with family members? With whom?
Where else has the victim been living?
In what type of neighborhood does victim live now?

4. Known Friends and Acquaintances

Diagram of friends and acquaintances made and attached?	yes/no
Nature or relationship and connections between victim and friends/acquaintances?	
Frequency of contact between victim and friends/acquaintances?	
Does victim have many friends? Were these loose contacts?	
Did friends have the same lifestyle?	
How did victim interact with coworkers?	
Did victim easily make contact with strangers?	
Did victim have friends/acquaintances with whom victim shared secrets?	
Did victim use cell phone? What was the usage?	
Did victim use chat boxes? Which ones?	
Did victim frequently use e-mail? E-mail address(es)?	
Does victim have enemies due to recent or previous conflict?	
Involved in any form of criminal behavior?	
Fellow suspects? Any relations from prison?	
Was victim part of a criminal network?	

5. Sexuality

Gender identity:	male/female
Sexual orientation:	hetero/homo/bisexual
Sexual preferences:	
Describe the sexual activity of the victim:	
What was victim's position toward people from the other sex?	
Has victim been sexually active just before the crime? In what way?	
Did victim behave sexually provocative? When/in what situation?	
Did victim use sexist language? When/in what situation?	

6. Physical

Describe victim's appearance:
Any unusual physical characteristics? Describe them.
Physical anomalies, limitations or disabilities? Describe:
Noticeable physical characteristics such as scars, tattoos, piercings, birthmarks, etc.? Describe them:
How did victim normally dress at work, in spare time, while going out, while sleeping, and while working out?
What was victim's preferred type of clothing?
What is the general opinion of people surrounding the victim on the victim's appearance?
Did victim like wearing noticeable clothes?
Did victim like wearing provocative clothes?
Did victim ever wear clothes from expensive brands?
Any particulars regarding the care victim put into physical appearance?
Left or right handed?

7. State of Health

What was the physical condition of victim?
Did victim have any particular disease?
Were there any recent changes in health?
Any noticeable weight loss or weight gain?

Provide an overview of all illnesses/medical conditions over the last 5 years:
What health institutions did victim frequent?
Sleeping habits? Any recent changes?
Alcohol use? What type, amount, and frequency?
Drug use? What type, amount, frequency?
Use of medication? What type, dosage, frequency?

8. Psychological Background

Did victim have any sexual deviances? Were they actively attended to/pursued?
Any fears or phobias?
Did victim grow afraid/scared about anything recently?
Noticeable personality traits?
Was victim ever diagnosed with any mental defects/illnesses?
Was victim ever admitted for a mental disease?
Did victim ever receive treatment from a psychiatrist or psychologist?
Tendency to self-destructing behavior?
Did victim ever talk about suicide?
How did victim cope with own emotions?
Did victim express emotions to people around victim?
Has victim ever been depressed, despondent, or strikingly negative?

9. Education

What educational programs did victim follow?
How did victim perform during education?
Any completed studies? Reasons why (not)?
How did victim interact with peers?
Was victim ever in military service?
If so, where, when, what rank, and in what position?
Any traumatic experiences?
Was victim part of an elite unit?
Did victim refuse to enlist? On what grounds?
Dishonorable discharge?
Did victim have trouble with authority? Describe how?

10. Mobility

Victim's mode(s) of transportation (and type)?
Describe the state of mode of transportation?
Describe victim's use of public transportation?

11. Work

What is the employment history of victim?
What is the current profession?
Does training/education/studies victim enjoyed match these professions?
How did victim perform at work?
Did victim need to interact with coworkers?
Was victim involved in social activities at work? In what role?
What would loss of job mean to victim?
How often did victim stay home sick during current career?
When was the last time victim stayed home sick, and for what reason?

12. Spare Time

Describe hobbies/skills?
Describe victim's nightlife/going out habits: pattern and frequency?
Did victim play sports? What sports? Which tasks did victim perform here?

Did victim work as a volunteer? Describe:
What stores or companies did victim frequent?
What places are connected to victim's lifestyle?

13. Finances

Did victim have any sources of income? Which ones, and how much?
What was victim's expenditure and what did he spend it on? Was this in line with victim's income?
Did victim carry money around? Describe the amount and the way victim carried it around:
Did victim have any debts? With whom and how much?
Did victim have a life insurance policy?
Did victim have any outstanding loans?
Did victim have an inheritance to leave behind?
Are there any striking aspects of victim's recent income and expenditure?
Did victim have a tendency to save? How much savings does victim have?
Did victim spend a lot of money on a certain item/items? What item(s)?

14. Behavior and Personality Traits

Was victim victimized before (and was this relevant to this crime)?
How would victim react to being attacked by a stranger?
How do others describe victim's behavior?
How do others describe victim's personality?
Did victim have ambitions? What were they?
Who/what did victim admire?
What setbacks did victim encounter?
What was important to the victim?
Did victim value privacy?
Did victim have an impulsive personality? How did this manifest?
Did victim have a tendency to compete/argue?
Did victim display emotions? At what occasion?
Did victim take risks?
Did victim have a tendency to lie?
How did victim behave under stress?
Did victim put trust in others, or mostly in him/herself?
Did victim have different moods (happy, afraid, upset, or angry)?
Did victim stick to principles?
Did victim find norms and values important?
Did victim have a daily routine or recurring activities?
Did victim have any unusual or striking habits?
Did victim have certain rituals?
Is there anything striking with regard to the victim's lifestyle?
Did victim make thoughtless decisions?
Did victim make any thoughtless purchases?
Did victim make any thoughtless statements?
Did victim often speak with raised voice? In what situations?
Did victim use coarse language? In what situations?
How did victim deal with violence?
Was victim violent or subdued?
In what situations, and in what way?
What is the estimated level of the victim's social skills?
Did victim allow him/herself to be easily pushed around? In what situations?
Was victim assertive?
Was victim compliant? In what situations?
Did victim have a certain reputation?

Was victim naturally curious?
Did victim have particular fears?
Did victim show any distrust to persons or institutions?
Did victim like to be the center of attention? In what situations?
Did victim often take charge? In what situations?
How did victim position him/herself relative to any authority that was exercised on victim?
Did victim have a negative attitude toward a certain race? Which race?
Did victim have a negative attitude toward a certain sex? What sex?
Did victim have a negative attitude toward a certain age? What age?
What type of music did victim prefer?
Did victim read literature? What literature?
Did victim have any technical knowledge/skills? How much?

15. Crime Scene

Were any dates of particular importance to victim? Which dates and why?
Was victim supposed to be at the crime scene? Why?
Was victim often at the crime scene? Was it part of victim's routine? Why?
Was there a special reason for the victim to be at the crime scene? What reason?
Are any items/goods of victim missing? What items/goods?
Did victim regularly use the same routes? Describe the routes.
Did victim have means of transportation on the day of the crime? Describe means.
Any other remarkable details prior to the crime?

The following questions are relevant only to the composer.

Approach, Attack, and Risk Assessment

What clothing did victim wear when victim was found?
What route was used by victim on the day of the crime?
What was the phase/moment of approach?
Remarkable characteristics of perpetrator during the approach?
Did victim notice the approach?
What actions did the perpetrator perform during the approach?
Are there any traces (etc.) that confirm this mode of approach?
Was this a familiar location to the perpetrator, or was this unknown territory?
In what way was the victim attacked by the perpetrator?
How much violence did the perpetrator use?
Were any tools/devices/other means used during the attack?
Did the perpetrator bring any means to gain/keep control over the victim?
Was any material used that was found at the crime scene?
How did victim react to the attack?
Any signs of resistance by the victim?
Any signs that the perpetrator was familiar with the crime scene?
Does evidence indicate that the perpetrator made the victim perform certain actions?
Was there a dialogue? What did it consist of?
What were the exact words used by the perpetrator?
Estimation of risk for victim based on lifestyle?
Estimation of risk for victim based on incident risk?
Estimation of risk for perpetrator based on MO risk?
Level of skill of perpetrator?
Victim risk level?

Appendix C: Suspectology: Case Study 2

Case Synopsis

On December 10, 1991, Mr. Bryan P. Ruff was reported missing from his place of employment at the Kennecott Smelter to the Salt Lake County Sheriff's Office by his supervisor at Burns Security, Mr. Michael Farnsworth. Authorities were told by Mr. Farnsworth that Mr. Ruff was checked in on at 1830 hours by Sergeant Todd Fallows and Shannon Hughes. At 2000 hours Sergeant Fallows contacted a Ms. Becky Westwood to inform her that the guard shack at the Beta Gate was unmanned and that she needed to cover the remainder of Mr. Ruff's shift; Ms. Westwood arrived at the shack at approximately 2050 hours.

At the guard post, Salt Lake County Sheriff's investigators discovered the following: an opened soda, an open bag of pretzels, and a cold cup of soup. There was no sign of a struggle. Additionally, Mr. Ruff had left his hard hat inside the guard shack, which he was required to wear if he had left to walk around the premises of the smelter, indicating he may not have left of his own volition. While the sheriff's investigators were perusing the guard post for further evidence, a woman claiming to be Ruff's wife, Jennifer, called the post and asked if Bryan was all right and if they had located him yet. Authorities were able to trace the number the woman was calling from back to one Dale Bradley, a coworker and friend of Bryan Ruff. When the woman posing as Mr. Ruff's wife called again, authorities asked if she was Christi Bradley, wife of Dale Bradley. She confirmed that she was and that she did not think she would be able to get any information if she used her real name. Authorities were eventually able to make contact with the real Jennifer Ruff who stated her husband should be at work and had no idea where he might otherwise be found.

As the investigation into Mr. Ruff's disappearance continued, contact with Mr. Dale Bradley was made to determine his whereabouts on the evening of Bryan's disappearance. Mr. Bradley stated that he was at home in his apartment with Christi and members of a band that she did hair and makeup for. Mr. Bradley stated he was very upset that Christi was leaving the following day to go on a tour to Austin, Texas. As such, Mr. Bradley left the apartment and decided to go for a drive before going to marriage counseling.

Mr. Bradley claims he went to the location of the marriage counseling office but it was locked so he went to the library at the University of Utah to listen to inspirational tapes about renewing relationships and marriages. Mr. Bradley then claimed he had a minor car accident in his red Camaro and called a friend, Bill Easton, to come pick him up. While waiting for Bill, Mr. Bradley became ill and threw up near his car. After Mr. Easton picked Mr. Bradley up, he claimed he went home.

Further into the investigation, it was discovered that Mrs. Christi Bradley was having an extramarital affair with Mr. Bryan Ruff. The spouses of both Mrs. Bradley and Mr. Ruff suspected infidelity; Mr. Bradley apparently confided in Mr. Easton that he had seen the love letters between Christi and Bryan.

Alas, without the body of the victim, and sound circumstantial and physical evidence to tie Mr. Bradley and/or Mrs. Christi Bradley to the crime, the authorities had little to go on. Fortunately, however, on July 10, 1993 (2 years after the crime), campers in the area known as "Five Mile Pass" in Utah discovered what appeared to be a human body. The Salt Lake City County Sheriff's Office responded and discovered that the remains found by campers were indeed human, and dressed in jeans, a shirt, without shoes, and the security jacket with Bryan Ruff's badge number on it would have been (before it was disturbed by the campers) over the head of the victim when he was buried. At autopsy, it was discovered that the victim had been shot five times in the chest and left forearm. The weapon used to dispense Mr. Ruff was estimated to be a .22 caliber. The body was positively identified via dental records provided by the family as well as through personal effects found with the body such as Bryan Ruff's wallet, and a cowboy boot that was identified by Mrs. Ruff as being her husband's.

In early 2005 Detective Todd A. Park initiated a cold case investigation into the abduction and homicide of Mr. Bryan P. Ruff. Detective Park reinterviewed several key witnesses in the case including the now ex-wife of Mr. Dale Bradley, Christi. As 14 years had passed since the crime and the former Mrs. Bradley had some ill-will toward her ex-husband, she was much more forthcoming with investigators about where Dale had been that day and what she and Bryan discussed on the phone prior to his disappearance. Christi stated that Dale cleaned out his car the night Bryan went missing, which he never does. Additionally, Christi stated that while she was on the phone with Bryan, Bryan suddenly stated that there was another employee that just showed up and he needed to go. Christi iterated that Bryan sounded very scared when he said this. From that moment Christi believed that Dale had done something to Bryan. This was confirmed later by Mrs. Jennifer Ruff, who stated Christi had called her in a panic the night Bryan disappeared and kept saying over and over, "I know Dale did it! I know Dale did it!" Another significant past interview examined by Detective Park was conducted with Mr. Dale Bradley, whose story about the night in question had conveniently changed.

As to the forensic evidence in the case, Detective Park wisely chose to view and examine each piece of physical evidence collected during the initial investigation as well as at the body disposal site at Five Mile Pass. While examining the boot that was positively identified as Mr. Ruff's by his wife, Detective Park noted a fairly obvious amount of red paint chips and smears adhering to the boot that Mr. Ruff had been wearing the evening of his death. It was determined via forensic analysis that the paint residue found on the boot belonging to Mr. Ruff was a match to the red paint that coated the exterior of Mr. Bradley's vehicle. Further, it was discovered via ballistic examination of one of Mr. Bradley's .22 caliber firearms (he had several) compared with casings and other projectiles recovered from the scene that there was a match to one of Mr. Bradley's firearms.

With all evidence in place against Mr. Bradley, he was tried and convicted for the abduction and murder of Mr. Bryan Ruff. The following section will classify the typology of the crime itself and subsequently delve deeper and provide pre-, peri-, and post-offense behaviors to support the assertion that Dale Bradley did, in fact, willfully abduct and murder Bryan Ruff as retribution for having an affair with his wife Christi.

Classification and Summation

Based on the peri-crime behavior as depicted in Table C.1, this crime is classified as a power-assertive offense. The classification of this homicide as a power-assertive offense is justified given the following factors: the decedent was shot five times in the chest, indicating that the sole purpose of the attack was to kill the victim, not hurt or torture him as we would see in the case of an anger-retaliatory or anger-excitation offender. Further, there was no additional damage to the decedent's corpse, again indicating that the attack was purposeful and involved little emotion. What we will do next in this segment is provide readers with a chart diagramming the pre-, peri-, and post-offense behavior in this case that all indicate the involvement of Mr. Bradley

Table C.1 Peri-Crime Behavior Outcomes for Case Study 2

1. Bryan Ruff reported missing at 2050 from Kennecott Smelter.
2. Nothing is disturbed inside the guard shack—lunch and hard hat.
3. Ruff said to Christi on the phone he had to go, someone was there and sounded scared.
4. Evidence: Red paint chips found on victim's boot match Bradley's Camaro.
5. Evidence: Soil samples from Bradley's vehicle matches soil samples collected at Five Mile Pass.
6. Evidence: .22 matches the projectiles that killed Ruff. Christi Bradley called Jennifer.
7. Ruff's face was covered with his jacket before burial at Five Mile Pass.

in Mr. Ruff's murder. However, before we begin, a caveat to this case must be made. In most cold case files, there are an abundance of suspects, and this process is ideally for narrowing the suspect pool to those who fit the classification of the crime (e.g., power-assertive, power-reassurance, etc.). With this case, it was fairly clear from the beginning that the suspect was Dale Bradley; that being said, although we could not whittle down our suspect pool, the exercise is still useful in identifying the perpetrator by combining his behaviors and the evidence recovered from the crime scenes. Now, let us proceed with the pre-, peri-, and post-offense behaviors that would be Mr. Bradley's undoing.

Theory of the Crime

Based on the aforementioned correlations demonstrated by the pre-, peri-, and post-offense chart derived from materials found within the case file, we can surmise that the crime occurred as follows: Mr. Bryan Ruff arrived for his shift as a security guard with Burns Security at the Kennecott Smelter. Phone records indicate he had several conversations with Christi Bradley that evening. Also during the course of the shift, Mr. Ruff opened a package of pretzels, a soda pop, and a cup of soup for his dinner. He was confirmed to be at his post at 1830 hours by Sergeant Todd Fallows and Shannon Hughes. At approximately 2000 hours Sergeant Fallows reported that the guard post was unmanned. The last telephone call from Mr. Ruff while at his post was logged at 1824 to Christi Bradley's home, and the call to report Mr. Ruff missing also came from the post and was logged at 1952 hours. Therefore, we can speculate that between 1830 and 2000 hours, an hour and a half time window, Mr. Ruff vanished.

From the crime scene we can postulate that one of two events occurred: Mr. Ruff went willingly with his assailant or he was coerced by the threat of a weapon. In either scenario, it is quite likely that Mr. Ruff knew his assailant, as there would be few random robbers that would happen by a guard post by a rural smelter in the evening hours. In the file, it was noted that the mileage from the guard shack to the gravesite was 54 minutes (46.4 miles). The call that Dale Bradley made to Bill Easton at Gino's Bar was logged at 2229 hours and lasted 2 minutes and 52 seconds—plenty of time for Mr. Bradley to commit the murder, dump the body, and return to the general vicinity of the smelter.

As to the forensic evidence in this case, Locard's principle of exchange never seems to fail in that paint from Mr. Bradley's car was found on the victim's shoe, the casings from Mr. Bradley's .22 matched those found in the victim's remains, and the soil samples taken from Mr. Bradley's trunk matched the chemical makeup of the soil near the grave site at Five Mile Pass.

Table C.2   Pre-Crime Behavior Outcomes for Case Study 2

1. Ruff and Bradley were initially good friends—went mountain biking, etc.
2. Bradley suspected Christi and Ruff were having an affair.
3. Bradley came into the possession of several firearms including .22s.
4. Bradley allegedly showed Bill Easton love letters between Christi and Ruff.
5. Jennifer Ruff discovers months after Ruff's disappearance through phone records that Ruff had been vacationing with Christi in California and Las Vegas.
6. The suspect vehicle was identified as a red Camaro belonging to Bradley.

Table C.3   Post-Crime Behavior Outcomes for Case Study 2

1. Bradley said they weren't that good of friends, just hung out sometimes.
2. Bradley got drunk and was throwing up outside his Camaro.
3. Christi Bradley called Jennifer Ruff and kept saying "I know Dale did it!"
4. Bradley repeatedly changed his story about the night Ruff disappeared (later admitted he was at the shack).
5. Bradley cleaned out his vehicle the night of Ruff's disappearance.

What most likely occurred was that Mr. Bradley had discovered Mr. Ruff was having an affair with his wife Christi (most likely via the love letters he had discussed with Mr. Easton days earlier). Mr. Bradley left his home to go see Mr. Ruff to straighten things out. Christi remained at home with her band members. Mr. Bradley most likely forced Mr. Ruff at gunpoint into his vehicle (the red Camaro), possibly with a struggle given the victim's shoe made a dent in the driver's side door (which Mr. Bradley tried to explain away as having backed into a gas station pole and bending the door backward). Once the two had arrived at File Mile Pass, Mr. Bradley shot Mr. Ruff five times in the chest and arm. One interesting thing to note is that Mr. Bradley placed Mr. Ruff's coat over his head before burial; this could indicate one of two things: remorse or shock on the part of Mr. Bradley; or, in keeping with the anger-retaliatory typology, this behavior could indicate that Mr. Bradley did not want Mr. Ruff to look at him as he left; that is, he wanted to have the ultimate control over his victim, even in death. Once Mr. Ruff was dead and buried, Mr. Bradley drove back to his stomping grounds, but became ill and called Bill Easton to come get him, and he returned home.

Correlations Between Pre-, Peri-, and Post-Crime Behaviors

Let us now examine how the correlations between pre-, peri-, and post-offense behaviors demonstrate that the unlawful killing of Mr. Ruff was committed by Dale Bradley. For pre-offense behaviors, let us begin with number one: "Ruff and Bradley were initially good friends—went mountain biking, etc." This behavior is correlated with post-offense behavior #1, peri-offense

Table C.4 Consolidated Pre-, Peri-, and Post-Crime Behavior Outcomes for Case Study 2

Pre-Crime Behavior	Peri-Crime Behavior	Post-Crime Behavior
1. Ruff and Bradley were initially good friends—went mountain biking, etc.	1. Bryan Ruff reported missing at 2050 from Kennecott Smelter.	1. Bradley said they weren't that good of friends, just hung out sometimes.
2. Bradley suspected Christi and Ruff were having an affair.	2. Nothing is disturbed inside the guard shack—lunch and hard hat.	2. Bradley got drunk and was throwing up outside his Camaro.
3. Bradley came into the possession of several firearms including .22s.	3. Ruff said to Christi on the phone he had to go, someone was there and sounded scared.	3. Christi Bradley called Jennifer Ruff and kept saying "I know Dale did it!"
4. Bradley allegedly showed Bill Easton love letters between Christi and Ruff.	4. Evidence: Red paint chips found on victim's boot match Bradley's Camaro.	4. Bradley repeatedly changed his story about the night Ruff disappeared (later admitted he was at the shack).
5. Jennifer Ruff discovers months after Ruff's disappearance through phone records that Ruff had been vacationing with Christi in California and Las Vegas.	5. Evidence: Soil samples from Bradley's vehicle matches soil samples collected at Five Mile Pass.	5. Bradley cleaned out his vehicle the night of Ruff's disappearance.
6. The suspect vehicle was identified as a red Camaro belonging to Bradley.	6. Evidence: .22 matches the projectiles that killed Mr. Ruff R3. Christi Bradley called Jennifer.	
	7. Ruff's face was covered with his jacket before burial at Five Mile Pass.	

behavior #2, and peri-offense behavior #7. As to post-offense behavior #1, Bradley had stated that he and Ruff were not good friends and had just hung out occasionally. This statement is contradictory to the pre-offense behavior and indicates that he is trying to distance himself emotionally from the victim. As to peri-offense behavior #2, that nothing was disturbed at the crime scene, this is correlated with pre-offense behavior #1 because the victim and assailant were good friends—meaning that nothing was disturbed at the scene because Ruff ostensibly may have gone willingly with whomever confronted him (or the individual had a weapon). Finally, as to peri-offense behavior #7, that Ruff's jacket was covering his face prior to burial, this indicates some level of remorse by the killer, indicating that there may have been a personal relationship between the victim and the assailant prior to the killing.

Moving on now to pre-offense behavior #2, that Dale suspected that Christi and Ruff were having an affair, this is correlated with post-offense behavior #3, that Christi Bradley called the victim's wife on numerous occasions saying that she knew that "Dale did it"—meaning that Christi had

Ruff Homicide
Person of Interest: Dale Bradley

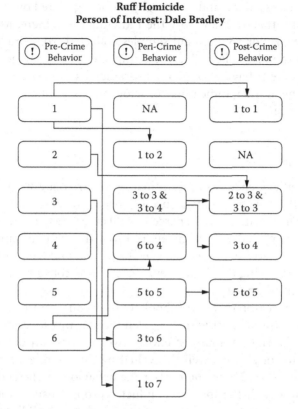

Figure C.1 Crime behavior correlations for Case Study 2.

knowledge of the motive behind the killing. As to pre-offense behavior #3, that Mr. Bradley was in possession of several firearms, including .22s, this is correlated with peri-offense behavior #6, that the .22 projectile found at the crime scene matched Mr. Bradley's R3. Finally, pre-offense behavior #6, that the suspect vehicle was identified as the red Camaro belonging to Mr. Bradley, is correlated with peri-offense behavior #4, that red paint chips found on the victim's boot belonged to Mr. Bradley's Camaro.

Next we will examine the correlations between the peri-offense behaviors and pre- and post-offense behaviors. Remember, peri-offense behaviors are those associated directly with the crime itself, and do not relate to any one particular individual, though in this case it was pretty evident who the perpetrator was from the initial reporting. The first behavior is #3, that Mr. Ruff said to Christi that he had to go and sounded scared, which correlates to post-offense behaviors #3 (Christi called Mr. Ruff's wife saying she knew that Dale did it), and post-offense behavior #4, (Mr. Bradley repeatedly changed his story about the night in question and finally admitted he was at the guard shack). These behaviors are correlated because Mr. Ruff appeared to have known his assailant, and further, by sounding scared on the telephone, one could infer that he knew why the individual was there. Moving on to peri-offense behavior #5, that soil samples collected from Bradley's vehicle matched soil samples collected at the dump site, this behavior is correlated with post-offense behavior #5, that Mr. Bradley had cleaned out his vehicle the night of the murder, indicating consciousness of guilt and the attempt to destroy evidence.

Conclusions

While physical evidence is so incriminating we are not always blessed with the silver bullet that pinpoints a specific suspect or perpetrator. In fact, as previously mentioned, nearly 70 percent of all cases are made without having that great element and are ultimately resolved through circumstantial evidence that cumulatively points to a specific person and frequently gets convictions. But gathering this "other" evidence is time consuming and requires a great amount of tenacity.

It is for that reason that in this book we have concentrated on the "other" evidentiary items that exist within a given murder investigation. An avenue where, with the right amount of effort, investigators can obtain sufficient information to convict by carefully evaluating the pre-offense behavior, the crime behavior (peri-), and the post-crime behavior. In the end it provides the investigator with the tools to conduct a proper suspect interview and reveals a lot of circumstantial pieces of the puzzle that will fit together. This process is not the only way to resolve a homicide investigation but is a valuable tool in the investigator's toolbox that should be fully explored.

Appendix D: Sample Cold Case Evaluation Report

April 6, 200_

Review and Analysis

This report was prepared based on a complete review of all of the associated case documents including individual police reports, statements, scene photographs, investigative notes, and other evidence accumulated during the course of this investigation as provided by the requesting agency. *The resulting analysis and opinions reached in this case were based solely on that material in conjunction with sound investigative principles. The receipt of additional materials, evidence, and/or information not previously provided may result in altered findings and opinions.*

Background

This review and analysis is based on the murder investigation of Sally SMITH, a white female, aged 54 years, initiated in 1993, by the Mitchell County Sheriff's Office and the State Police. On this date Mrs. SMITH, hereinafter referred to as JANE, was shot to death, by two rounds from a 12-gauge shotgun, inside her residence located at 61 Vincent Road, Mitchell County.

On April 5, 2006, the scene was revisited by the undersigned, for additional scene establishment photographs and possible reconstruction type activities. Figure D.1 is the crime scene, as found in 1993. Figure D.2 is the scene April 2006. The house structure is basically the same as noted during the crime scene examination; however, the front enclosed screened area has been removed and the exterior has been repainted.

Opinion

The physical, testimonial, and circumstantial evidence accumulated during this investigation are all indicative of a staged domestic homicide, wherein

Figure D.1

Figure D.2

the offender murdered the victim and then staged the scene to resemble an *"interrupted burglary scenario"* in an attempt to steer suspicion and the investigation away from the real criminal act of homicide.

This opinion was reached following careful review and analysis of all aspects of the incident including: the victim, the crime scene, the crime itself, possible motives, and other criminal behavior and dynamics noted during the review process and is explained in detail in the following report.

Victimology

One of the first steps in the Review and Analysis process is to conduct a Victimology assessment relating to the victim. The purpose of a Victimology assessment is to determine what, if anything, elevated an individual's potential for becoming the victim of a violent crime and then to place the victim on a risk continuum from low to moderate to high. This assessment is based on both factual and subjective criteria about the victim, but generally speaking it is the overall lifestyle of the victim and the situational dynamics present at the time of the crime that are the primary focus in making the assessment.

The Victimology assessment is based on such factors as JANE'S age, overall health and physical characteristics, marital status, maturity level, education, work and employment history, socioeconomic level, childhood family background, current family living conditions, strong ties to the local community, residence type and location, general overall life experiences, ability to handle stressful situations, and other personality characteristics. All of JANE'S reported physical, social, and personality characteristics were coupled with the fact that she was not a drug or alcohol abuser, was not otherwise engaged in criminal activity or other high-risk behaviors such as alcohol or drug usage, and at the time of the murder she was at her own residence, engaged in routine domestic activity. She was slightly physically disabled with an underdeveloped left arm due to polio as a child, but this did not appear to play any part in this crime whatsoever. Based on all of these factors as described above, JANE should be assessed as a low-risk type victim.

There are two important factors for low-risk type victims to take into consideration. First, because there is little chance they should ever come into contact with an offender in their routine lives, low-risk victims are often specifically targeted by an offender. Second, the lower the risk factors for the victim, then the higher risk factor for the offender. This means the offender must take more risk in order to victimize this person rather than others who may be more vulnerable or accessible.

The Crime and Crime Scene

The next stage of the Review and Analysis process is to conduct a thorough and detailed review of all of the facts and circumstances surrounding the crime itself and the crime scene. The crime scene initially appears to be one where the victim arrives home and unsuspectingly interrupts a crime in progress. The obvious conclusion sought by the offender in this case is that once the crime was "interrupted," the "burglars" must have murdered the victim and then fled the house.

The offender contemplating committing a crime and then staging a crime scene to avoid detection typically believes it is necessary to do so because without it, they would almost immediately be considered as the prime or most logical suspect. There are hundreds of different possibilities of staging scenes; most methods used are dependent upon the intelligence and capabilities of the offender and overall availability of other methods. Non-criminals who stage crime scenes, however, typically do so in a criminally unsophisticated manner and generally tend to stage a scene based on uncomplicated themes such as an accident, suicide, interrupted burglary, or home invasion type scenario.

The offender alters the scene by changing, adding, replacing, removing, or even creating some type of physical evidence that establishes what *they think* should, could, or would happen or result if the criminal act being staged actually occurred. Because they typically do not know what real crime scenes look like, their knowledge is limited to what they have seen on TV and in the movies and read in crime novels or newspapers. With most of the staged scenes revolving around very basic themes, they are usually quite discernable from real crime scenes because of the inconsistent nature with much of the forensic and behavioral evidence presented by the offender. Some examples of the inconsistent circumstantial and behavioral evidence found in this investigation follow:

First is the fact that the only crime that was really *completed* during this entire event *was the victim's murder.* Other than the movement of the weapons to appear as if they were the interest to the offender, nothing else of value was reportedly taken from or disturbed in the scene excepting the removal of the murder weapon. The one item that was apparently stolen from the house was a shotgun that was likely used as the murder weapon. This means that the "thieves" only took from the house the one item of evidence that could positively link them to the crime scene.

Second is the limited amount of time that would be necessary for the offender to actually stage the scene. Because the staging consisted of only obtaining a blanket, collecting the weapons from wherever they were located, moving them into the living room area, and then breaking the window to simulate forced entry, the entire scene could be staged in just a few minutes, giving the offender ample time to escape and try to establish his alibi. Figure D.3 shows that other than the broken window, the guns found in the living room are the only signs that anyone else was in the house and the only evidence of any crime other than homicide.

Third, for profit-type burglars by nature are generally nonconfrontational. They tend to commit their crimes during times and at locations where

Figure D.3

people are not likely to be at home or around. They do not want to confront a home or business owner during the course of their crime. This is why businesses are most frequently broken into at night after they are closed, or on the weekends when there is no one there. By the same token, this is the reason why most home burglaries are actually committed during *daylight hours on work days* while the resident is at work or away from the house, or take place during the late evening/early morning hours as to not "confront" the residents. *Therefore, the general time of day and day of week for the incident make this event highly unlikely to have occurred as staged.*

This is the type of information that is known by the police, but not necessarily understood or is common knowledge to the "non-criminal" attempting to stage a scene. The same thing is true about the actual murder. While burglars can and will react in a violent way if they are surprised or challenged by a resident during the commission of a crime, generally speaking they will avoid such personal confrontation if at all possible, usually only resorting to attacking if their route of escape out of the building/residence has been blocked or the resident somehow presents a physical barrier to their escape, or if the victim knows the offender.

Based on information supplied by family members in their earlier statements, JANE would likely be non-confrontational to the offender(s) if she did happen upon them in the act and therefore would present no threat to them or their escape potential. What would have been more consistent with interruption of this type of offender would be a physical assault, use of restraints to immobilize the victim; even forced sexual assault would be a possibility. The "ambush" or execution style of assault using a firearm under these circumstances is *not generally consistent* with these types of offenses.

In this particular situation, it is unlikely that JANE'S arrival would actually "surprise" the offender(s) in the act. This is based on the statements of Vicky Smith and Michael Peters, who reported that following the discovery of JANE, they could hear the ambulance and other vehicles driving toward the house on the gravel road. If this is the case, it is likely that the offender(s), if inside the house, would also be alerted to JANE'S vehicle as it drove toward the house, giving them warning and allowing them to escape prior to her entrance into the house. Figures D.4 and D.5 depict the residence as it appeared in April 2006 during the revisit of the scene. These photographs depict the gravel type circular driveway that leads to the house. A vehicle could clearly be heard as it entered the graveled driveway to the house. This was verified by the undersigned in April 2006.

If they (the suspect(s)) did not hear the vehicle approach, then they certainly would have heard her arrive at the house, exit her car, interact with the dogs, and then open the master bedroom door. Again, all of this activity outside should have alerted the offender and given him ample chance to avoid any confrontation with the homeowner and thus escape out the back door

Figure D.4

Figure D.5

without being seen. This would be the expected non-confrontational result. It is also clear that JANE had actually entered and exited the house several times while carrying in the various packages and her suitcase from her car. Each time she exited the house, it would give an offender another chance to make a clear escape and thus avoid any confrontation. *Again, this would be the expected course of action.* Once inside, JANE apparently set out several items of clothing on the bed and got some wrapping paper, probably to wrap presents. It is only then that she was "confronted" by the offender(s) and shot.

Figure D.6 is an original crime scene photograph depicting the master bedroom. Note the suitcase on the floor and recent purchases in plastic bags adjacent to the bed. Based on her physical condition, all witnesses confirm that the victim would have made several trips bringing everything inside.

It is also very important to consider that the master bedroom where JANE was murdered was not in the line of travel to the rear door and possible escape. Therefore, it was not necessary for the offender(s) to "go through" the master bedroom in order to facilitate their escape. So the entry into the master bedroom by the offender was really for only one purpose, and that was to kill the victim.

Fourth, unless the burglar was acting on specific knowledge about the activity of the homeowner/resident, it is almost inconceivable that a burglar would approach a house, especially in the rural part of the country, where most residents are armed, and that is illuminated with exterior and interior lights on, particularly if the exterior lights were the automatic motion sensor type (see Figures D.7, D.8, and D.9). Additionally, the fact that the interior lights were left on, as emphasized by Robert SMITH, and the venetian blinds were pulled down, preventing anyone from actually looking inside,

Figure D.6

Figure D.7

would again almost eliminate this house being chosen at random for a break-in, as the offender could not be certain that there was not someone inside. *Therefore, the presence of lights on inside the house would likely make this an unlikely target of opportunity.*

Fifth, few actual burglars attempt to break into a house where there is any evidence of dogs, unless they are especially prepared in some manner to

Figure D.8

Figure D.9

contain, incapacitate, or otherwise deal with them. It is not only the aspect of being bitten or physically injured, but there is also the danger that barking dogs would alert residents or neighbors. If somehow the offender managed to get inside the house without raising the attention of the dogs, it is almost inconceivable that the dogs would not respond to movement inside the house while the offender was inside rummaging around for the weapons. Certainly they would have picked up the offender's scent from around the house and upon JANE'S arrival at the house. It is just as likely, based on family statements, that JANE normally let the dog inside once she came home, and in fact the dog actually slept inside at night. Therefore, it is reasonable to assume that on this evening she would have also let the dog in the house. Once inside, it is inconceivable that the dog would not have noted the presence of a stranger inside the house and reacted accordingly. Even if JANE did not allow him easy access to the house normally, it is likely that the dog would have insisted on entry to the house to search out the intruder that he knew was inside, or would have noted the presence of a stranger inside the house once JANE opened the door. *Therefore, the mere presence of dogs at the scene, with no effort to deal with this threat, makes the house a highly unlikely target of opportunity for any burglar. Further, the normal actions of the victim to allow the dog entry into the house upon her arrival would have certainly resulted in a stranger being immediately "found out."*

It is also interesting to note that upon their entry into the house and after discovery of JANE, Michael and Vicky did allow Bosco (the Rottweiler dog) into the house specifically for protection. There was no mention of Bosco detecting any foreign scent inside the house, as there was no attempt on his part to go from room to room to follow the scent and thus find the intruder. This effort, usually a very frantic, intense search by a protective dog to locate the source of any strange scent, would be a normal reaction, but was absent during this event. Figure D.10 is the Smith's dog Bosco, taken outside the residence during the crime scene examination. Bosco was not normally placed on a chain or leash outside, and was free to roam around the surrounding area.

Sixth, there are several important inconsistencies, improbabilities, and/or impossibilities associated with the breaking of the rear window in order to gain entrance into the house. The supposed method of entry by

Figure D.10

breaking out the dining room window, although effective, was rather amateurish. Most experienced burglars know that the sound of breaking glass is very loud and very distinct. It is a sound that if overheard by anyone would likely gain their attention and cause them to investigate. Also, after the glass is broken, one must then reach inside the house, not knowing if someone is home, whether there is a dog inside, or even what method of locking the front door was used. The increased sound of the venetian blinds moving as the person reached through the broken window to open the front door should also be taken into account.

As described in crime scene notes, and visible in the scene photographs, the window itself was not completely shattered. Rather, only portions of the lower sash window were actually broken out, leaving some portion of glass still inside the window frame; thus the actual opening, or missing portion, was measured at 12″ at the base, curving up to an opening of 16″ at the top. A recent visit to the residence in April 2006 concluded that it was still possible for a perpetrator, once having broken the window, to reach through and unlock the door and unlatch the sliding bolt lock, thus allowing access to the house. This did take considerable effort, but it was possible. Figures D.11 and D.12 depict the reconstruction of the event, simulating the suspect reaching inside to unlock the rear door. The crime scene photographs from Nov. 6, 1993, showed a chair turned over in front of the window (Figure D.13). The location of this chair could have precluded the suspect from getting close enough to the window to stretch inside, as depicted in Figure D.14. This chair was likely placed in this position by JANE, who according to Nancy Woods placed a chair under the window to get access to the house when she was locked out approximately 1 month before her death.

Figure D.11

Figure D.12

Figure D.13

Figure D.14

It would actually be more consistent with a forced entry type burglary if the rear or other main entranceway door would have been forced open through kicking or ramming. As long as sound was not a factor, this method is just as certain, but it also eliminates the chance of being injured through broken glass. This method of creating evidence of forced entry is not generally used when staging a scene because the offender does not really want to cause serious or expensive damage to something he might have to repair at a later time.

Whether the window was used as a point of entry becomes almost moot when Deputy Jones' observations are taken into consideration. Deputy Jones reported that upon his initial arrival at the scene he went to the dining room area of the house where he observed broken glass on the carpet floor, broken out from the dining room window. Jones reported that he pulled back the blinds to look at the damage and was able to look in the backyard. According to Jones, there was heavy dew present that evening but he noted no foot-prints or obvious trail in the grass leading up to the window. If there were no footprints or foot tracks in the grass leading up to the window and back door area, the question then becomes how was the offender able to get to this point without making such tracks? The absence of foot tracks in the dew makes this scenario of forced entry at this point almost an "impossibility" to have occurred as staged by the offender. Figure D.15 depicts the rear door on April 5, 2006. At the time of the crime, this area consisted of a grass lawn with no steps or other plants. Figure D.16 depicts Deputy Jones at the rear door on November 6, 1993. Also note that the blinds are in the closed position.

Window glass found inside the dining room would be consistent with the force originating from outside. However, in this particular situation it is

Figure D.15

Figure D.16

also possible to stage the scene by opening the rear dining room door, walking outside onto the small steps, and then leaning over to break the window without having to actually step onto the ground first. This is the likely explanation as to how the window was broken from the outside, with no signs of tracks on the wet grass leading up to the window. It is just as important to note that in addition to no human footprints in the area, there were also no indications that the dog walked around this area. Again, this is almost inconceivable that the dog, even if he were away at the time of the break-in, once he returned to the house would not detect the scent of the person and follow it around to the rear of the house.

Again, this is often what happens to non-criminals who are attempting to stage a scene. The window is broken out to offer evidence of forced entry, but no thought is given to the wet grass outside and the lack of tracks leading to the window.

Seventh, the final aspect of the window being used as the entry point comes first from Ragan Smith's statement. She reported that after his arrival, Robert Smith eventually made his way from the master bedroom into the dining room area and was actually the first person to spot the broken glass on the floor and then pull back the blinds to see the broken window. He then opened the dining room door and walked briefly outside onto the steps and then returned and closed the door. This action is very important because Vicky stated very clearly that **she heard her father moving the latch on the door, prior to its opening.** She was very familiar with this sound and was able to describe it clearly in her statement. This is important because it provides clear indications that the door latch was **in place** and locked upon **Robert Smith's** arrival at the scene and neither Vicky nor Michael indicated they had locked the door after discovery of JANE'S body. Figure D.17 depicts the slide bolt that appeared on the rear door; as the slide moves to the left to unlock, there is a very distinct and loud metallic click as mentioned by Vicky in her statement. The current occupants reported that this was the same door and slide bolt that was in place the night of the homicide.

Confirmation comes from Robert Smith's own statement. He states unambiguously that prior to his departure from the house, he made sure the **dining room door was latched.** The significance of this statement is clear. The door latch was locked as he departed and was in place when he returned hours later after the alleged break-in. However, once access to the house was made by the offender, **it is inconceivable** that the *offender then relocked the latch.* This is absolutely counter to normal *"burglar or offender"* type activity, which is to go around and **first unlock all** of the entrance/exit ways to facilitate their escape in case they are surprised or interrupted. Therefore, relocking of the "latch bolt" by the offender(s) is highly improbable. This is one of the best examples of something that someone staging a scene would

Figure D.17

not necessarily know or think about, and a good example of the type of commonly made mistakes.

It is surmised that after Robert Smith opened the dining room door to break the window out, he then closed the door and either "subconsciously" relocked the door latch or intentionally locked it to validate his later statement that he secured the entire house prior to his departure, without thinking about the glaring inconsistency of a thief locking the door behind himself.

Eighth, it is also very normal for the person staging the scene to actually be the one to initially find the evidence to support their efforts, such as Robert Smith's finding the broken window. This ensures two important things: first, they make certain that the evidence is brought to the attention of the police, and second, they place themselves at a location that any physical or trace evidence found in the area originating from them can be attributed to the fact they were legitimately in the area and had discovered some important evidence themselves.

No event happens in a vacuum, however. There are always events leading up to the homicide (particularly in premeditated events), and then there are events that take place during the actual homicide or acts of murder, and finally events that take place afterward. It is those events before, during, and after the homicide that are used to determine and identify the consistencies and inconsistencies in the circumstantial, physical, and testimonial evidence collected in the investigation.

Once establishing that the scene was staged, the next step is to begin to identify likely suspects. Part of any homicide investigation and analysis is the identification of likely suspects. For this analysis three factors were used to identify possible suspects. These factors are known as the *Motive*, *Opportunity*, and *Means*. Simply put, we are looking for a person who has a reason or motive to murder, who has the chance to commit the crime, and who has the ability or tools necessary to commit the crime. Each of these areas is discussed in detail below.

Motive

The motive is the actual underlying cause or reasons behind the death of the victim. There is always a reason (motive) behind the perpetrator's actions. Some of the more common motives for homicide include monetary gain, revenge, jealousy, love, sex and marriage, and/or some other interpersonal conflict between victim and offender. Often, especially in personal conflict-type homicides, there are multiple motives in play.

(*Note:* There are some crimes in which the actual or underlying motive is only understood by the perpetrator himself and may never be clarified until he is captured. Such better known examples would include the well-publicized Son of Sam, the Tate-Labianca murders committed by the Manson family, and the Zodiac murders.)

Robert Smith: There are several obvious motives present when considering Robert Smith as the likely suspect in this case, as addressed below:

1. Robert Smith had separated from his wife several years earlier and was currently living at another location. Although they were supposedly still openly communicating, there were multiple mentions of problems between the two, especially over money and the victim's spending habits. *(Note: The exact nature and extent of the problem was not fully covered in the investigative report.)* It appears that the Smiths were remaining married because of the children.
2. Robert Smith was seeing or having an affair with a much younger female, Virginia Paul, who had earlier worked for Smith at his pharmacy. It is not clear exactly when this "friendship" turned more intimate but at the time of the homicide it was an active, intimate, physical and sexual relationship. The importance of this aspect of potential motives is the fact that Robert Smith was still married to the victim at the time when this relationship was ongoing. The love, affection, and attention of a younger woman could have a considerable impact on an older middle-aged man.
3. Virginia Paul, the younger woman, was attending state college and was contemplating an upcoming graduation and employment in an overseas hotel. This type of employment would put her offshore and thus out of contact with Robert Smith for considerable periods of time. Note also that in her own detailed statement provided in 1993,

she indicates that she really had no long-term plans that included Smith, likely because at the time he was already married. Basically, this relationship was about to end in the foreseeable future because Virginia was going to graduate and move away.

4. Robert Smith was the policy holder of several large insurance policies on his wife. His wife was still the beneficiary on his life insurance, but following her death he stood to collect from several different policies. The exact amount of money received by Smith has not yet been fully and accurately determined. It is estimated that the various insurance policies were in excess of $500,000. Additionally, there was a smaller policy with Allstate, through Sears. There was money from her retirement fund from her private school, and money from the possible sale of all of the property from the various real estate holdings in their joint possession at the time of her death. A full accounting of all of the insurance, retirement, and real estate sales would be necessary in order to fully establish this aspect of motive, but indications are this would be a considerable amount, enough to get him firmly established in a new life without JANE.

5. Because of the presence of several juvenile children remaining living with his wife, if Robert Smith attempted to file for divorce, it is certain that he stood to lose a considerable amount of money. He would be liable for child support and perhaps alimony or spousal support, as well as a split of other marital property and assets. This would certainly include the monies from the sale of the pharmacy and any other assets jointly held. Further, it is likely that if he filed for divorce, his relationship with Virginia Paul would be revealed and according to her own statements this might be troublesome for her own family.

6. There is also brief mention in the report that JANE may not have been willing to give Robert a divorce for whatever reason. This needs to be explored further to validate before it can fully be appreciated as part of the motive for her murder.

An affair with a younger woman, a large amount of potential insurance money, and a dying marriage make very powerful motives for someone to commit murder. In many instances, only one of these factors is ever present.

Other Possible Offenders/Motives

As previously indicated, the scene, with the forced entry and layout of the weapons in the living room, was clearly staged to resemble a "for-profit" type burglary. Therefore, the motive for such an offender would be to steal some item of value in order to sell it or keep the item for themselves. However, what discounts this from being an actual for-profit burglary is the fact that nothing except the weapon used to murder the victim was actually stolen. Once the victim has been murdered or eliminated, what would stop the perpetrators from actually completing the crime they started?

Opportunity

Opportunity refers to the chance or ability to actually commit the crime. For instance, if the homicide occurs at a specific time at a specific place yet the suspect is known to be at another location and thus does not have the opportunity to commit the crime, they must be eliminated as a suspect, no matter the motivation. The only other way possible was if the suspect was involved with a coconspirator who agreed to kill the victim while the main suspect established an alibi.

For this case, Robert Smith had more than ample *opportunity* to commit the crime and still return to his house in order to attempt to establish an alibi, or verify his presence during the commission of the crime. His opportunity can be established in the following:

1. Documenting Robert Smith's activity in conjunction with other events helps to establish a substantial window of opportunity to commit this crime. JANE arrived back at the Peters residence at about 2100 following their return from the city. All witnesses agreed that JANE immediately loaded her packages from the Peters's car into her own vehicle and then departed for home. *Peters estimated that she should have arrived home at approximately 2115.*
2. Robert Smith further acknowledges he was at his daughter's house until 2120–2130 that evening and then departed to go to his pharmacy apartment where he lived.
3. Tracy Butler, the oldest daughter, stated that she called her mother's house at 2145 to make arrangements to bring her little sister home, but there was no answer. Since JANE should have been home at approximately 2115, the fact that she did not answer the phone is consistent with her time of death being prior to 2145.
4. At 2204, Robert Smith makes a phone call from his apartment to Virginia Paul, as verified through phone records; however, he has remained unaccounted for and has no actual alibi from 2120–2204 (over 45 minutes).
5. Even if we take the best estimates of everyone involved as to their arrivals, departures, or driving time from one place to another, *this still places the victim at the scene of the crime during the same time that Robert Smith has no independent alibi and no confirmation as to where he was during the time of the murder.*

6. Based on the relationship between Robert and JANE there would likely be no problem in Robert coming directly into the house and interacting with JANE for a few minutes. This would allow him a chance to make sure no one else was at home, locate and load the weapon, and then shoot her. There did not appear to be any signs of a struggle, intermediate means used to control or threaten, or any physical trauma to JANE. Based on the locations of injuries to her arms and chest, it is likely that JANE never saw the attack coming and had no chance to react, flee, or even try to defend herself before she was killed.

7. Further, the amount of staging found at the scene would take no longer then a few minutes to arrange, and then Smith could be on his way home to attempt to establish his whereabouts and alibi through the long distance phone calls. The distance from the crime scene (residence) to the apartment pharmacy is only 5 miles. Thus a driving time of approximately 5 minutes or less is consistent.

8. It is likely that Robert Smith may have gone by the house even earlier that evening, perhaps to see if JANE was home or not. As provided in his statement, Robert Smith stated that he was at his daughter's house and that he initially went home around 2030 because he was suffering from diarrhea. After using the bathroom he then made a phone call to Virginia Paul (noted in phone records at 2034). She was not home so he then returned to his daughter's house. *Note that he returned, but stayed less than 30 minutes before he departed again.* **This may be interpreted as trying to establish an alibi for his presence that evening**.

9. Further, because JANE traditionally worked and then came home and was usually in the company of her children, there were not a lot of opportunities for her to be murdered and not involve the kids. It is for this reason that November 6, 1993, was not necessarily the first instance when Robert may have gone to her house in order to kill her. There was another incident that was very similar to events earlier in 1993 when JANE was away at a game and was supposed to be home late. The events are described in Robert Smith's recorded statement given to detectives in 1993. The following is a direct quote from a portion of that interview transcript:

SMITH: Ah it was on a Friday night when the Academy played in the City.

Grant: Okay.

SMITH: And ah … JANE had told me, you know, to check on the house and so forth as usual and ah that BILLY was gonna spend the night with **DOUG ANDREWS**. That was the understanding that I had. Well sometime around 9 or 10 that night, ah I rode over to the house. I found BILLY's truck parked under the carport and I thought well DOUG came and picked BILLY up. Then I saw some lights change in the house and I knew somebody was in the house. Well I opened my console ... I was in my car. I opened my console. I took a 45 out and an extra clip and dropped it in my pocket. And sometimes I have guns in the trunk and sometimes I don't and I popped the trunk and the shotgun was in the trunk. I don't know how long it'd been there. BILLY said he may have put it there, you know, back in September sometime.

Grant: Um hum.

SMITH: We had ... We had been out shooting some. And ah ... And you'd have to see the trunk of my car to know that it could be there that long without anybody noticing it but I ... Anyway I ... I moved some stuff and there it was and I took it, I broke it down, it was loaded, I closed it up and I went to the carport door, the bed bedroom door.

Grant: Do you remember that it was loaded what kind of shots you was using?

SMITH: It was just two shells is all I know.

Grant: Okay.

SMITH: I mean it ... Ah ... In other words, I didn't take 'em out and look or anything and ah bit when ...

Grant: And you still had the 45 (inaudible).

SMITH: And I went to the door, and ah it was locked. Since I was checking the house, I did have my key with me that night. I unlocked the door and when I walked into the bedroom, PHYLLIS JOHNSTON, BILLY's girlfriend, came out of the dining room into the and she liked to have a heart attack when she saw me standing there. I mean they knew I was there, cause they were getting ready to leave and ah ... BILLY was several seconds behind. PHYLLIS went ahead and went outside. In other words, they both saw the shotgun (inaudible) And ah ... Ah ... I told BILLY that we needed to have a long discussion and he assured me that his mother knew that he was there watchin' movies with PHYLLIS. He had asked her before she left. Well ... I know this is a let's say falsehood. That sound ... Ah that's not JANE.

Grant: Yeah.

SMITH: I mean she doesn't believe in unchaperoned teenagers bein' anywhere by themselves much less at this house. And I said well we're gonna have a serious discussion about this. I think it's time for you to take the young lady home. And he assured me again oh yeah, she knew I was goin' to the video store ... But anyway that ... And ah ... I ... Checked the rest of the house and I left the gun there, cause it's really BILLY's gun. I gave it to BILLY years ago ah ... but ...

Grant: So you left the shot gun ... So that's been ... they played ... you're talking about playin' ball in the last month or two.

SMITH: Within the last month probably.

Grant: Yeah Okay. So that's the last time you saw it?

SMITH: It ... whatever night that was. I mean, like I said, I'd have to look at the schedule but I ah ...

Grant: But it was the night of the big game in the city?

SMITH: That was the only night that JANE stayed out of town, you know. And I was out at the house, you know, that late. Ah ... it ...

Grant: Did BILLY come back there and stay there that night?

SMITH: Yes.

Grant: Did you go back there with him?

SMITH: Ah ...

Grant: And tend to ...

SMITH: No JANE got home that night.

Grant: Oh Okay. Alright.

SMITH: I mean she was ... But she told me that they was probably gone be after midnight before they got home and they did get home before that. Ah ... But ah ... And BILLY's curfew is at midnight. Ah but Ah ... JANE was gone be home that night and she was home that night, but I was checkin' on it in the mean time to check it, you know, on BILLY. Like I said, that's kind of my job when she's out of town ...

Grant: Un hum.

SMITH: And I'm at home is ... I check on BIL ... Matter of fact, if I'm not gonna be at home, she makes BILLY stay with someone else, you know.

Based on the facts and circumstances, it is surmised that the actual murder event was not the first time that Robert Smith may have attempted to murder his wife.

Means

The "means" or ability to commit the murder and stage the scene in this particular investigation was centered on several very important factors. As stated previously in this report, nothing happens in a vacuum. There is always a before, during, and after for every event. No one wakes up one morning out of the blue and decides to kill his wife, rob a bank, or commit any other crime. There are usually a series of things that happen over the course of their life to bring them to that particular point.

The "means" in this case would refer to the actual weapon used to inflict the fatal injury. This was the most difficult element to evaluate because the actual weapon used was never found following the incident. It is assumed that the weapon used was the missing Browning Over/Under 12 gauge shotgun.

Figure D.18

As stated before, this was actually the only item that was ever reported as missing from the house. Since the weapon originated in the house and Robert Smith knew its location and the location of ammunition, it is clear that he would have the means available to commit the murder.

The weapon reported missing was located in Billy Smith's room prior to the event. Also present, according to witnesses, were shotgun shells found on the dresser inside this same bedroom. Robert Smith admittedly had recently placed the shotgun inside Billy's bedroom himself. This admission in Robert Smith's taped statement is very important when viewed as part of the "totality of circumstances," especially when the circumstances of how the gun came to be in the house were explained. Figure D.18 is a crime scene photograph that shows some of the ammunition that was readily accessible in the house.

What is also considered as "means" information contained within the investigation file documenting several other instances when SMITH may have been involved in criminal conduct and "staged" a crime. Examples include:

1. Intelligence reports from the State Narcotics Unit indicating that SMITH was believed to have staged burglaries inside his pharmacy as a way to explain away some 13,000 missing "pills" or controlled substances. The complete report is not available for review, but there is mention of a complaint from the Board of Pharmacy that they suspected this was going on. Furthermore, there are other intelligence reports that indicate that SMITH may have been involved in controlled substances distribution within his local area.

2. There is a further report completed in 1987 detailing an arson fire that supposedly destroyed some buildings owned by SMITH. There are indications that these buildings were insured for $50,000 and were totally destroyed during the fire. There is no follow-up on the initial report continued in the investigative file to determine the actual outcome of the investigation. But again, such crimes would follow along a pattern of "staged" scenes and contribute to the "means" aspect of the offender because it shows that he had experience in arranging evidence to suit the crime he was trying to depict.

Event Dynamics

Forensic Evidence

As part of the event analysis, a review was also conducted of the various reports from the Crime Lab covering the forensic examination of the physical evidence recovered. From the material provided for review there was no physical or forensic evidence presented that could positively link Robert Smith to JANE'S murder.

This, however, is not or should not be a surprise, as many times when interfamilial homicides are committed most of the traditional crime scene evidence becomes moot. For example, finding Robert Smith's fingerprints at the house or even on the guns found in the living room would be explainable since he had normal everyday access to the house as well as access to the guns. The same is true for any hairs and fibers, and even a small amount of blood from Robert Smith, if they found it at the scene, would be meaningless for the same reason—that he had normal access to the house, so any such evidence could be explained away through normal living.

Due to the circumstances surrounding the event, even if Robert Smith's clothing from that night was examined and glass fragments were found that matched the broken window, this could easily be explained away because he was allowed unescorted access to the house by the police because initially he was considered as a suspect. Therefore, any of that type evidence would be negated through actions of the suspect himself and overall dynamics of the event.

In this particular case, even potential firearm evidence is just about meaningless because the weapon used was a shotgun. This means there is very little chance that gunshot residue (GSR) would have been deposited on Robert Smith's hands or even clothing, even if he was checked the night of the incident. Further, because of the physical characteristics of a shotgun (that being a smooth-bore type barrel) and the use of "shot" or pellets, it would be impossible to actually match up the pellets recovered during autopsy to *any particular* weapon because they would not have picked up any of the striations that mark normal bullet projectiles as they pass through a rifle barrel.

Therefore, for this case, forensic type evidence is going to be of limited use or importance. The importance of the physical evidence found and documented at the scene, and there is actually a lot of it, is going to be in the general nature of the scene itself and how it relates to the overall dynamics of the event.

Event Dynamics

Offenders involved in staged crime scenes also tend to go overboard when they talk to the police, to place themselves in the best possible light. Often this will consist of positive statements regarding their relationship with the victim and emphasizing their effort to protect or care for the victim prior to the incident. Evidence of this sort is documented in several areas in this case:

First, Robert Smith was emphatic during both his written and oral statements to police that he did his best to make certain the house was safe and secure before he departed for what he thought was only going to be a few hours (as his wife was due home that evening sometime). He was also emphatic that every door was locked prior to his departure. In his written statement he makes a detailed point of listing every entrance/exit to the house, and what he did to make sure each was secured.

Second, Robert Smith made every effort to portray himself as a loving, attentive father, and a good husband, emphasizing the amount of time spent with his youngest daughter the night of the homicide. This is interesting because of Tracy's statement that she was surprised to see her dad come back to the apartment because she assumed that he would come back, honk the horn, and she would go outside and retrieve the books for the youngest daughter.

Third, Robert Smith commented several times as to the overall good relationship he had with JANE including the fact that he would come to the school two or three times a week to have lunch with her. This contrasts with other statements that this was not true or at least was a newer development.

Fourth, Robert Smith denied any physical confrontations with his wife, although there are several mentions in the reports of the children supposedly commenting on the physical violence.

Additionally, interviews with the Woods provided information to the effect that to their knowledge there had been no previous break-ins or attempted break-ins at the house previously or subsequent to the homicide.

Conclusion and Recommendations

This is an extremely difficult but prosecutable case. While there is no forensic evidence, there is an overwhelming amount of circumstantial and behavioral type evidence that if properly presented paints a very clear and damning picture of what really happened in 1999.

Accepting the premise that this was a staged crime scene, one has only to review the file to identify the one person who is likely involved.

Robert Smith had very strong motives for murdering his wife. No suspects have been identified who may have any motive to murder Jane.

Robert Smith had the means in which to kill her.

Robert Smith had the opportunity to murder his wife.

Robert Smith is the only one who could be seen as actually benefiting from his wife's death. He collected a great deal of insurance, collected monies from the sale of real estate and other funds, retained custody of his children, and was able to marry his girlfriend.

No other suspect has ever been identified.

No other similar case has been reported within the same area. There was no break-in before, no break-in afterwards.

Recommendations

Some basic recommendations are presented here. (A detailed investigative plan has been prepared under separate cover.)

1. A firm commitment by district attorney, sheriff's department, and state police to work and complete this investigation.
2. Formulation of a task force-type operation that includes all agencies that wish to participate, with all original documents, evidence, and information maintained by one agency for later prosecution.
3. Scheduling of meetings to review progress of the investigation, ensuring all leads are being identified and completed.
4. A complete analysis of the financial windfall experienced by Robert Smith, to include all insurance, sale of real estate, retirement, social security, and any other financial gains by Robert Smith.
5. Complete the investigative plan.
6. Add to the investigative plan as new information is developed.

Review and Analysis completed by:

Arthur S. Chancellor
Director, Cold Case Unit

Appendix E: Cold Case Scholarly Sources— Annotated Bibliography

Addington, L. A. (2007). Hot vs. cold cases: Examining time to clearance for homicides using NIBRS data. *Justice Research and Police, 9*(2), 87–112. http://jrsa.metapress.com.logon.lynx.lib.usm.edu/content/2r7pk7588p505395/.

Abstract: Very little attention has been devoted to studying factors associated with how quickly murders are cleared. This dearth of knowledge is mainly due to a lack of available data, especially at the national level. Currently the Uniform Crime Reporting Program is undergoing a large-scale conversion from its traditional summary system form of data collection to the National Incident-Based Reporting System (NIBRS). One benefit of NIBRS is that it enables law enforcement agencies to report incident-level clearance information, including the incident and clearance dates. The present study utilizes NIBRS data to compare characteristics of homicides that are cleared quickly with those cleared over a longer period of time and those that are not cleared. Findings from this exploratory study confirm the conventional belief that murders are cleared quickly if at all, as a large drop in the percentage of cleared cases is observed one week after a murder occurs. The present research also suggests that incident characteristics play a dynamic role in predicting not only whether a murder is cleared, but how quickly. These findings provide new insights for studying clearance and suggest policy implications. (p. 87)

Allsop, C. (2013). Motivations, money and modern policing: Accounting for cold case reviews in an age of austerity. *Policing and Society: An International Journal of Research and Policy, 23*(3). http://www.tandfonline.com.logon.lynx.lib.usm.edu/doi/abs/10.1080/10439463.2013.782211#.Ue1CDo2kpAE.

Abstract: Over the past two decades "cold case review conferences" have become an established component of how police forces respond to long-term unsolved major crimes. This article examines the place of cold case major crime reviews in UK policing in an age of austerity. In particular, it focuses on examining how police justify expending resource on these reviews, considering why particular motivations have been advanced and in turn what these reveal about modern policing. Informed by empirical data collected during an eight-month ethnographic study of a Major Crime Review Team and interviews with key actors involved in managing and conducting cold case reviews, the article suggests a typology of motives used to justify the continued investment in reviewing historic unsolved major crimes. The discussion concludes by considering what these motivations and their invocation reveal about the current policing practice.

Caglia, A., Stefanoni, P., and La Rosa, A. (2011). Cold cases: New technologies for DNA analysis allow the reopening and solution of unsolved cases. *Forensic Science International: Genetics Supplement Series, 3*(1), 230–231.

Daggett, M. (2007). Emerging forensic identification technologies: Heat shock for cold cases. NCSTL.org. http://www.ncstl.org/news/DaggettApril07.

Abstract: On any given day, there are as many as 100,000 active missing persons cases in the United States. Every year, tens of thousands of people vanish under suspicious circumstances. Viewed over a 20-year period, the number of missing persons can be estimated in the hundreds of thousands. More than 40,000 sets of human remains that cannot be identified through conventional means are held in the evidence rooms of medical examiners throughout the country. But only 6,000 of these cases, or 15 percent, have been entered into the FBI's National Crime Information Center (NCIC) database. Locating and identifying missing persons remains one of the most challenging aspects of forensic investigation. Several Federal programs have implemented procedures, guidelines, law enforcement tools, and resources for solving missing persons cases. A few main programs are summarized, including Combined DNA Index System (CODIS), the National DNA Index System (NDIS), National Center for Missing Adults (NCMA), National Crime Information Center (NCIC), and Integrated Automated Fingerprint Identification System (IAFIS). A newly-compiled cold case toolkit created by the National Clearinghouse for Science, Technology and the Law (NCSTL) at Stetson University of Law is an interactive component of the NCSTL Web site, and includes a series of links to cold case resources in the following categories: NIJ Resources, Law Enforcement Technology Used in Investigating Cold Cases, Police Department Web sites that Solicit Information from Visitors About Cold Cases, Cold Case Forms, Cold Case Investigation Training Opportunities, Psychological and Medical Resources for Families, Regional Cold Case Web Resources, General Cold Case Web Resources, and a Cold Case Bibliography. Each resource listed in the Cold Case Toolkit includes a direct Web site link, as well as information on the content of the resource and its applicability to solving cold cases. (p. 1)

Davis, R. C., Jensen, C. J., and Kitchens, K. (2011). Cold case investigations: An analysis of current practices and factors associated with successful outcomes, executive summary. Santa Monica, CA: Rand Corporation. https://www.ncjrs.gov/App/Publications/abstract.aspx?ID=260008.

Abstract: The study involved a national survey of law enforcement agencies that documented the range of ways that cold case work is conducted and how the various strategies affect cold case clearance rates. This national survey was followed by research in four jurisdictions that conduct large numbers of cold case investigations. At each site, hundreds of case files of solved and unsolved cases assigned to cold case squads were examined in order to identify factors that influenced the outcomes of cold case investigations. The study identified three types of cold case investigations that involved distinctive approaches. The identification of factors related to the success of cold case investigations was impeded by the failure of agencies to keep records on court filings, convictions, sentences, or the time spent on cold case investigations relative to the number of clearances obtained. This failure in recordkeeping is due largely to detectives switching back and forth between active and cold case investigations, such that data on case processing does not distinguish between active and cold case investigations. Two recommendations are offered for future research on cold case investigations. One recommendation is to conduct cost-effectiveness analysis of investigator time spent on cold cases compared to new cases. The second research recommendation is to assess the conviction rate for cold cases and determine whether involvement of prosecutors in investigations leads to a higher rate of convictions. 2 tables and appended table with data abstracted from cold case files. (p. 1)

Fuller, D.S. (1999). New crime-solving technologies help close "cold cases." *CLU (Criminal Law Update)*, *7*(4), 4–7. https://www.ncjrs.gov/App/abstractdb/AbstractDBDetails.aspx?id=187273.

Abstract: Until recently, when an unsolved case grew old the trail grew cold, and perpetrators went unpunished. With the 1990s came widespread use of high-tech crime-solving methods such as national databases, DNA testing, and the Internet. One advantage of cold case investigations is more time to track down witnesses and review evidence. A disadvantage is that the cold case detective must find fresh leads in cases that have long since gone stale. The San Antonio (Texas) Police Department posts cold cases on the Internet and their website invites tips via e-mail. In at least one case, this procedure contributed to solving the murders of two high school students—more than 1,000 days after the murders. While technology can help solve cases, much progress in solving cold cases still involves painstaking reexamination of evidence from case files and the efforts of seasoned, experienced investigators. The Texas Attorney General's Cold Case Unit is available, upon request, to assist and coordinate with local authorities, to establish multi-jurisdictional resources, and to provide training on cold case investigation. (p. 4)

Heurich, C. (2009). Helping local police departments solve cold cases. *Police Chief*, *76*(9), 42–47. https://www.ncjrs.gov/App/abstractdb/AbstractDBDetails.aspx?id=250776.

Abstract: NIJ's program entitled, "Solving Cold Cases With DNA" is dedicated to getting DNA science to the field for solving cold cases that have lacked the evidence needed to identify a suspect and/or build a case for prosecution.

Since 2005, NIJ has awarded almost $50 million to State and local police agencies for the purposes of identifying and reinvestigating older, unsolved rape and homicide cases that can be solved with modern DNA technology. Many agencies that have sought NIJ funding intend to establish a dedicated unsolved case unit or, in some cases, keep an existing unit operating. In 2007, NIJ funded the RAND Corporation in a project to identify key factors in developing a successful cold case unit. In addition to conducting a national survey of police and sheriffs' departments in determining what policies and procedures are most effective in solving cold cases, RAND is also focusing on four jurisdictions. Study results are expected by the end of 2009. Still, this article offers some advice from law enforcement agencies that have benefited from NIJ's funding of cold case efforts. Advice offered includes assigning detectives full-time to cold case units and developing a checklist for prioritizing which cold cases to pursue. Cases advised to rank high on the solvability scale include those not prosecuted because suspects or witnesses could not be located or were uncooperative in the original investigation; cases that might yield compelling evidence if new DNA techniques were used; and cases with latent fingerprint, ballistic, or DNA evidence that could be submitted to expanded relevant databases. (p. 42)

Innes, M., and Brookman, F. (2013). Helping police with their enquiries: International perspectives on homicide investigation. *Policing and Society: An International Journal of Research and Policy, 23*(3). http://www.tandfonline.com.logon.lynx. lib.usm.edu/doi/abs/10.1080/10439463.2013.771542?journalCode=gpas20#. Ue1Co42kpAE.
Innes, M., and Clarke, A. (2009). Policing the past: Cold case studies, forensic evidence and retroactive social control. *The British Journal of Sociology, 60*(3), 543–563. http://onlinelibrary.wiley.com.logon.lynx.lib.usm.edu/doi/10.1111/j.1468-4446.2009.01255.x/full.

Abstract: In this article an empirically grounded study of the police practices used when conducting cold case reviews of unsolved homicides is used to illuminate the key features of what is termed "retroactive social control." It is suggested that this mode of social control, that works by placing past events under new descriptions, is an increasingly important feature of how social control is being imagined and delivered, and is predicated upon the capacity to de-stabilize and re-write previous official definitions of a situation. Retroactive social control it is posited encompasses two intertwined dimensions: the social control of collective memory, in terms of what is remembered and how; and social control through memory, wherein the shaping of the past influences the enactment of control in the present. The focus upon police cold case reviews suggests how forensic evidence and new investigative technologies have played an important role in shaping the development of these innovative aspects of contemporary policing. As such, the empirical focus illuminates a broader trend relating to how developments in science and technology are affording new possibilities in ways that social control is conceptualized and conducted. (p. 543)

Johns, L. G., Downes, G. F., and Bibles, C. D. (2005). Resurrecting cold case serial homicide investigations. *FBI Law Enforcement Bulletin, 74*(8), 1–13. http://www.fbi.gov/stats-services/publications/law-enforcement-bulletin/2005-pdfs/august05leb.pdf.

Keel, T. G., Jarvis, J. P., and Muirhead, Y. E. (2009). An exploratory analysis of factors affecting homicide investigations—examining the dynamics of murder clearance rates. *Homicide Studies, 13*(1), 50–68. http://hsx.sagepub.com.logon.lynx.lib.usm.edu/content/13/1/50.short.

> Abstract: This study seeks to examine the practices of law enforcement agencies in attempting to solve cases of homicide. Five key dimensions, as determined from the extant literature, are examined using data from a recent law enforcement agency study of homicide investigative practices and policies. These include management practices, investigative procedures, analytical methods, demographics of the population served, and the extent of political influences that might affect agency effectiveness in clearing homicides. As expected, the results show some factors that enable effective agency investigations and other factors that hinder such processes. Some results can be interpreted to support contentions of victim devaluation by the police. However, an alternative interpretation, and perhaps more viable notion, is offered suggesting that police devaluation by the community may also contribute to explanations for the variance found in homicide clearance rates. (p. 50)

Kirkpatrick, M.D. (2001). Solving cold cases with digital fingerprints. *Sheriff, 53*(4), 14–17. https://www.ncjrs.gov/App/Publications/abstract.aspx?ID=189295.

> Abstract: The Integrated Automated Fingerprint Identification System (IAFIS) was conceived in 1989, developed by the Federal Bureau of Investigation beginning in 1993, and put into operation in July 1999. The system's 10-print identification services and criminal-history records information are particularly useful for solving cold cases using latent fingerprint evidence. The system includes an "unsolved latent file" and a corresponding search feature. Every month more than 8,000 fugitives, arrested in a jurisdiction different from that of the original booking agency, are identified by IAFIS. Where once they all would likely have been released on bail, now many are held for extradition. The article concludes that, as more law enforcement agencies obtain and use the technology to electronically submit latent fingerprints to the database, latent fingerprints lifted at crime scenes may be the critical factor in solving hundreds of cases and shrinking agencies' cold case files. (p. 14)

Lord, V. B. (2005). Implementing a cold case homicide unit. *FBI Law Enforcement Bulletin, 74*(2), 1–8. http://www.fbi.gov/stats-services/publications/law-enforcement-bulletin/2005-pdfs/feb05leb.pdf.

Magni, P. A., Harvey, M. L., Saravo, L. and Dadour, I. R. (2012). Entomological evidence: Lessons to be learnt from a cold case review. *Forensic Science International, 223*(1), 31–34. http://www.sciencedirect.com.logon.lynx.lib.usm.edu/science/article/pii/S0379073812004380.

Abstract: Insects are known to be useful in estimating time since death, but this is only possible if samples are collected and preserved correctly according to best practices. This report describes a case where an 18-year old female was found dead and during the first medico-legal investigation which determined it was a homicide, entomological samples were collected but not considered. The case was then closed with no suspect. However, 9 years after the first investigation the courts decided that the case needed to be re-examined. In doing so the new review team decided that although the remaining entomological evidence was poorly preserved some extra information may be gained from its analyses. On inspection of the remaining samples of larvae no normal morphological analyses could be conducted. Molecular analyses were combined with an unorthodox morphological analysis to provide an estimate of the post-mortem interval based on insect evidence, indicating the value of multidisciplinary approaches to both cold and contemporary cases. (p. 31)

Marks, K. (2009). New DNA technology for cold cases. *Law and Order, 57*(6), 36–43. https://www.ncjrs.gov/App/Publications/abstract.aspx?ID=249525.

Abstract: DNA analysis was first used to solve a crime in 1986. At that time, it was necessary to obtain a relatively large sample of evidence for DNA testing, and the sample was often used up in testing with the older DNA testing, called Restriction Fragment Length Polymorphism (RFLP). With newer techniques, RFLP is no longer used because of its limitations. Current DNA testing is anchored by Short Tandem Repeat (STR) technology, which is part of a larger type of analysis that involves polymerase chain reaction (PCR). PCR can make millions of exact copies of DNA from a biological sample. This DNA amplification allows DNA analysis to be conducted on biological samples as small as a few skin cells. DNA technology that further refines STR is imminent. Mini-filer or mini-STR is being used for testing previously untestable DNA samples, and it looks at one to three loci, or locations, on the DNA strand. Being able to test for even 1 location at a time instead of all 13 loci on the DNA strand has allowed minute or degraded DNA samples to yield results. YSTR or Y-chromosome analysis is useful in testing for only male or female DNA, which is often the case in sexual assault cases or missing persons cases. Mitochondrial DNA (mtDNA) analysis can be used to examine the DNA from samples that cannot be analyzed using STR. Although older biological samples that lack nucleated cellular materials—such as hair, bones, and teeth—cannot be analyzed with STR, they can be analyzed with mtDNA. (p. 36)

Mouzos, J. and Muller, D. (2001). Solvability factors of homicide in Australia: An exploratory analysis. *Australian Institute of Criminology*, 1–6. http://www.aic.gov.au/documents/6/B/8/%7B6B8439DA-5190-441D-8F7C-9DFDF9880D3D%7Dti216.pdf.

Phillips, A. (2007). Praying for a breakthrough: Solving cold case investigations without DNA evidence is not impossible. *Law Enforcement Technology, 34*(8), 20–25. https://www.ncjrs.gov/App/Publications/abstract.aspx?ID=241842.

Abstract: When a "cold" case is reopened, it is usually because a new circumstance has arisen that provides a reason to reopen the case. The Toledo murder case was reopened because an initial suspect in 1980 was implicated in a sexual molestation case in 2003. When a case is reopened, one of the first steps is to go to the property room and re-examine all the evidence for fresh insight. Every witness who is still alive should also be contacted. As time passes and relationships between witnesses and suspects change, witnesses may be more willing to share information that was withheld in the initial investigation. Other options include an examination for DNA and fingerprint samples in retained evidence. In some cases, matches can be found in CODIS (for a DNA match) and AFIS (for a fingerprint match). This is possible because these databases are being continually updated as suspects from a "cold" case may have committed new crimes in which their identifying DNA and fingerprints were collected and added to these nationwide databases. The development of new directions in a "cold" case can also be developed by enlisting the aid of "cold" case experts, who may have particular expertise relevant to the evidence in a case, such as the analysis of bloodstain patterns and techniques for linking murder weapons to crime scenes. The Toledo "cold" case was solved through a combination of these "cold" case investigative methods. (p. 20)

Reese, A. and Prabhaunnithan, N. (2012). Analysis of the cold case survey of law enforcement for the Colorado Bureau of Investigation. http://cdpsweb.state.co.us/coldcase/doc/Cold%20case%20report%20Updated%202013.pdf.

Regini, C. L. (1997). Cold case concept. *FBI Law Enforcement Bulletin, 66*(8), 1–6. http://www.fbi.gov/?came_from=http%3a//www.fbi.gov/stats-services/publications/law-enforcement-bulletin/leb-old.

Scerra, N. (2011). Impact of police cultural knowledge on violent serial crime investigation. *Policing: An International Journal of Police Strategies & Management, 34*(1), 83–96. http://www.emeraldinsight.com.logon.lynx.lib.usm.edu/journals.htm?articleid=1912279&show=abstract.

Abstract: This paper aims to examine the influence of police cultural knowledge on the investigation of violent serial crimes. Specifically, it aims to identify whether such knowledge impacts the way in which investigative techniques are implemented. Of particular interest is the police knowledge specific to victims of violent serial crimes. (p. 83)

Schuster, B. (2008). Cold cases: Strategies explored at NIJ regional trainings. *NIJ Journal, 260.* http://www.nij.gov/journals/260/cold-case-strategies.htm. http://www.securitymanagement.com/archive/library/confess_fbi1105.pdf.

Spraggs, D. (2003). How to ... open a cold case. *Police: The Law Enforcement Magazine, 27*(5), 28–31. https://www.ncjrs.gov/App/Publications/abstract.aspx?ID=200718.

Abstract: Federal Bureau of Investigation (FBI) Uniform Crime Reports show that under 20 percent of all crime in the United States is cleared by arrest or exceptional means. Violent criminals face significantly higher statistics, but almost half of all murderers and rapists nationwide are still roaming the streets. There appear to be an ample number of cold cases that are just waiting to be re-opened and solved. The cold case investigation process involves assigning detectives to examine cases that went unsolved for various reasons. These reasons include the lack of available technology to analyze evidence, hostile witnesses, and not enough time allocation to properly work the case. Police agencies of all sizes can form cold case squads, either permanently or temporarily, to examine old cases. No department has unlimited time, personnel, and resources so it is important to carefully select the cases for review. Because homicides and sexual assaults tend to yield the most evidence, they are well suited to cold case review. It is important to define the parameters for selecting specific cases. A crime analyst can sort through and filter all reported crimes and give a list of cases that meet the criteria. A few factors, such as physical evidence and available witnesses, can determine whether a case is too old to re-open. Re-opening a cold case requires patience, diligence, and strong deductive reasoning abilities. The first step is the review of all existing case material; this is the most time-consuming step. The most important components of cold case investigation are the people—victims, witnesses, and suspects—and the physical evidence. Inventory of the available evidence is one of the most important steps in a cold case investigation. Biological evidence may degrade over the years, poor storage of items can result in ruined fingerprint evidence, poorly developed and fixed negatives and photographs may fade, and evidence may have been destroyed or lost by evidence technicians. (p. 28)

Turner, R., and Kosa, R. (2003). *Cold case squads: Leaving no stone unturned.* Washington, DC: BJA Bulletins. https://www.ncjrs.gov/html/bja/coldcasesquads/199781.pdf.

Abstract: A cold case squad may be a viable option for a jurisdiction that is plagued by a significant number of unsolved murders. Some cold case squads are formed because the volume of new cases or police initiatives prevents any work from being done on old cases. Some squads are formed out of convenience when a decline in new murder cases provides departments with the personnel and other resources necessary to begin investigating old cases. The specific duties of cold case squads vary among law enforcement agencies. Nearly all of these squads review and continue the investigation of unsolved homicides or suspected homicides in which the lead detective initially assigned has retired, transferred, or otherwise left the case. Cold case squads can be useful in locating and working with past and potential witnesses and reviewing physical evidence to identify suspects. Cold case squads also perform an outreach and networking role by assisting other jurisdictions with homicide investigations as appropriate. The most important component of cold case squads is personnel; the squads must have the right mix of investigative and supervisory talent. Cold case squads can consist of a single full-time investigator, occasional squads, or interdepartmental partnerships. Cold case squads usually include at least a supervisor or team manager, a supervisor to coordinate daily operations, and investigators. Squads may also use the services of agencies such as the Federal Bureau of Investigation, coroner's office, or internal and external specialists. Not all cold case squads reside in municipal police departments. The branches of the military investigate cold cases involving homicides that occurred on military bases or involved military personnel. Traits considered essential for cold case investigators include seniority, strong communication and interpersonal skills, strong research skills, patience, creativity, persistence, high motivation level, and enthusiasm for the job. The process by which cases are reviewed and considered for referral to the cold case squad varies. Cases are reviewed and prioritized according to the likelihood of an eventual solution. (p. 1)

Walton, R.H. (2007). Evidence issues in cold-case homicide investigation. *Evidence Technology Magazine, 5*(3), 36–41. https://www.ncjrs.gov/app/abstractdb/AbstractDBDetails.aspx?id=240768.

Abstract: Time which was once considered an enemy in homicide investigations is now a friend to those evidence teams working on unsolved cases. Close relationships are found to change as years pass. Because of maturity, distance from the crowd previously associated with or the result of a religious experience, people with knowledge of murders that occurred years ago may now come forward. In addition, advances in technology today have provided the ability to learn more from physical and biological evidence, such as DNA technology and automated fingerprint identification systems (AFIS). Today, modern cold-case homicide investigations are a team effort. It is a joint undertaking carried out by dedicated investigators, evidence and laboratory personnel, and prosecutors who join forces, as the evidence team, in an attempt to solve cold cases. Understanding the sequence of cold-case investigative events provides an insight into the role evidence personnel play during the early stages of an investigation and the hurdles they face. (p. 36)

Walton, R. H. (2010). *Cold Case Homicides: Practical Investigative Techniques*. Boca Raton, FL: CRC Press.

Abstract: (Stein) This text includes three sections: Investigation, technology, and investigative tools. In the first section, Walton discusses the etiology of the cold case concept, investigative techniques for cases, the prosecution of cold cases, various databases to assist with investigations (e.g., ViCAP, HITS, etc.), and various interview techniques (particularly relevant is the interviewing of senior citizens as they are frequently the age demographic represented when considering cold cases). In the second section of the text, Walton (2010) examines the utility of fingerprints, mtDNA, nuclear DNA, and ballistics evidence when presented in a cold case investigation. In the third section, Investigative Tools, Walton (2010) presents various fields in forensic science (e.g., forensic anthropology, forensic dentistry, etc.) and how they can be of value in a cold case investigation.

Wellman, A. P. (2013). Grief in comparison: Use of social comparison among cold case homicide survivors. *Journal of Loss and Trauma: International Perspectives on Stress & Coping.* http://www.tandfonline.com.logon.lynx.lib.usm.edu/doi/full/10.1080/15325024.2013.801306#.Ue1Br42kpAE.

Abstract: The current qualitative study examines the use of social comparison among cold case homicide survivors as a method of defining their grief. Twenty-four (n = 24) cold case homicide survivors completed in-depth interviews about the trauma of living with an unsolved homicide. Survivors compared themselves to individuals coping with non-homicidal deaths and fellow homicide survivors. Results indicate survivors of unsolved homicides utilize downward elevation, lateral comparison, and upward contacts in their journey of grief and coping. The direction and type of comparison can have both positive and negative effects on the survivors' views of self and progress made towards emotional recovery. Implications are discussed.

Wexler, S. (2004). Cold cases are getting hot. *Law Enforcement Technology, 31*(6), 18–20, 22, 23. https://www.ncjrs.gov/App/abstractdb/AbstractDBDetails.aspx?id=206160.

Abstract: The article opens with a description of two murder cases, one from 1957 and one from 1968, that were only recently solved thanks to advancements in information collection and dissemination (databases) and DNA fingerprinting technology. Over the past few years, for a multitude of reasons, cold case squads have been forming in police forces around the country; cold case units are in operation in Boston, Chicago, Los Angeles, and New York, among others. It is estimated that 30 to 35 percent of murders go unsolved and that each year, another 6,000 unsolved murders occur. Cold case investigators now have access to tools police officers did not have in decades past. DNA fingerprinting technology has advanced to the point where DNA information can be obtained from microscopic pieces of evidence. Plus, the development of national databases, such as the FBI's Integrated Automated Fingerprint Identification System (IAFIS), allows investigators to search through more than 46 million prints to find possible matches. The article describes how cold cases are identified for renewed investigation efforts; cases that were not properly investigated the first time are moved to the top of the list. Cold cases in which new information is provided are also given top priority by cold case investigators. While new DNA technology, including STR testing, and national databases provide treasure troves of information, old-fashioned detective work is still heavily relied upon when investigating cold cases. Interviewing past witnesses may lead to new information or reviewing old case files may provide fresh leads. Finally, simply reminding the public about past crimes may serve to jog the memories of those with information. (p. 18)

Index

A Call for Authors

Advances in Police Theory and Practice

AIMS AND SCOPE:

This cutting-edge series is designed to promote publication of books on contemporary advances in police theory and practice. We are especially interested in volumes that focus on the nexus between research and practice, with the end goal of disseminating innovations in policing. We will consider collections of expert contributions as well as individually authored works. Books in this series will be marketed internationally to both academic and professional audiences. This series also seeks to —

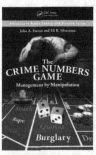

Police Reform in China

- Bridge the gap in knowledge about advances in theory and practice regarding who the police are, what they do, and how they maintain order, administer laws, and serve their communities
- Improve cooperation between those who are active in the field and those who are involved in academic research so as to facilitate the application of innovative advances in theory and practice

Mission-Based Policing

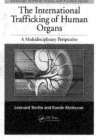
The International Trafficking of Human Organs
A Multidisciplinary Perspective

The series especially encourages the contribution of works coauthored by police practitioners and researchers. We are also interested in works comparing policing approaches and methods globally, examining such areas as the policing of transitional states, democratic policing, policing and minorities, preventive policing, investigation, patrolling and response, terrorism, organized crime and drug enforcement. In fact, every aspect of policing, public safety, and security, as well as public order is relevant for the series. Manuscripts should be between 300 and 600 printed pages. If you have a proposal for an original work or for a contributed volume, please be in touch.

Series Editor
Dilip Das, Ph.D., Ph: 802-598-3680
E-mail: dilipkd@aol.com

Dr. Das is a professor of criminal justice and Human Rights Consultant to the United Nations. He is a former chief of police, and founding president of the International Police Executive Symposium, IPES, www.ipes.info. He is also founding editor-in-chief of *Police Practice and Research: An International Journal* (PPR), (Routledge/Taylor & Francis), www.tandf.co.uk/journals. In addition to editing the *World Police Encyclopedia* (Taylor & Francis, 2006), Dr. Das has published numerous books and articles during his many years of involvement in police practice, research, writing, and education.

Proposals for the series may be submitted to the series editor or directly to –
Carolyn Spence
Senior Editor • CRC Press / Taylor & Francis Group
561-317-9574 • 561-997-7249 (fax)
carolyn.spence@taylorandfrancis.com • www.crcpress.com
6000 Broken Sound Parkway NW, Suite 300, Boca Raton, FL 33487

Advances in POLICE THEORY and PRACTICE

Books in this Series:

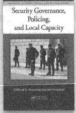

Honor-Based Violence
Policing and Prevention
Karl Anton Roberts, Gerry Campbell, and Glen Lloyd
Catalog no. K15429, November 2013
227 pp., ISBN: 978-1-4665-5665-2

Security Governance, Policing, and Local Capacity
Clifford D. Shearing and Jan Froestad
Catalog no. 90143, December 2012
257 pp., ISBN: 978-1-4200-9014-7

Policing and the Mentally Ill
International Perspectives
Edited by
Duncan Chappell
Catalog no. K13821, May 2013
381 pp., ISBN: 978-1-4398-8116-3

Policing White-Collar Crime
Characteristics of White-Collar Criminals
Petter Gottschalk
Catalog no. K20530, December 2013
339 pp., ISBN: 978-1-4665-9177-6

Financial Crimes
A Threat to Global Security
Edited by
Maximillian Edelbacher, Peter C. Kratcoski, and Michael Theil
Catalog no. K13172, June 2012
488 pp., ISBN: 978-1-4398-6922-2

The Crime Numbers Game
Management by Manipulation
John A. Eterno and Eli B. Silverman
Catalog no. K10516, January 2012
282 pp., ISBN: 978-1-4398-1031-6

Police Integrity Management in Australia
Global Lessons for Combating Police Misconduct
Louise Porter and Tim Prenzler
Catalog no. K14262, April 2012
296 pp., ISBN: 978-1-4398-9598-6

Most titles also available as eBook

Series Editor

Dr. Dilip K. Das is president of the International Police Executive Symposium, IPES, www.IPES.info. He is also human rights consultant to the United Nations. Dr. Das has over 40 years of experience in police practice, research, writing, and education. He is founding editor-in-chief of *Police Practice and Research: An International Journal*.

Advances in POLICE THEORY and PRACTICE

is **Advances in Police Theory and Practice** series encourages the contribution of works coauthored by police
actitioners and researchers. Proposals for contributions to the series may be submitted to the series editor
. Das, at **dilipkd@aol.com** or directly to:

Carolyn Spence, Senior Editor
CRC Press / Taylor & Francis Group
carolyn.spence@taylorandfrancis.com

Published

lice Corruption
eventing Misconduct
d Maintaining
tegrity
n Prenzler
alog no. 77961
rch 2009

mmunity Policing
ternational Patterns
d Comparative
rspectives
ted by
minique Wisler and
kwoaba D. Onwudiwe
alog no. 93584
e 2009

mmunity Policing
d Peacekeeping
ted by
ter Grabosky
alog no. K10012
e 2009

curity in Post-
nflict Africa
e Role of Nonstate
licing
ce Baker
alog no. 9193X
gust 2009

licing Organized
ime
telligence Strategy
plementation
ter Gottschalk
alog no. K10504
gust 2009

e New Khaki
e Evolving Nature of
licing in India
ind Verma
alog no. K10722
ember 2010

Mission-Based
Policing
John P. Crank,
Rebecca K. Murray,
Dawn M. Irlbeck, and
Mark T. Sundermeier
Catalog no. K12291
August 2011

Police Reform in
China
Kam C. Wong
Catalog no. K11036
October 2011

The International
Trafficking of
Human Organs
A Multidisciplinary
Perspective
Edited by
Leonard Territo and
Rande Matteson
Catalog no. K13082
October 2011

Los Angeles Police
Department
Meltdown
The Fall of the
Professional-Reform
Model of Policing
James Lasley
Catalog no. K14343
August 2012

Police Performance
Appraisals
A Comparative
Perspective
Serdar Kenan Gul and
Paul O'Connell
Catalog no. K11803
September 2012

Forthcoming Titles!

Police Investigative
Interviews and
Interpreting
Context, Challenges,
and Strategies
Sedat Mulayim, Miranda
Lai, and Caroline Norma
Catalog no. K23394
October 2014

Crime Linkage
Theory, Research, and
Practice
Jessica Woodhams and
Craig Bennell
Catalog no. K14634
August 2014

Women in Policing
An International
Perspective
Venessa Garcia
Catalog no. K16281
June 2015

Democratic Policing
Darren Palmer
Catalog no. K20353
June 2014

Islamic Women in
Policing
A Contradiction in
Terms?
Tonita Murray
Catalog no. K10720
March 2015

Female Criminals
An Examination and
Interpretation of Female
Offending
Venessa Garcia
Catalog no. K16301
June 2014

Policing in Hong
Kong
History and Reform
Kam C. Wong
Catalog no. K14267
December 2014

Civilian Oversight of
Police
Advancing
Accountability in
Law Enforcement
Edited by
Tim Prenzler and
Garth den Heyer
Catalog no. K22986
September 2014

Policing Terrorism
Research Studies into
Police Counter-terrorism
Investigations
David Lowe
Catalog no. K22506
January 2015

Police Leadership in
the 21st Century
Responding to the
Challenges
Jenny Fleming and
Eugene Mclaughlin
Catalog no. K12766
September 2015

Corruption Fraud,
Organized Crime,
and the Shadow
Economy
Edited by
Maximillian Edelbacher,
Peter C. Kratcoski, and
Bojan Dobovsek

Collaborative
Policing
Peter C. Kratcoski and
Maximillian Edelbacher

Most titles also available as eBook

Printed in the United States
by Baker & Taylor Publisher Services